685-A-B3-173

19

An Introduction to the Politics
of Tropical Africa

An Introduction to the Politics of Tropical Africa

Richard Hodder-Williams

London
GEORGE ALLEN & UNWIN
Boston   Sydney

633449

George Allen & Unwin (Publishers) Ltd,
40 Museum Street, London WC1A 1LU, UK

George Allen & Unwin (Publishers) Ltd,
Park Lane, Hemel Hempstead, Herts HP2 4TE, UK

Allen & Unwin, Inc.,
Fifty Cross Street, Winchester, Mass. 01890, USA.

George Allen & Unwin Australia Pty Ltd,
8 Napier Street, North Sydney, NSW 2060, Australia

First published in 1984.

British Library Cataloguing in Publication Data

Hodder-Williams, Richard
 An introduction to the politics of tropical Africa.
1. Africa, Sub-Sahara—Politics and
government——1960–
I. Title
320.967   JQ1872
ISBN 0-04-320162-8
ISBN 0-04-320163-6 Pbk

Library of Congress Cataloging in Publication Data

Hodder-Williams, Richard.
 An introduction to the politics of tropical Africa.
Bibliography: p.
Includes index.
1. Africa, Sub-Saharan——Politics and government.
2. Africa, Sub-Saharan——Constitutional history.
I. Title.
JQ1872.H63 1984   967   84-9273
ISBN 0-04-320162-8 (alk. paper)
ISBN 0-04-320163-6 (pbk. : alk. paper)

Set in 11 on 12 point Plantin by Getset (BTS) Ltd., Eynsham, Oxford
and printed in Great Britain by
Billing and Sons Ltd, London and Worcester

for JOHN-PAUL

who might otherwise never be a dedicatee, and
whose cheerful presence has been a constant source of joy
but no constructive assistance at all to this enterprise

Contents

Preface

The politics of tropical Africa is so vast a subject that no single volume can hope to be comprehensive. Inevitably, therefore, this book must be something of a personal testimony. Yet it would not have been written without the unwitting help of many friends and colleagues in Africa as well as in Europe; if they recognise one of their favourite phrases here, I hope they will take it as a compliment.

My aim has been to provide for students and the general reader interested in contemporary tropical Africa an introduction which provides some basic information, an analysis of some of the central factors of political life in the continent, and enough issues to fuel many discussions. To those experts whose knowledge of sections of this book is deep and extensive I admit that the complexity of problems and the subtlety of arguments have often been simplified. I do not see how it could be otherwise.

That the book ever saw the light of day owes more than usual to Anne Merriman, whose patience and accuracy at the typewriter have as usual been so much appreciated.

Introduction

The study of Africa arouses many passions and many pre-judices. Even listening to educated British professionals talking about the continent and contrasting that with articulate Africans discussing their own politics and the world they live in is a curious experience. Inhabitants of the same world, commenting with earnestness on the same geographical region, they often seem to be living on quite different planets talking about quite different phenomena. It is not difficult to see why the people of the 'North' – the rich, industrialised states of Europe, North America, Japan and Australia – should hold the views they do. After all, it *is* the exotic aspects of tropical Africa that impinge upon their consciousness.

The travel brochures emphasise the white beaches and palm trees of the ocean shores, the dramatic backcloths to the game parks, the curio sellers and the hotels of international quality. The television programmes reproduce much the same vision of Africa, perhaps spicing the glorification of sun and sand and the fascination for the last great concentrations of wild life with some comments on the possible disadvantage to African societies of the tourist explosion or with dire prognostications for the demise of game before the twin pressures of poaching and food requirements. While the picture so presented contains no falsehoods, it badly distorts the true picture of the African continent. In so vast an area, stretching over 4,000 miles from North to South and nearly 3,000 miles from eastern extremity to the most westerly shoreline, the variety of natural habitat, economic activity and physical limitations on what is possible is truly enormous.

There still remain many thousands of square miles of un-tamed land, from mountain forests to mangrove swamps and the desolate inhospitality of desert land, of course, but there are many more thousands of square miles where African farmers cultivate their fields and herd their cattle, sometimes on rich land well endowed with rainfall, sometimes on thin sandy soil where only a scanty living can be eked out. There are tiny trading posts with extremely limited ranges of goods; there are fine shops filled with French perfumes. Magnificent office complexes are found cheek by jowl with squalid temporary houses of corrugated iron. Traffic jams feature in many a capital, whose hinterland often contains villages without a single track on which a car could drive. The contrasts between affluence and poverty, between modernity and tradition, are more blatant, perhaps, but they are a truer reflection of the political milieu than coral lagoons and browsing antelope.

In the realm of politics itself, the same concentration on the exotic dominates the presentation of news in the Western media. Military coups, small wars, bizarre governmental actions and events which supposedly satisfy Western audiences by their peculiarities, make up the vast majority of information which is made available. For most people, the heart-rending pictures of young children suffering from kwashiakoor during the Nigerian Civil war, the atrocities of Idi Amin's Uganda, or the absurd posturing of a Bokassa make up the primary images of the continent's politics. Again, there is no denying the facts to which these pictures draw attention. But to see African politics merely in these terms is as grotesque a parody of the reality as it is a sad reflection on the news values of the North.

Through much of Africa, by contrast, politicians and officials are grappling with a host of difficult governmental decisions, negotiating with local leaders, listening to spokesmen for representative groups, trying to create programmes which express their visions of the good society within the financial and technical constraints that lie so heavily upon them. Political parties operate in many countries, by no means always the oppressive arms of an authoritarian regime, as it is sometimes commonly supposed outside the continent. Villagers discuss seriously the problems of locating a new school or the different qualities of rival candidates for office; administrative officials wrestle with the conflicts that often arise between local preferences and the bureaucracy's ideas of rational policy. In short, the sort of political activity familiar to any observer of politics elsewhere has its counterpart in the African continent.

This does not mean that those who already live in Africa will necessarily see their continent's politics more clearly. They may well know the details of their local community power structure extremely well; but that is no sure basis for understanding why it operates as it does, much less how local politics in a distant African country function. The North is frequently confused by myth and partial vision; but so, too, is the South. The history that is taught (and the history that is remembered still more) is often distorted; the assumption that 'our ways' are universal ways is as familiar a pitfall to the understanding of others in Africa as it is in Europe and North America. So, while students in Africa should rightly feel aggrieved at the oversimplified and exaggerated portrayal of their continent in the North, they should not assume that indignation leads inevitably to true knowledge; they, too, must question their assumptions and the too easy shift from personal experience to continent-wide generalisations. There is a saying in Britain that sometimes 'one cannot see the wood for the trees'; in other words, too intimate an acquaintance with the parts (the trees) obscures the shape and significance of the whole (the wood). Two dangers, therefore, have to be guarded against: the assumption that local experience means knowledge of the whole political system and the belief that generalisations for the whole continent can be made from an understanding of one. Tanzania is not Nigeria; the Ivory Coast is not Guinea.

The size and variety of the African continent, which makes any generalisation difficult, is perhaps too obvious a point to labour. But it is the necessary starting point. Along the Mediterranean littoral lie a string of states with long and close links to Europe and to Asia; at the foot of the continent lies a country colonised by emigrants from Europe and ruled under principles of racial separation to be found nowhere else now in Africa. Both extremities have a very special brand of political activity, as is to be expected from their very special historical experiences. Between these two extremes, roughly demarcated by the tropics of Cancer and Capricorn, lie more than forty states; apart from Liberia and Ethiopia, these have all emerged very recently from a period of imperial overrule into sovereign states whose boundaries rarely, if ever, correspond to single national groupings or to political units of an earlier historical era. It is with these states that this book is concerned.

There is, of course, something slightly artificial in concentrating only on tropical Africa, for the lines of such a demarcation do not mark impermeable zones. Trade and travellers, and with them ideas, have for centuries linked the Mahgreb to the northernmost countries of tropical Africa; indeed, Northern Nigeria in many ways looks more naturally to the Islamic states of Algeria and Libya than to its own non-Islamic fellow citizens in the South. Similarly, although white-ruled South Africa is unquestionably distinct from its northern neighbours by the very fact of its institutionalised racial discrimination, ties of trade and ideas also cross the Limpopo River in both directions and the very existence of South Africa's peculiar political system profoundly affects the politics of the rest of the continent. It may be that tropical Africa is merely a residual category, a convenient shorthand for countries which cannot be as easily categorised as South Africa or the Mahgreb states. But it is a category commonly used and statements made about African politics generally are usually held to apply, more or less, to the whole bloc of states which make up the category. There is, therefore, a sound reason for treating them at the outset as a group of states which might usefully be analysed as a single group.

But any journey of discovery cannot advance far before the apparent differences between the individual members become noticeable. The Sudan and Zaire cover more than 900,000 square miles each, ten times the size of the United Kingdom and large enough to incorporate the European Community, Spain, Portugal and much of Scandinavia; at the other extreme the Gambia covers a mere 4,000 square miles for its half a million inhabitants. The emirates of Northern Nigeria contrast vividly with the scattered villages of Zambia; the densely populated hillsides of Rwanda contrast with the apparently unoccupied savannah of Upper Volta; the sophisticated conversationalists of Abidjan cafés contrast with the more robust leisure activities of the Zambian copper miners. Tall, short, broad, slim, Nilotic, Bantu, ebony skinned, pale-chocolate skinned, the peoples of tropical Africa represent a kaleidoscope of types. Generalising about its inhabitants is as sensible and as useful as generalising about Europeans as an undifferentiated group.

Observing the differences between the citizens of tropical Africa serves also to highlight fundamental differences between the experiences and culture of Africa and Europe. In tropical Africa, 85 per cent of the population live in rural areas; few of these have access to running water or electricity; literacy, although increasing, remains low; many villages, themselves more a collection of individual farmsteads scattered over the countryside than the nucleated settlements of Europe, have no access to roads; the roads themselves are more likely to be of murram than of tar and turn to slippery quagmires in heavy rain; most countries contain people of many and varied languages, over 100 in Tanzania, more than 200 in Nigeria; the problems of communication are therefore formidable, both physically and intellectually. Nature, too, can be singularly unhelpful. Rain, which is frequently inadequate, is normally so heavy that the effective rainfall is much less than that measured; disease is rife, not only such perennials as malaria, but the debilitating and widespread bilharzia; life expectancy, although rising, remains appreciably lower than in Europe; the demographic profile of these states shows half their populations under 16 years of age. Politicians are, therefore, operating in a singularly hostile environment where so much that the industrialised world takes for granted is largely absent.

For some students in the rich industrialised world, this awareness of the continent's utterly unfamiliar environment and social history can easily produce a despairing conviction that understanding peoples so alien is impossible. Students of mine have said that their total unfamiliarity with the life of a subsistence farmer or with the social and familial networks of an African village prevents them from understanding, let alone passing judgement on, the politics they are supposed to be studying. Such a lament is understandable; but it is unnecessarily defeatist. It also negates the central principle of the social sciences; by observation, careful probing and empathy, good scholars can extricate themselves from the confines of their own experiences and enter into the perceptions and prejudices of those they study. It is not easy; and mistakes are to be expected. But to deny the possibility is effectively to sentence us to the stifling ghettos of our own tiny personal worlds. There is no real alternative for the peoples of the North to visiting Africa, to talking to a wide range of people there, to living – if only for a brief while – an active life within an independent state, to seeing the land over which governments attempt to rule, to soaking up, in short, the smell of the dusty highveld, the enervating weight of the sea-level humidity, the physical proximity of normal social contact, the concern for courtesy as well as the desperate struggle for survival. What they can do instead, and what they ought to do, is to absorb their contacts with African novelists. There is a long, often distinguished, and still growing tradition in Africa of writing about personal experiences and beliefs, often in the guise of novels. A week-end relaxing on some European beach with a couple of novels by Achebe or Ngugi wa Thiong'o, an autobiography or two, and a collection of French African poetry is a week-end conducive to pleasure and comprehension simultaneously. Good non-academic literature, the product of highly articulate and often extremely perceptive Africans communicating visions of their own heritages and societies, sharpens our perceptions and illuminates our understanding with a degree of authenticity, despite the inevitable exaggeration and simplification of the novelist or poet, unmatched by most more traditional and overtly academic or educational introductory works.

For the North, then, the study of Africa requires the rigour of the good social scientist and the empathy of the novelist. For the South, too, the same needs apply, although they may not seem so obvious. Yet British and American students, brought up in a specific social system to perceive the world about them through largely pre-set lenses, are constantly surprised by the new data and fresh analyses offered to them of their own countries by the probing of political scientists. In Africa, likewise, the study of the continent's politics must allow the possibility of human fallibility and the likelihood that the conventional wisdoms of the day are simply conventional and not necessarily wise. Since the politics of Africa are so clearly linked to outside peoples and forces, there is a special need – if the aim of inquiries is to explain and understand rather than simply to pass judgement – to get under the skins of those outsiders, to comprehend their motives and passions, and to recognise that they, too, may be as human and fallible, as human and noble, as the men and women of Africa.

Similarity of approach does not mean that the African condition has no special qualities of its own. It was a consciousness of the difference between the environment of African political life and the environment of the industrialised and affluent liberal democracies of Europe and North America which much influenced the writing of American academics in the 1950s and early 1960s. It fitted snugly into the growing emphasis on comparative politics and offered exciting challenges to those scholars who believed in the possibility of a science of politics. Furthermore, it appeared to leaders within the American academic community that the study of Third World states would be conducive to wider national interests, since the end of Empire coincided with Cold War tensions and the loyalties of the new states were as yet uncertain. British academic writing on politics generally tended to focus on the fundamental institutions of states, on Constitutions, parties, parliaments, local government organisation, elections; this was true for the most part of Africanists too. The distinction between academics on different sides of the Atlantic, however, can be exaggerated; British writers were fully aware of the importance of social and economic factors in giving shape to political disputes, just as American writers in fact became enmeshed in the institutions of individual states. But it encapsulates a basic truth. Early African studies were dominated by American scholars, greater in numbers and better provided with research funds, who tended to assume that the new states of Africa constituted a single category within which a further process of categorising could take place. African scholars, because of the paucity of indigenous institutions of higher education, in the early days of African studies contributed little to the debate. Like so much of the continent, it was overrun by foreigners. In time, however, Africans began to contribute more, but disappointingly little that was unique emerged. Trained formally in the United States, Britain, or France, they generally learned, and perhaps even internalised, the perspectives and methodologies of those states' intellectuals. Even in the 1980s, twenty years after independence for most of the continent, the academic dominance of the North over the study of African politics remains a central feature.

Initially, both British and American traditions had shared an essentially optimistic vision of Africa's future. From one perspective, it was assumed that the process of modernisation, defined largely in terms of a progression towards the model of a differentiated and participant political system associated with the industrialised states of Western Europe and North America, would gradually draw the African states out of their much more traditional practices. From the other perspective, it was expected that the transplantation of the institutions associated with French and British politics would create in Africa new democratic societies in the image of their former political masters. There were, even in the heady days immediately after independence, a few observers who doubted these hopeful scenarios, but they were a minority.

In time, these perspectives came under attack, in part for their failure to cope with the reality of African politics and in part for their thinly veiled ethnocentrism. The resolute refusal of African states to tread the modernisation path and espouse liberal democratic forms of government persuaded scholars to address a different set of problems. An influential American response was to argue that the transformation of society was still the fundamental function of the governments of the new states and that order, together with strong and decisive government, was probably a necessary precondition for this desirable development. British scholars, less concerned with the purposes of government and the public positions of the new states in the world community, turned both to the consequences of democracy's failure, most notably the rise of the military, and to its supposed causes, the incongruence between peasant and bureaucratic values and democracy's needs. The second criticism of the modernisation school in time became an intellectual support for a quite different set of assumptions about politics in Africa. The very idea that development was necessarily the essentially quantitative measure adopted by some commentators (a higher GNP, greater participation in parties, more cars and consumer durables, and so forth) was challenged and qualitative criteria, especially those concerned with an egalitarian distribution of resources, became fashionable. A much more clearly articulated concern for a socialist society, itself still a largely ethonocentric concept nevertheless, began to dominate much of the literature (Phillips, 1977).

All these perspectives raise important questions. Attacking the paramountcy of one over another does not exclude the likelihood of each perspective offering suggestive insights. The pains of rapid change associated with the process of modernisation are real enough; the factors underlying the collapse of parliamentary democracies remain telling influences on contemporary institutions; differing notions of development turn attention to different data and pose different problems. At any one time a fashion seems to dominate Africanists as new ideas, and often new states, command a disproportionate amount of attention. But that is the way of intellectual advancement, especially when the problem being tackled is as awesomely ambitious as an all-embracing analysis of tropical African politics.

By the middle of the 1970s it seemed that a new orthodoxy had emerged. As scholars became disenchanted with the focus on modernisation and development, they began to see the new states as essentially peripheral parts of an international capitalist system upon which they were dangerously dependent. The resurrection of analyses in the Marxist tradition, as well as a widespread disaffection among radicals and liberals from what Edward Heath in Britain once referred to as the unacceptable face of capitalism, encouraged this new emphasis on dependency. The general tenor of this approach cannot easily be gainsaid; indeed, recent historical research makes it abundantly clear how closely tied to their old imperial masters, economically and culturally, are the new states of Africa. But the stress on dependency should not obscure the very real autonomy that nevertheless remains. The leaders of Africa are not political eunuchs; and many of the areas of governmental activity, such as educational curricula or health care programmes or social welfare priorities, remain primarily subject to domestic choices.

Sketching out the intellectual fashions of the last two decades inevitably oversimplifies and creates the illusion of greater uniformity than was actually the case. But it conveniently raises two important points. First, much of the study of Africa has consciously attempted to establish a uniformity, which the variety of historical experiences and economic developments suggest is extremely unlikely. There is no single path of modernisation; nor is there any single model which accurately reflects the diverse forces at work within the states of tropical Africa. The scholarly concern to establish order out of the disordered universe observed is a dangerous habit. In seeing African politics as a single category about which theories ought to be constructed, variety is emasculated to create a spurious order. Instead of searching for uniformities (which are, in any case, likely to be so broad as to be applicable to politics anywhere), the emphasis should perhaps be placed on diversity. The point is not that tropical Africa lacks any shared conditions or problems; it does. The point is that individual states – and this is one fascination of the continent's politics – respond to common problems in diverse ways.

Secondly, African studies, like most academic endeavours, have enjoyed fashions. What these have often represented have been ideological preoccupations. The geographically fashionable foci (Ghana in the 1950s, Tanzania in the 1960s, Southern African liberation in the 1970s, Mozambique and Zimbabwe in the 1980s) indicate clearly enough the extent to which many scholars have productively linked their personal interests to their own research areas. One of the consequences of such a tradition is the extent to which writing on African politics is often intended, and more often used, to make a political judgement rather than merely an advance to our understanding. Neutrality is not a quality commonly accepted among students of African studies, which are dominated by those who are in some way *engagé*. There are understandable reasons for this in a continent where some of the major conflicts of our time – between white and black, between alien and indigenous rule, between capitalism and socialism, between rich and poor, or North and South – are actually being, or have very recently been, fought. Africa is still unsettled, its political form uncertain, its experimentation not yet concluded. It is virtually impossible, therefore, not to get involved in the great issues being played out in the continent. Whether one likes it or not, a scholar's findings or analysis will most likely be used by some group or other as support for their normative position. In African studies more than in European studies, explanation is often interpreted as justification. Furthermore, a passionate involvement in African affairs, in which the forces of good and evil seem constantly to be in conflict, results often in work which justifies and strengthens the author's own position.

It is therefore necessary to indicate from the outset the assumptions upon which this book is written. It was Pliny, more than two thousand years ago, who wrote that there is always something new emanating from Africa. Travellers and natural historians might share that perception; students of politics should not. Although the environment in which the politics of tropical Africa takes place is markedly different from that of Western Europe or North America, it does not follow that those politics are unreplicated elsewhere. Things may not be what they seem, admittedly; the functionalists were important if for no other reason than for their concern to stress that organisations commonly, and often arbitrarily, designated by similar names – such as single-party regime or bureaucracy – were frequently functionally different. Fred Riggs attempted to create an entirely new vocabulary to deal with the politics of the Third World precisely to ensure that the connotations of words in common Western political currency did not influence interpretation of those politics (Riggs, 1964). It did not catch on; but it made the central point that, taken as a whole, the politics of the Third World are qualitatively different from those of the industrialised nations of Western Europe and North America while, at the same time, their constituent parts are perfectly recognisable to political historians and students of contemporary politics. Perhaps an analogy might illustrate this. Classical music had a form and harmonies peculiar to itself; modern music has spectacularly different forms, rhythms and harmonies, but the same notes.

How, then, should the politics of tropical Africa be examined? My own approach is unashamedly eclectic. The most appropriate conceptual framework depends entirely upon the question posed; in short, there are horses for courses. I take it for granted that the new states of Africa, although formally independent, are constrained, as are all states, by the international environment. Within the limitations of these constraints and those dictated by physical resources and human capabilities, there remains a degree of discretion to politicians to choose their government's policies. The simple framework set out by David Easton for a political system still seems a convenient organising schema and implicitly underpins much of my analysis (Easton, 1956 – 7). As the focus shifts further and further from the international context through analyses of whole political systems to the operation of their parts, the level of theorising becomes more specific and the units of analysis smaller and more manageable. A different range of concepts which seems useful for the analysis of African politics comes into play at this stage as patrons and clients, spiralists, and brokers, for instance, enter the scene. Ultimately, however, politics is about the behaviour of individuals in discrete situations and here I have assumed that people have multiple roles and their actions can only be understood and explained if those actions are carefully situated in the precise context of the peoples themselves. So there is no unifying theory here to explain all; political activity is too human, too subject to a multiplicity of causes as well as chance, for that to be possible. And tropical Africa is, in addition, itself no monolithic and undifferentiated political system, but a composition of around forty individual systems, which have much that is common to one another but also much that is distinct.

The structure of the book implicitly clarifies my assumptions about the subject. There is no doubt that the past lies heavily upon the African present and no comprehension of contemporary affairs would be complete without some examination of the legacies of imperial rule. But the past pre-dates the European occupation. Pre-imperial Africa not only affected the precise form and extent of imperial rule; it has also survived the imperial years, partly as myth and partly as reality. The first two chapters of this book, therefore, attempt to draw out of the past those ideas, institutions, values and relationships which deeply affect current politics. But there was one distinct period in the past which particularly affected post-independence politics. This was the years immediately surrounding the transfer of power from imperial rule to African rule. The third chapter of the book examines in slightly more detail the heritage of these years. The ideas then prevalent and the institutions set up at the outset of independence provided the benchmark against which later changes were in many ways a response or a development.

The last four chapters of the book trace the variety of ways in which the independent states of tropical Africa have attempted to organise their political lives, to manage the tensions within their own societies, to respond to the demands of both internal requirements and external pressures, and to establish frameworks within which the universal activity of politics could take place. It is essentially a thematic, rather than a chronological, treatment, since different paths have been followed by different states at different times. Its focus is deliberately institutional, since the central interest of students of politics revolves around the power of the state. Who gets what, when and how, as Harold Lasswell once summarised the heart of political studies, is as valid an initial set of questions for tropical Africa as for the United States of America.

In writing an introductory book to explain the politics of tropical Africa, it is inevitable that there must be some simplification and a great deal of selectivity. It can only be one person's guide to a complex and constantly changing mosaic. And it cannot, if it is to cover the failures as well as the successes, escape from expressing disappointment at the performance of so many governments. The reasons for what has gone wrong are often beyond the powers of any politician to influence, but it would be naïve not to recognise also that tropical Africa has had its share of knaves. Emphasising the exotic does not create a fiction; it merely distorts the balance between the publicised disasters and the less openly acknowledged successes. I hope, therefore, that this book goes some way to creating a balance. Above all, I hope it begins to suggest the fascination of African politics, the variety, the seriousness, the often overwhelming difficulties, the vibrancy of politics in the continent.

1 The Acquisition of Empire

It is a truism to say that the present is rooted in the past but, as with most truisms, it captures an essential truth. The politics of Northern Ireland can only be understood in the context of the province's historical experience, just as the politics of the southern states of the United States make sense only with an awareness of the American Civil War and the peculiar phenomenon of American populism. Tropical Africa is no different. Furthermore, what is now the present will soon become the past; there is, therefore, something artificial in abstracting current practices from the seamless web of change and adaptation that marks the human experience. The student of contemporary politics, however, must indulge in this abstraction but, in doing so, there must be a realisation that what is being examined is, as it were, a single frame of a moving picture whose meaning depends on countless frames that have preceded it.

Inevitably, therefore, there must be an arbitrary element in choosing which aspects of the past to emphasise. In the case of tropical Africa the choice is comparatively simple. Its incorporation into the European empires is generally held to have been not only the most significant process of recent decades in a relative sense but also significant in an absolute sense with its radical, indeed revolutionary, impact on society, economics and politics. But there is a paradox; as one historian has expressed it: 'Looking back, one may see now that the colonial period was no more than a large episode in the onward movement of African life: in another sense, it was an unexampled means of revolutionary change' (Davidson, 1964, p. 20). The extension of European empires had mixed motivation; the peoples with whom the Europeans came into contact responded in different ways, as their own political necessities and values

1

dictated. The impact of European expansion, therefore, is a complicated equation, being a function both of European motivation and African response. But the consequences of that differential impact are crucial to any understanding of the complexities of contemporary tropical African politics.

This equation, it should be said, is no more than a starting point, a necessary but not a sufficient condition for comprehending the present. Although the early days of imperial incorporation represented, and indeed created, forces which came to dominate the unfolding structures of African countries, the years that followed introduced new developments which sometimes accentuated and sometimes softened them. Imperial motives altered; African responses changed; external factors such as depression and war sent shock waves through the whole continent; new technologies radically influenced what was possible; the dominant ideas and philosophies of Europe underwent important transformations. Which was cause and which effect, it is not always easy to decide. But the corollary of conceptualising the initial imperial acquisition as a frame in a dynamic process of change and adaptation is the acceptance that further changes and adaptations are still to come. Chapter 2 considers these post-acquisition developments and their impact on contemporary politics; in this chapter, it is the initial acquisition of imperial possessions in Africa which is the focus.

Imperial Expansion

The causes of imperial expansion, especially that extraordinary scramble for control of the African continent in the last decade of the nineteenth century, remain matters of dispute. Few now accept the judgement of Sir John Seeley, Professor of History at Cambridge University, whose 1881 lectures, published later in his celebrated *The Expansion of England*, included this striking observation: 'We seem, as it were, to have conquered and peopled half the world in a fit of absence of mind' (Seeley, 1883, p. 152). Yet this striking assertion is a good starting point, for it draws attention to two important aspects of the whole question of imperial expansion. Before the last decade or so of the nineteenth century, Europe's interest in tropical

Africa was almost entirely commercial; that is to say, independent traders visited Africa to buy produce – gold or slaves from West Africa, for instance – and transhipped them to Brazil, the West Indies, or some other part of the New World. Ports may have been controlled and garrisoned, but very little of the hinterland was. The imperial presence was felt only when the interests of imperial traders were manifestly hampered by disorder, violence, or brigandry; gunboats usually sufficed to ease the traders' problems, but occasionally there was physical occupation as well. British policy, two distinguished scholars of this period claim, did not change throughout the Victorian age; it 'followed the principle of extending control informally if possible, and formally if necessary' (Gallagher and Robinson, 1953, pp. 12 – 13). In other words, the British government was drawn into – it did not seek – expansionary activities.

Secondly, Seeley's observation refers directly to people. It is important at this stage to indulge in some conceptual clarification. The word 'colony' is derived from classical Greek and referred to a place where nationals from the home country settled to form a permanent extension of their country of origin. North America and Australia provide obvious examples of this phenomenon. Colony, colonisation, colonials should properly refer only to aspects of this process of settlement. Among the countries of tropical Africa only in Kenya, Zimbabwe, Angola and Mozambique did anything approaching a true colony develop and these countries had special problems, and advantages, as a result. For most of tropical Africa, the European powers extended their 'imperium' or rule and did not populate them with permanent settlers from among their own people. Colonialism inevitably involves imperialism; imperialism does not necessarily require colonialism, for the domination of a people does not demand the occupation and settlement of land. What happened in the late nineteenth century was a massive expansion of imperial control rather than a spread of colonial occupation. In the various depressions that struck Europe in the latter part of the nineteenth century, millions of people emigrated; the disruptive process of industrialisation also drove many Europeans to seek their fortune and future in foreign lands; but they did not choose, on the whole, to go to Africa. They followed their predecessors to North America and Australia.

Imperial expansion, the extension of European rule, differed in extent and intensity. Those parts of the continent which were known to have natural resources desired by metropolitan powers, were climatically attractive for white occupation and which were comparatively easily accessible, felt this new imperial rule most pervasively; those parts which lacked the sought-after resources, were climatically unattractive to people from Europe and were difficult of access, retained a much greater degree of independence. The mines of Southern and Central Africa attracted the imperial powers strongly; the mosquito in Ghana, as Kwame Nkrumah was later to observe, saved his country from being truly colonised; the difficulty of reaching Western Tanganyika or Northern Mali left these parts hardly touched by the imperial presence for many years. Seeley's implicit assertion that imperial expansion was, in many ways, a haphazard enterprise is partly true; certainly, there is little evidence that Britain, at any rate, consciously sought to extend its already considerable empire still further into Africa. Yet, such an expansion was obviously not entirely accidental; there were forces which pushed and pulled the European powers into the continent.

It has become the conventional view that imperial expansion was essentially the product of the imperatives of the economic system in the industrial states of Europe. This is, in fact, largely a misreading of the commentators who are supposed to have advanced this theory (Etherington, 1982). In the nineteenth century investment and trade was channelled overwhelmingly to the growth points of the globe, to the Americas, Australia, India and South Africa, not to the barely discovered and wholly undeveloped central portion of the African continent. The European powers were drawn into this part of the world by a different set of factors although, once drawn in, they tried in their various and often half-hearted ways to gain economic benefit from their new imperial possessions.

It is difficult in the essentially democratic and rational intellectual climate of the 1980s to capture the very different mood of the nineteenth century, when European statesmen saw little wrong in dividing the African continent into different metropolitan powers' spheres of influence, when a nation's military resources were unselfconsciously used for the extension of the nation's power, when belief in the essential virtue of a wealth-creating capitalism and a Christian morality was rarely challenged publicly, when Cecil Rhodes's heartfelt thankfulness that he was Anglo-Saxon caused no embarrassing blushes. The Jubilee of Queen Victoria in 1896 provided a dramatic opportunity for the extraordinary confidence and general pride in the British Empire to be expressed publicly (Morris, 1968). Expansion was, in these days of Herbert Spencer and Charles Darwin, inevitable and good; bringing the civilisation of Victorian England, narrowly and selectively defined though it may have been, to 'lesser breeds without the law' was accepted widely as a noble enterprise; Kipling's white man's burden was not a joking matter. In short, the spirit of the times was entirely in tune with imperial expansion.

But that spirit was mainly supportive, rather than causative. Each acquisition tended to have a history of its own; sometimes the initiators were well-placed individuals; sometimes they were the governments of rival European powers. In the British case, three of the currently most significant countries in tropical Africa came into the empire as the result of the initiatives made by imaginative and thrusting individuals. The *laissez-faire* capitalism of the day and the financial constraints on metropolitan countries combined to ensure that the opening up of parts of Africa to Europe was sometimes achieved through companies, not governments. In 1886 Sir George Goldie's Royal Niger Company was granted a charter to trade and set up the necessary administrative structures in what is now Nigeria; in 1888 Sir William Mackinnon's Imperial British East African Company was for similar purposes granted a charter over what is now Kenya; in 1889 Cecil Rhodes, richer but unknighted, was granted a royal charter for the British South African Company to develop what is now Zimbabwe. The right to grant these charters was self-created and provided, so it was hoped, a cheap way to extend British control. But Goldie and Mackinnon failed in their economic enterprises; however, their positions in society and their well-placed friends were influential in persuading the British government reluctantly to absorb their areas of operation into the empire. Rhodes all but failed, too; revolts, pestilence, war, the sheer magnitude of the costs of establishing the infrastructure of a modern state in central Africa, nearly overwhelmed his company. Indeed, some British military assistance in 1896 – 7, an extraordinary faith in his genius which allowed the company to raise more capital on the London stock market, and remarkable patience on the part of the shareholders kept the company afloat; it took thirty-five years before the first dividend was paid. Hard-headed investors looked elsewhere. But there were always some optimistic folk at the time who gambled on the future, more visionaries than rational actors. Few at the time profited from it; their time was yet to come.

The late nineteenth century was also a time of rivalry between the European powers. This had two distinct effects on imperial expansion; on the one hand, states sought to preserve what they already possessed and structured part of their policies on strategic calculations. For Britain, the strong points of the empire were east of Suez, in the Indian subcontinent and the Far East, in Australasia. Africa's significance lay in its geographical position between the metropolitan power and Asia; its strategic importance emphasised the ports and refuelling stations of South Africa, the Suez Canal which had been opened in 1869 and, above all, Egypt, not the high savannah grasslands of the central plateau. Yet it was, curiously enough, this concern for Egypt which brought Britain firmly into that highveld, for the headwaters of the Nile, assumed bizarrely to be of strategic significance, lay in what is now Uganda (Robinson and Gallagher, 1961).

On the other hand, the rivalry was represented by intense competition for new possessions. France was in some ways the obvious instance of this; the defeat at German hands in 1871 had shattered the national self-confidence and the empire became a means of re-establishing her credibility as a great power. France's manifest destiny as the purveyor of a distinctive culture was largely dictated by a felt need to reassert the greatness of France. But Germany, too, sought out her sphere of influence and attempted to acquire imperial possessions as the symbol of a great power. Only recently united into a single state and lacking the old mercantilist history which gave other

European powers a natural entrée into Africa, Germany started late in the scramble for Africa. But what she lacked in experience she made up for in single-minded determination. Where France, Germany and Portugal sought to expand their territorial sovereignty, Britain sought to contain. Botswana and the Rhodesias were embraced within the empire largely to prevent the Portuguese creating a single possession joining the Indian and Atlantic oceans. There was always the danger that the great powers would actually come to blows over their respective spheres of influence, as indeed they did in 1898 when British soldiers confronted French soldiers at Fashoda in an attempt to prevent any further expansion of the French Empire westwards. A few years before, from November 1884 to February 1885, the great powers had met in Berlin, with the United States and Russia ironically looking on as non-participants, precisely to limit the dangers of such confrontations.

The present map of Africa was drawn in Berlin. The consequences of these meetings remain to this day, in many cases a burden to the independent governments. The boundaries that were then established did not always follow natural lines of division. In West Africa, for instance, the borders tended to run north – south, exaggerating the region's heterogeneity, for they divided peoples of a common language and heritage and incorporated into a single state peoples of very different culture and sometimes long-standing antagonisms. In East Africa, too, the borders divided peoples. The Somali found themselves in five different states, a division which their politicians and people still resent and try to undo; the ruler-straight boundary between Kenya and Tanzania has a logic only in the politicians' need to delimit the spheres of influence of Britain and Germany. The Cabinda enclave, cut off from the rest of Angola to permit the Belgian Congo (Zaire) to have an outlet to the sea (an outlet which the fearsome rapids of the mighty river made virtually useless), and the Gambia's total encirclement by Senegal (they finally created a confederation in 1982) provide two further examples. Perhaps one of the strangest eccentricities of this delimitation process was the Caprivi strip, a long finger of scrubland intruding from German South-West Africa (Namibia) to the Zambesi River. Count von Caprivi, the German Foreign Minister, was determined that his possession should have access for a German gunboat on the great Zambesi River; perhaps he did not know that a few miles below that slender extension of the German Empire were the Victoria Falls and a few miles upstream a series of impassable rapids. It is not difficult to catalogue a host of examples of curious state boundaries, but it is easier to recognise unnatural divisions than to recognise natural ones. A continent of many hundred political units was forced into a continent of forty-seven states. Acute problems have arisen as a result; much of the process defied rational defence; yet it is difficult not to feel that the small political units of nineteenth-century Africa were inappropriate to the developments of the twentieth.

Since acquisition at the turn of the century was still often no more than a paper acquisition, the product of politicians apportioning the continent between their respective countries in Berlin, the actual degree of contact between imperial power and new subjects could be negligible. From the very beginning of this imperial era, uneven impact was a central feature and it continued this way for some time. In settler societies, in the colonies proper, the impact was sharper and deeper than in, say, the remoter regions of Mali or upper Zaire, or the deserts of Somalia, or the dry savannah land of Upper Volta. Treasury parsimony was one major reason. Most civil servants and politicians were opposed to unwarranted adventurism (indeed, they enjoyed living 'in splendid isolation') and were suspicious of the overenthusiastic advocates of imperial involvement. To take a single example from many possible instances, a senior Foreign Office official in 1883, faced with formulating policy on the partition of Africa west of the Niger, minuted: 'Protectorates are unwelcome burdens, but in this case it is . . . a question between British protectorates, which would be unwelcome, and French protectorates, which would be fatal' (Davidson, 1964, p. 271). So they tried hard to release little money; where they did release some, they attempted to limit it to areas of potential economic growth and thus aggravated the already increasing inequalities in the continent. Investment in the settler colonies in particular, but by no means exclusively, went where economic returns were expected to be highest – for instance, to the transport routes needed to link the plantation sectors to metropolitan markets. The Treasury at the turn of the century was no more generous then than it is now.

Administrative caution, however, was always fighting a publicly expressed pro-imperialism. As the music-hall song of the time went:

> *We don't want to fight,*
> *But by Jingo if we do,*
> *We've got the men, we've got the guns,*
> *We've got the money too.*

It was difficult for politicians to be restrained in their actions. Gladstone felt strongly that Gordon had acted against his instructions in pushing down the Nile towards Khartoum in pursuit of the Mahdi and he hesitated to send an expeditionary force to assist him. Ultimately, he did and Sir Garnet Wolseley arrived fractionally too late to save Gordon from his death. Overnight Gladstone ceased to be called the GOM (the Grand Old Man); the initials were reversed and he was faced with cries of MOG (murderer of Gordon). This jingoism is thus reflected in the heroes of the age, in the popular literature of the day, in an unacknowledged seepage into the European consciousness that the imperial mission was noble and civilising. The leaders of educational thought now saw one of their functions as the preparation of young men to serve the empire. The strength of imperialism in the metropolitan countries lay as much in its moral defences, in the belief among the educated political classes that it was right and proper to extend to Africa law and order where there was supposed to have been none, Christianity where paganism was thought to have denied the people the one true religion, and a system of economic activity which was seen as a liberating and enriching force in a continent whose energies were trapped in the backwardness of an outdated system of production and exchange. It was arrogant; it was often unthinking; it was ignorant of Africa; it was probably racist; but it was real and deeply held.

Each addition to an empire, then, had its own special cause. In one case, it was acquired for later use as a pawn in international bargaining, in another for the expropriation of its gold or timber; yet others would have been acquired to defend trade routes to existing possessions, to deny them to a rival, to bale out people of substance at home, and so on. Once they had been acquired and controlled, a difficult process which will be described later, they still had to be justified. Some of these initial motives died; others weakened; economic interests and calculations came increasingly to be matters of extreme importance. But the precise form the consequences of imperial expansion took depended not only on the uneven nature of acquisition but also on the African responses to that intrusion.

Traditional Society

Whatever caused the scramble for Africa, it is generally accepted that the consequences for the peoples of Africa were profound. The enlargement of political scale represented by the instant creation of two score states, the introduction of more advanced technologies, the involvement of the Christian churches in educational and health developments, the spread of new economic systems and new ideas all made a major impact. Yet the revolutionary nature of this impact and the ultimate demise of pre-colonial practices and values can be too easily assumed. As the Nigerian historian Ajayi once wrote: 'Change is the essence of human history . . . Under colonialism, just as in the ages before, some institutions changed while others continued; and as always men and women had to adapt themselves and their institutions to change' (Ajayi, 1969, p. 498). Tropical Africa's experience of imperial rule was, except in some of the coastal enclaves, comparatively short in the perspective of a people's history, rarely extending beyond seventy years and frequently covering a shorter span. Jomo Kenyatta, for example, was old enough to recollect the first physical manifestation of the imperial presence and young enough to be Kenya's first Prime Minister and President; and Félix Houphouet-Boigny was 4 years old when his own people, the Baoulé, were finally subjugated by the French in 1909, yet in 1984 he was still President of the Ivory Coast. Such men grew up alongside the gradual extension of European empires, partly rooted in a traditional society which survived in many of its old forms, partly influenced by the new forces of the alien overrule. Tropical Africa thus has a dual heritage, for imperialism did not bury pre-colonial society like Mount Etna buried Pompeii.

To talk simply of pre-colonial society or traditional society is to torture the reality of the African past. Traditional society cannot be singular and universal; such a belief denies the African continent its very history, its changes, developments and varieties, or else it assumes that certain patterns of organisation and values are racially exclusive. African history is full of examples of migration, incorporation, dynastic rise and fall, changing trade patterns, and contact, both economic and intellectual, with Arab and European cultures. There are no unalterable, inbuilt sets of values which are uniquely, uniformly and eternally African. Traditional society, in that sense, never existed. Political organisations and values in Africa differed in time and space and the picture of traditional society which is conjured up by African myth-makers as much as by European commentators is, in reality, specific to a particular time, usually the last decade of the nineteenth century, and to a particular people. Nevertheless, there is a need for a concept such as traditional society, if only to provide a benchmark against which to measure the imperial impact and to trace the continuities of pre-colonial times. In using the phrase 'traditional society' here, what is being referred to is the variety of institutions and values which had developed among the African peoples by the last decade of the nineteenth century.

At the same time, it is important to distinguish sharply between the myth and the reality. The myth is an idealised, simplified, even purified version of reality; it is related to, but rarely if ever a precise mirror of, that reality. Such myths are important in contemporary politics and not only in the African continent (see Lipset, 1964). They can be potent sources of political support and many African leaders have attempted to appeal in part, at any rate, to their vision of the pre-colonial past in order to unite their people and to legitimise their governments' actions. Nyerere's writings in the 1960s were particularly full of references to traditional society; but he was not alone. African socialism, the African personality, *négritude*, Zambian humanism, even Nkrumah's conscientism, all have included ideas derived from politicians' pictures of days long gone. Such pictures, harking back to a golden age that did not really exist, are poor guides to reality, although they are indispensable for an understanding of many contemporary ideologies.

What, then, was the reality? The simple answer is that there was not one, but many. A starting point is to describe two diametrically opposed caricatures which have each had, in their time, influential adherents. One simplification was that Africa was endemically authoritarian; the chief spoke, so it was supposed, and the people obeyed. Such a perception was based upon convenience and also experience. It was convenient in two ways. On the one hand, it facilitated the making of treaties granting European rights over large tracts of land; if the chief's personal authority were assumed to extend over a large area and over many peoples, as Cecil Rhodes was happy to let Lobengula claim in the 1880s, the complication of making agreements with many political units was avoided. On the other hand, the actual administration of territory was significantly eased if there was an obvious, single authority through whom the imperial powers could operate. This was a peculiarly British perception, however, born perhaps of the ascriptive values which were still prevalent in ruling circles; in the more democratic culture of post-revolutionary France, chiefs did not enjoy the same instinctive respect they enjoyed in British circles. The caricature of chiefly dominance seemed, in addition, entirely congruent with many of the indigenous political structures met by whites in the late nineteenth century. The Zulu and Ndebele peoples in the South, the Baganda in Central Africa, and the Hausa in what is now Nigeria all gave the impression of states structured in this way. European visitors to Mengo, the capital of Buganda, in the 1860s would have instantly recognised an embryonic monarchical state distinctly reminiscent of the Europe of the Middle Ages described in their history books.

But this caricature was hopelessly inaccurate as a generalisation. Indeed, it misunderstood even those societies which seemed most authoritarian (Cobbing, 1977). More significantly yet, a great many African polities were not structured in a hierarchical fashion at all and had no dominating chief. Some, the chiefless or acephelous societies, had no single figure as their political head but divided responsibilities among several individuals; others, such as the Tiv or the Luo, had a pyramidal political structure composed of several chiefs of equal status and no 'chief chief' (see, generally, Colson, 1969). Even among the hierarchical societies, the chiefs, as among the Shona-speaking paramountcies of Zimbabwe, were essentially the legitimators of a group decision taken by the community's headmen and thus enjoyed a power more symbolic than real. The appreciation that African societies were more varied, and more democratic in their decision-making, than the early caricature had allowed for gave rise, in its turn, to a second, contrasting caricature.

This later view held that African societies, far from being authoritarian, were essentially democratic. Three aspects of this perception call for comment. First, there is an implicit assumption that every adult was involved in the decision-making; but this was just not true. In most societies women, although important in certain clearly defined spheres, participated hardly at all in public affairs; there were clear status differences which gave to certain people, headmen, elders, or particular age-sets, the responsibility for making decisions for the community. As Oginga Odinga recalled: 'In the village the authority of the elders was much respected; indeed, it was never challenged' (Odinga, 1967, p. 12). And Julius Nyerere, quoting approvingly Guy Clutton-Brock's observation that in traditional society the elders sit under the big tree and 'talk till they agree', unconsciously underlined the limited extent of participation (Nyerere, 1966, p. 104). While it is unquestionably true that in many polities wide consultation and discussion took place, it would be wrong to see this as a universal talk-in.

Second is the point exemplified again in Clutton-Brock's formulation that discussions tended to unanimity or, at least, an acceptance of a consensus. This notion is well expressed by the Ghanaian philosopher, Willi Abraham, when he was writing of the Akan society: 'The time to express one's eccentricity was in the period of deliberation. To persist in one's individual opinion, when this deviated from the public opinion deliberately arrived at and publicised, was a piece of malice' (Abraham, 1962, pp. 75–6). This view became influential in the years after independence when the single-party state was sometimes justified in terms of its traditional legitimacy; but this view, too, is something of an over-simplification. There was organised dissent, as branches of a family competed for office, or, as among the Tswana, rivals manipulated genealogies (Comaroff, 1974 – 5). On other occasions, a community would divide and the losing faction would exercise its right of 'nomadic self-determination' by moving off and establishing a new polity (Mazrui, 1967b).

Third is the implicit feeling that it is the community, rather than the individual, which is the most important social unit. Sekou Toure often spoke of the 'communaucratic' nature of traditional society, implying that individuals receded before the group and that their lives took meaning essentially from the role assigned to them within the group. 'The family members thought of themselves as one', Nyerere stated in September 1967, 'and all their language and behaviour emphasised that unity' (Nyerere, 1968, p. 337). The notion of the sovereign individual which lies at the very heart of liberal democratic theory is thus alien to the organic conception of society to which many African peoples adhered. Again, there is much truth in this perception; but there are too many counter-examples, too many innovatory individuals, to permit this caricature to enjoy the status of undisputed fact. Yet the concern for the family, defined to include a very wide range of relations, is very real. The co-operative practices of much of tropical Africa, in building houses, reaping crops, hunting, and so forth, have not died. Communal economic activity, however, did not mean that the fruit of the activity was distributed equally (Kopytoff, 1964). Nor were status differences thereby eliminated; on the contrary, the richer and more important members of a village were often expected to express their position publicly in the spirit of the proverb that 'a man who lives by the Niger does not wash himself in spittle'.

Vestiges of these three aspects of the democratic claim have survived into the present day. Studies of voting behaviour in rural villages, for instance, illustrate the process of public discussion within the village, the development of a consensus, and the communal decision to support one candidate rather than another. In those villages in the West Lake Region of Tanzania which had been least touched by the tentacles of imperial rule and its accompanying economic and social changes, 90 per cent or more of the voters would cast their ballots for one candidate (Hyden, 1968). In the Nigerian election of 1959, too, there were signs of communal decision-making. 'They say we shall vote for the NCNC', one voter said, while another told his interviewer: 'The only person we know in our constituency is Azikiwe and he is our candidate. We have all raised our hands for him' (Post, 1963, p. 377). But where the bonds which hold a traditional community together had weakened and the monied economy had permeated, the villagers were divided and individualism began to break down the community consensus.

The response to imperial rule also depended upon a people's general mode of dealing with the outside world and managing tensions. Kofe Busia, who was for a short time Prime Minister of Ghana, wrote a small book on democracy in Africa in which he reminded his readers that 'the contemporary problems of Africa must be seen in the context of Africa's own cultural heritage. That heritage is intensely and pervasively religious' (Busia, 1967, p. 1). In writing this, he was drawing attention to the fact that behaviour in many societies was dictated by custom, the basis of which was the wish to keep on good terms with ancestors, whose spirits were thought to be able to influence the contemporary world. Among people as distinct as the Acholi of Uganda and the Malagasy the imagery of life was that of the pumpkin tree, in which the roots (the past), the trunk (the present) and the branches (the future) were inextricably intertwined. Damage to any one part would destroy the whole. Just as current behaviour was validated by appeal to traditional norms, so current events were explained by reference to the intervention of others, often the spirits of dead members of the family. Thus there was a tendency to externalise causation, to explain individual or communal disasters on the failure to follow the procedures and behaviour patterns established by past generations. No society was so wholly self-contained that it excluded innovation; but many societies were held together by a set of beliefs antithetical to widespread innovation. There was, in other words, a continuum stretching from societies where a very high proportion of actions was validated by reference to immemorial norms, the consummatory societies, to societies where there was much greater leeway for innovation, the instrumental societies (Apter, 1965).

There are, therefore, two dimensions to take into account when considering African responses to imperial rule. The first is the organisational structure; the second is the orientation of values.

There are thus six ideal types of African polity and they can be conceptualised as occupying particular locations in space bounded, on one side, by a continuum of values from consummatory to instrumental and, on the other, by a hierarchy of political structures (Apter, 1965). These are, of course, ideal types and the fact that the consummatory – instrumental axis is, in reality, a continuum means that locating individual peoples on this map is a complicated task. Its utility lies in the suggestive interpretation it provides to explain the different responses to the European intrusion by various African peoples. The more consummatory and less hierarchically organised a society, the more likelihood there was for repudiation to be chosen as the response. The more instrumental and hierarchically organised a society, the more likely that collaboration with the Europeans would be chosen.

But conceptualising traditional society in this way does not explain the differences between African peoples or the essential values themselves. Ideas and values do not appear instantly out of a vacuum; they grow up from within a society. Whether they can be transmitted from generation to generation despite changes in the environment of a society is a debated point. Is socialism, as Nyerere claimed, an 'attitude of mind' and thus theoretically transmittable through the process of socialisation (Nyerere, 1966, p. 162)? Certainly, traditional wisdom is transmitted through the generations, linguistically through the use of proverbs and illustrative stories, practically through the education provided to children by their mothers. The role of women, the proper respect for relations of different generations, the norms of marriage, and so forth, have survived the passage of time, to a surprising degree unscathed by the massive changes in the political and economic world of which the rural people have become part. What has developed is a syncretic response, a borrowing from the new alongside the retention of the old, not an inevitable transition from the 'traditional' to the 'modern'.

The democratic and socialist aspects of traditional society, which politicians besides Nyerere have attempted to conjure up, developed out of necessity. Most of Africa provided a hostile physical environment in which to live. Poor soil, erratic rainfall, disease and pestilence, not to mention competition between peoples for land and cattle, meant that survival could never be taken for granted. Co-operation was essential, equality the inevitable result of poverty. Where peoples had settled and had managed to create a surplus, then stratification could take place (Goody, 1971). Among the interlacustrine Bantu, for example, the courts of the kings could only be supported because the economy produced enough to absolve the kings and their agents from occupying themselves fully in the productive process. The nomadic peoples in the most hostile environment, by contrast, retained a very egalitarian and unhierarchical form of political organisation. The imperial intermission radically altered the whole environment in which life was lived. The tradition of nomadic self-determination which defused internal quarrels was limited by the defiantly immobile boundaries established by the European powers in the 1880s; the Pax Britannica, and its French and Belgian equivalents, limited the threats from neighbouring peoples; the exchange economy and the growth of cash crops fundamentally altered the basis of the economic system. Co-operation became less essential and poverty less widespread. The very basis of the old values was being eroded.

The erosion of values has not meant their extinction. The essential point about the African continent is its syncretic nature; alongside the procedures and supporting assumptions of modern organisations there remain the beliefs and priorities of an earlier day. The extended family, for instance, which in times of disaster provided a safety net for the unfortunate, remains an important ingredient in the contemporary political environment. Urbanisation increased its significance; as migrants entered an alien and often frightening milieu, they sought out a relation to provide support and guidance in the difficult process of integrating into the city environment. The first nationwide political parties were agglomerations of clan and tribal unions, which had been established on the basis of familial and regional links. At another level, however, the extended family has been a problematic factor. Villagers had often clubbed together to provide the money to educate one of their sons and they looked upon this sacrifice as a form of investment. The returning graduate, perhaps posted to a high bureaucratic position in the local administration, was expected not only to use his good fortune to assist his extended family but also to reward his village by allocating benefits and resources to it. The steady stream of family beating a path to a minister's door seeking favours is a problem all politicians have to face. Their modernised vision of the nationally oriented and rational public servant clashes with their familial links so strongly inculcated in them through their socialisation in the village.

The present and the past are thus indissolubly tied. At one level, the search for uniquely African structures which the acquisition of political independence encouraged turned political ideologues to the pre-colonial era and to a vision of the past which was often more idyllic than the reality. At another level, the values of the past, shifting slowly in the face of major alterations in the objective conditions and necessities of contemporary rural life, survived in part. The vast majority of Africans still live in the countryside; the vast majority of mothers, the chief agents of socialisation, remain illiterate and tied to the smallholding on which they make a precarious living. Old ideas die hard. In times of stress, people revert to the practices and ideals with which they were brought up. It is no accident that in the vast sprawling cities of Africa, where so many inhabitants are still unconfident migrants, there has been a growing tendency to turn to the old sources of explanation and comfort, the spirit media, witch doctors and diviners. As Ajayi implied, Africa is still in the process of adaptation.

Occupation and Pacification

Before the massive distribution of land that the Berlin Conference and other subsequent conferences allocated to the European states, some of the continent had already passed under the control of imperial powers. Apart from the true colonisation at the Northern and Southern extremities, two methods were generally employed. The simpler, and preferred, method was to sign treaties with African political leaders, so that an element of voluntarism underpinned the imperial relationship. Sometimes these arrangements were entered into with a full understanding of the political consequences; more often, however, the intricacies of the agreements were barely comprehended and the extent to which political autonomy had been relinquished was frequently unrealised. The second method, so much messier and more expensive, was to invoke the military strength of the imperial power to force recalcitrant African peoples into a subordinate position. The messes of many regiments in the British army are decorated with the insignia of campaigns fought to win, or preserve, a part of the African continent for the monarch's domains. The few defeats, and there were some, are less publicly recalled. In the last analysis, the much more advanced technology of the European powers proved ultimately too powerful against those movements which challenged imperial overrule.

The conferences at the end of the century, however, bestowed upon European powers through their own self-granted authority massive tracts of land in which their agents had negotiated no treaties nor subdued by force of arms the local inhabitants. To lay claim to territory is not to occupy it. The European powers did not instantly advance into the interior of the African continent with their national flags aloft and their bayonets at the ready. Africa was too big, the terrain too harsh, European treasuries too limited; Africa was gathered into the administrative bosom of its imperial masters more stealthily and over a longer period of time. The Nigerian novelist, Chinua Achebe, caught this process exactly in his earliest novel, *Things Fall Apart*. 'The white man is very clever', his hero Okonkwo says. 'He came quietly and peaceably with his religion. We were amused at his foolishness and allowed him to stay. Now he has won our brothers, and our clan can no longer act as one. He has put a knife on the things that held us together and we have fallen apart' (Achebe, 1964, p. 160). Interestingly, the very same sentiment was expressed on the other side of the continent by an old man recalling the 1890s. 'We saw you come with your wagons', he told a white official, 'and horses and rifles. We said to each other: "They have come to buy gold, or it may be to hunt elephant; they will go again." When we saw that you continued to remain in the country and were troubling us with your laws, we began to talk and to plot' (Hodder-Williams, 1977, p. 44).

The European presence was not always heralded by political or military servants of the metropolitan countries. Traders and missionaries often preceded formal administration and the tradition of hospitality so widespread in the continent frequently permitted such outriders of European expansion to establish roots in the rural areas. The very slowness of administrative control served to mask the reality of imperial overrule and Africans in many instances only came to realise that the individual impermanence of itinerant missionaries, traders and prospectors had given way to the communal permanence of white overrule when it was almost too late to respond effectively. In choosing how to respond – and the imperial intrusion was the catalyst which demanded some response, if only acquiescence – the African peoples exemplified their variety and autonomy by favouring different courses of action. The precise response depended upon a range of factors. One was closely linked to the fundamental values of their society. It is noticeable that consummatory societies, especially acephelous ones, tended to turn quickly to violent opposition; the threat to their self-contained, internally consistent and intensely spiritual societies was immediately evident and the populist nature of their political organisations provided no chiefly buffer between them and the newcomers. Among the more instrumental societies, especially the hierarchically organised ones, the readiness to collaborate was more frequent (Apter, 1965).

Apter's attempt to link African responses to the values of the various polities is suggestive, but there are fundamental problems with it. The notion of instrumental is defined almost necessarily to mean a willingness to incorporate aspects of the European offering, so that the link is not causative but tautological; to reject European offerings is itself part of the definition of non-instrumental. There is, as it happens, another way to look at the differential response, without altogether jettisoning the cultural explanation. The African societies of the late nineteenth century had their own politics, both domestic and foreign, and the European presence, itself appearing in a range of guises from Christian catechist to red-coated soldier, was evaluated rationally to see whether it might be harnessed to local needs, opposed as a fundamental attack on cherished values and power, or acquiesced in as the only practical option open. In other words, the precise response was a function of the African politics of the time.

This can be illustrated by examining one small part of Zimbabwe in the 1890s. The formal occupation of Mashonaland was not followed with the immediate infusion of white settlers on to the land; for most Africans, the first sign of the new situation was the appearance of a lone trader or transport rider, the passing through of a prospector, the arrival of a Christian catechist. Among the Nhowe at this time there were deep internal divisions and their chief saw the black catechist who asked to stay close to his village as a possible ally in the political struggle of the time. The catechist, and his white superiors, seemed to have skills and powers which could usefully be harnessed to his own interests. Close by the Nhowe, the people of Nengubo felt themselves under great physical pressure from two competing paramountcies on either side of their territory. To their leaders the black catechist and his white superiors seemed to offer some possible protection in a position of some tension. Both the Nhowe and the Nengubo people accepted the catechists into their polities, although there were doubting voices in both societies. After a few years, however, the reality of colonisation had become clearer and a series of natural disasters prompted the Africans into formulating a response to the realisation that their independence had been surreptitiously taken away and to the recent natural catastrophes. Among the Nhowe, the anti-chief faction continued its opposition to the catechist and blamed his presence for the misfortunes befalling the people; after prolonged and bitter debate, it proved victorious and the Nhowe paramountcy became a major centre of the struggle against the Rhodesian settlers in the war of 1896 – 7. In Nengubo, by contrast, although there was also a bitter debate about the catechist (and a small fraction of the inhabitants expressed their position by killing him), the chief and the majority of his people remained neutral in the war, seeing their own preservation and position being best served by not antagonising the white forces. So they did not join the uprising (Hodder-Williams, 1977).

There were, then, broadly three types of response. The first was a firm rejection of the newcomers in a context of a perceived competition for power. Nowhere is this rejection more exquisitely expressed than by the Yao chief, Macemba, writing in 1890 in Swahili to Herman von Wissman, the German who had ordered him to submit.

> I have listened to your words [Macemba wrote] but can find no reason why I should obey you − I would rather die first. I have no relations with you and cannot bring it to my mind that you have given me so much as a *pesa* [a fraction of a rupee] or the quarter of a *pesa* or a needle or a thread. I look for some reason why I should obey you and find not the smallest. If it should be friendship that you desire, then I am ready for it, today and always; but to be your subject, that I cannot be . . . If it should be war you desire, then I am ready, but never to be your subject . . . I do not fall at your feet, for you are God's creature just as I am . . . I am sultan here in my land. You are sultan there in yours. Yet listen, I do not say to you that you should obey me; for I know that you are a free man . . . As for me, I will not come to you and, if you are strong enough, then come and fetch me. (Davidson, 1964, p. 363)

Von Wissman was strong enough. Indeed, whenever there was a direct clash of this kind, which occurred when the European presence was clearly seen as a threat to an African state's power and position, the ensuing fight was one-sided. Often, the powerful states with their local dominance were smashed; on other occasions, their very resistance persuaded the European conquerors to treat them with some magnanimity. To reject the imperialists, therefore, while never successful ultimately, sometimes resulted in the retention of considerable autonomy; sometimes, however, it humbled a formerly powerful people.

The second response has been categorised as a negative retort, a refusal to accede to the demands of the imperial authorities, without the conscious and willing confrontation represented by Macemba. Nomadic societies, in particular, were likely to move off outside the reach of the imperial arm, snipe at its agents, and generally obstruct the extension of ordered administration. They rarely sought out a confrontation, but they involved many troops for many years as they refused to come willingly within the ambience of the European empires. In 1915, for instance, there were thirty armed operations in the Belgian Congo alone. Neither the French nor the British had completed the task of pacification by the end of the First World War. Indeed, British troops were still occupied in carrying out punitive expeditions in the Sudan in 1929 against the consummatory, nomadic Nuer. An attempt to use aeroplanes in December 1927 to overawe the prophet Guek Ngundeng and his followers failed. Thus, a generation after a bureaucratic administration had provided the framework for the peaceful expansion of education and economic activity in some parts of Africa, other areas were still ravaged by small wars. The consequence was to disadvantage still further these recalcitrant people. Inhabiting remote and inhospitable lands, lacking the modern skills of reading, writing and trading, they found themselves at independence unable to compete with their fellow Africans in the new political situation of the 1960s, where these modern abilities mattered so much. It was no consolation to be praised for the valour of past opposition to the imperial power; that gained no material benefits in the 1960s.

Resistance of these kinds, Henri Brunschwig has shown, was a minority response (Brunschwig, 1974). Most African societies, after an initial period of antagonism perhaps, collaborated with the European powers (Robinson 1972). Some embraced the new opportunities willingly; others did so as the lesser of two evils. Certainly, it soon became clear to most Africans that the rewards for collaboration were better than the consequences of resistance. This is graphically illustrated by the fate of two powerful chiefs in Uganda. The kingdom of Bunyoro-Kitara was an expanding, thrusting state at the end of the nineteenth century and its king saw the European intruders as a threat to his hegemony and challenged them. The kingdom of Buganda, by contrast, was being weakened by internal dissension. The British, guided by Lord Lugard, lent their support to the Protestant faction in Buganda, established a new king, or kabaka, in the land, and backed this new political organisation in its battle with the kingdom of Bunyoro. The kabaka of Buganda was given a baronetcy and the Baganda came to dominate Uganda's political and economic life. The omukama of Bunyoro, as was Archbishop Makarios also fifty years later, was exiled to the Seychelles, where he died, and some of the territory claimed by the Banyoro was firmly allocated to the Baganda. The rewards of collaboration could not be clearer.

Conclusion

The prevailing impression of this chapter should be variety. The mixed motives for white involvement in Africa, the variety of societies with which contact was made, the consequent variations in the processes of incorporation into the European empires, and the far from uniform response on the part of Africans to this incorporation, all had an impact on later generations. It should not be thought, however, that these aspects of the contact between continents need no further examination. The motives for imperial expansion will clearly colour the intentions of decolonisation; but new motives, and the re-ordering of the importance of old ones, will be as significant. The individuality of societies will continue to explain some of the differential responses to the accompaniments of imperial rule but the very individuality of societies, and of their members, means that new perceptions, new needs, new interests develop over time. While the differences in the speed and extent of incorporation had profound consequences for the future, this initial phase did not entirely lock societies into predetermined development paths.

Nevertheless, despite the fact that the patterns of interaction established at the beginning of the century did alter in the following decades, there is little doubt that these early years established three conditions of long-term significance. First, the involvement of Europe in Africa, whatever the motives may have been, introduced an exchange economy and new economic opportunities into the continent. Private property, trading for profit and the accumulation of capital were not unknown aspects of African history, but the encouragement to these developments was now great. In so far as the phrase has any precise meaning, Africa was firmly locked into a capitalist path of development. Secondly, the creation of states incomparably larger than most polities of the 1890s altered the political forum and thus the appropriate structures and institutions through which political disagreements were mediated. The problems arising from 'unnatural' units spanning many peoples under the overarching authority of an alien power were entirely new and prompted new African organisations and ideas which reached their apogee in the years of nationalist opposition to imperial rule. Thirdly, the uneven incorporation produced an uneven pattern of development and ultimately cumulative inequality. It is generally the case that those peoples most deeply caught up in the exchange economy, most readily devoted to schooling and modern education, and most widely involved in the bureaucratic structures of the imperial state, tended to dominate the political and economic spheres of their states in the initial years of independence. In some states, they retained their advantaged position; in others, a resentful backlash swept them from power. Whatever the ultimate resolution, the seeds of differentiation which fuelled political competition had been sown by 1914, and in a soil where such differentiation was likely to grow.

2   The Imperial Intermission

Most of tropical Africa was ruled by European powers for less than a century. But in that time massive changes took place in the continent, as indeed they did in most of the rest of the world. These changes established the environment for the politics of the new states at independence. The methods by which the metropolitan powers administered their possessions themselves created identities and loyalties as well as a particular experience of government; these were realities with which the successor governments had to deal. The economic transformation of the continent produced new interests and new classes, greater inequalities, as well as richer resources available to those who inherited the power of the state. Underpinning the imperial occupation were a set of ideas, some explicit, some implicit, which coloured the priorities and the perceptions of reality entertained by Africans. Thus, in Africa as in every other part of the globe at every time in history, political actors behaved not as individuals uncontaminated by a past and enjoying the absolute liberty of a totally free choice, but as human beings, limited by the constraints of what was possible as well as by the constraints derived from the values and conceptions of each individual's unique experience.

The imperial intermission implies two things. It draws obvious attention to the impact of the years of imperial rule, but it also assumes an element of continuity, a degree of initiative and autonomy, on the part of those subject to foreign rule. This inevitably means that there will be variations between countries and within countries just as it also asserts a variety of responses to imperialism, chosen by, rather than imposed upon, Africans. For all its undoubted importance, imperial rule did not leave behind an Africa in the image of Europe, or even an Africa such as Europeans might have hoped to create. There is much of

Europe in Africa; but there is a good deal of Africa still in Africa too.

Control

Occupation and pacification were only the start of imperial rule; control and administration had to follow. Looking back at the 1920s and the 1930s, it is difficult to escape a certain surprise at the general ease with which the imperial powers retained control over their tropical African possessions. The ratio of administrators to subjects in the 1930s was very high: 1:19,000 in settler Kenya, 1:27,000 in French West Africa, 1:35,000 in the Belgian Congo, and 1:54,000 in British Nigeria. It was indeed, a thin white line (Kirk-Greene, 1980). These white administrators were interlopers in an alien world, integrated very little with the communities amongst whom they lived, and confidently asserted their authority over the indigenous inhabitants of the continent. From the perspective of the 1980s, it seems inconceivable that such arrogant domination, inegalitarian and profoundly undemocratic as it was, could be tolerated. For some Africans, of course, it was not; yet, for the most part, the new order was not overtly challenged. When the protonationalist, Harry Thuku, did issue a ringing challenge to the whole imperial system in Nairobi in 1922, his call for widespread opposition to the system itself generated little support. Part of the reason for this lay in the very facts that the unspoken assumptions of the 1980s were not the unspoken assumptions of the 1920s and 1930s and that the ability of the imperial authorities to enforce their writ remained, so long as there was no co-ordinated challenge to it, supreme. But fear of reprisal, although certainly part of the story, was not all.

There are three ways of looking at this, which bear a certain similarity to Max Weber's three types of legitimate authority. The first administrators and missionaries were, as they had to be, self-confident men, confident not only in the rightness of their actions but in their ability to control their new environment. It was Pandit Nehru who once said that the British Empire largely rested on a confidence trick; 'the calm assurance of always being right', so noticeable among whites in Africa, produced a caste of thought among subjects which for a long time accepted as real the European assumption of superiority. Whites had a technical competence and a capacity to survive which made a profound impact; local religious taboos and rules apparently could not touch them. As one historian of Tanzania has written, the representatives of the stronger outside power 'were first considered as themselves strangers with charismatic power, so that early administrative measures were accepted with little resistance' (Austen, 1968, p. 41). Consummatory societies, more impressed by magical powers and the ability to defy the cosmic world, were probably more likely to feel this way.

A second dimension is to observe that in some places the imperial powers took to themselves the legitimacy of the existing rulers. This was a common practice in the British Empire; it is found in the sheikdoms of the Persian Gulf, the princely Indian states, in Egypt, in Northern Nigeria, in Zanzibar, among other places. All that was required in these instances was the acquiescence of the ruling classes and demands on them that did not materially diminish their power and status. Where there were hierarchically organised states, the existence of imperial rule could be largely disguised. In these societies, whether the collaborators were old ruling classes, as in Nigeria, or a new élite assisted into traditional positions of authority, as in Southern Uganda, it helped if the 'premise of inequality' applied (Maquet, 1961). The anthropologist, Evans-Pritchard, noted that the Azande, where the premise of inequality held, treated him as a superior; among the Nuer, where such a premise did not exist, he was treated as an equal. Provided the intermediaries retained a popular following, they effectively transferred their own legitimacy to the imperial power. It was only in the 1940s and 1950s, when the Ganda chiefs lost popular support in Buganda, that violence flared up and police stations, for the first time, were located there. Where inequality had been traditionally sanctioned, a new form of inequality was not necessarily seen as oppressive. These systems of inequality usually involved the superordinate groups in obligations – to defend their subjects, adjudicate disputes, distribute land, look after the general welfare. When these obligations ceased to be fulfilled satisfactorily, the imperial powers faced problems.

The practice of ruling through existing political leaders was peculiarly British. Most of the other imperial powers administered their possessions more directly and this needed a much more obvious expression of power. Conquest, however, can produce its own legitimacy. The African continent had seen plenty of examples of strong political groupings subjugating weaker ones and incorporating the defeated into the enhanced state system of the victors. The right to rule, therefore, in the short run could be conferred through conquest. However, where incorporation and integration did not take place and the superordinate – subordinate relationship between peoples became fixed, tensions developed which ultimately burst out in violent opposition to the inflexibility of the unequal system. This ultimately happened in Ruanda and Burundi between the dominant Tutsi and their Hutu subjects. More obviously, it happened in those territories where white victors lost their earlier legitimacy through their refusal to integrate their defeated subjects into a new political and social order. Race remained an unyielding classification which structured society, the economy and the political process.

In the third place, time itself came to give imperial rule a certain legitimacy. The 'inertia of loyalty', the acceptance as one decade slipped into the next that the new system had come to stay, the growth of vested interests who had gained in power and wealth as a result of imperial rule, and the realisation that imperial rule had its beneficial side, all played their part. There were often positive reasons for collaborating with the imperial powers and their agents from the outset, since advantages in the short run frequently accrued to those who signed up the powerful newcomers to assist them in their own political struggles (R. Robinson, 1972). The Pax Britannica was very real and it freed men in many societies to cultivate more or involve themselves in trade, thus providing opportunities for the acquisition of items which added a little at least to the comfort of living. Although the best educated colonial administrators in the British Empire went to India (the Colonial Secretary, Joseph Chamberlain, noted at the turn of the century that 'we take inferior men for West Africa and they are not good enough for other colonies'), the vast majority of district commissioners and district officers were extremely competent, fair, and usually genuinely interested in and concerned for 'their' people (Allen, ed., 1979). They were paternalistic and they assumed a natural superiority; but they also established an order which was reliable and in many ways beneficent. As the years passed and new generations were born and grew up, the only reality that many Africans knew came to be imperial rule. The effect of a gradual penetration was virtually to eliminate issues round which oppositions could rapidly gather. The history of the 1930s for most Africans was the routine of living, the labour of fetching water, growing crops and preparing food alongside the social continuities associated with the fundamentally important issues of birth, marriage and death. Where imperial rule was not directly oppressive – and this covered a very high propor- tion of the continent – the pressures which lead to revolt were absent. Africans, in the same way as underprivileged peoples throughout mankind's history, learned to live with the world in which they found themselves. It may have been a hard life, as it had been before, but it was the only life they knew.

There is another way in which this meeting of ruler and subject has been analysed, a conception which has angered many commentators but which is usefully provocative none the less. Octave Mannoni, a French psychologist of distinctly Freudian sympathies, abstracted from his examination of Mad- agascar what he thought was a theory of general applicability (Mannoni, 1964). He argued that the imperial situation wit- nessed a meeting of two personalities. The Malagasy's per- sonality was essentially dependent, in that the basic principle underlying behaviour was the need to conform to the rules and norms established by past generations rather than to innovate and bend the world to personal wishes. Interpersonal relations, with the living and the dead, were at the core of behaviour so that respect for the truth could on occasions be replaced by considerations of what the person addressed would like to hear. The European's personality was marked by an inferiority com- plex, born of a competitive society which stressed failures and inadequacies and a vision of a world in which a man could do without both the help and the authority of others. Colonialists were extreme versions of this type, makers rather than accep- tors of relationships. On contact, Mannoni argued, each met the psychological need of the other. The dependent Malagasy found a powerful figure on whom he could depend in a hostile world and who replaced the less effective ancestral spirits; the colonialist found pliant subjects on whom he could work out his inferiority complex. But in time these bonds began to weaken; the Malagasy increasingly found that the white colonialists did not protect and patronise them as the powerful figure of their imagination was supposed to do, while the colonialists became increasingly irritated by their clients' importunities and by a dependency which valued suppleness to the truth and which ignored that very independence of action which whites valued so highly. In time the tensions became too great; the Malagasy felt a deep sense of abandonment, of being let down and rejected by the powerful patron, and turned to violence. In 1947 there was a major uprising in Madagascar against French imperial power. Mannoni's paradigm is not a theory of general applicability and, by its very nature, is more apposite for consummatory societies than others. But it does point both to three stages in the development of relations between imperial rulers and their subjects, which scholars of quite different perceptions share, and also to the paramount significance of the intensity of imperial rule.

The first stage covered the process of incorporation which has already been described. In some parts of the continent, this was smoothly achieved through the process of collaboration; in others, protest was overcome by superior military force. The focus of these relations, however, whether peaceful or violent, was essentially parochial; indeed, the inability of African societies to enlarge their scale of operations by combining forces with neighbouring political units offered imperial troops the unrivalled opportunity to pick off communities one by one. There were occasions – the Maji-Maji uprising in Tanganyika from 1905 to 1907 and the Shona uprisings in Southern Rhodesia from 1896 to 1897 are the classic examples – when the focus of participants was wider than their immediate communities, but these were extremely rare. The communicators between imperial power and the African peasantry were few; the scale of societies was small, their horizons narrow and their political focus diffuse (Lonsdale, 1968).

The second stage is marked by three developments: the increasing acceptance of imperial overrule as the basic order of things; the widening of focus among many Africans; and the establishment of organisations aimed at criticising and adjusting the political system of imperial rule without actually challenging its foundations. In this period a more intensive administration and the fruits of missionary education increased the points of contact between ruler and ruled and enlarged the channels of communication. The political focus now became district-wide as the politically aware sought to develop organisations to express their disquiets and to cope with the process of industrialisation; essentially they sought to use what the imperial powers had brought, but at the same time to disengage from central control by building up the authority and power of the local councils. What anti-government feelings there were became expressed by taking up positions on local issues. The dominant development in this second phase is the willingness to operate within the structures laid down by the imperial powers, whether the local councils of the British Empire or the wider canvas of the French.

The experiences gained during these years coloured expectations and behaviour after independence. Imperial rule was bureaucratic, rather than political; it was authoritarian, rather than participant; it was centralist, rather than devolved. Above all, there was no doubt where power lay; it lay firmly with the imperial authorities. There may have been only a thin white line of administrators; but there was a line of steel behind them to back them if, and when, it was necessary. The bluff was rarely called; but the readiness of the imperial authorities to use their powers, whether legislative ones permitting detentions and limiting political protest, or the physical one of troop involvement, was rarely called into doubt. Thus, when independence came, the inheritance which the new leaders enjoyed was an essentially authoritarian one in which the compromises and negotiations central to the bargaining traditions of Anglo-Saxon democracy were absent. The emphasis on central control, whether of the party or the state, became a central feature of the post-imperial world, and it was buttressed by the politics of the third period, which covers the transition from imperial overrule to sovereign political independence. This nationalist phase, to which attention will be given later, represented an expansion of the points of contact, a widening of the focus and a broader base to political movements.

The Administrative Heritage

One of the first problems to face the imperial powers was the formulation of a general policy to guide administrators. Two contrasting ideals emerged. The philosophy of indirect rule, which is associated closely with the name of Lord Lugard, became dominant in British imperial thinking between the two world wars. It held that the most appropriate way to administer the newly acquired territories was to operate through existing political authorities rather than to act directly upon the people; in this way, the impact of imperial rule was less obvious to ordinary Africans and much of the day-to-day political activity of the rural areas was left apparently undisturbed. This philosophy had a threefold origin: the parsimony of the British Treasury, which necessitated a cheap method of administration; a genuine belief in the sanctity of local institutions and a fear of the social and political ills which might follow their decay; and, finally, Lord Lugard's own experience in Northern Nigeria where easily discernible political rulers had been the obvious tools for his administration (Perham, 1960; Kirk-Greene, 1966).

The philosophy of direct rule, by contrast, minimised the importance of existing political organisations. The paradigm for this essentially French conception was a bureaucratic state in which officials were appointed at every level, each level being related in a hierarchical pattern to the level above it and ultimately to the imperial government itself. There were domestic reasons for such a preference. The French state was a centralised, bureaucratic state in which the *préfets* in *départements* were powerful agents of the central government; the French motives for imperial expansion were more positive than the British and thus more easily attracted government funds; and there was not in France the tradition, and approval, of local government autonomy. Thus, the governors-general of French West Africa and French Equatorial Africa, for instance, who were themselves subject to control from Paris, were the heads of centralised hierarchies descending through the governors of the individual territories, through the appointed *commandant de cercle* and *chef de subdivision* (roughly equivalent to the district commissioner and district officer in the British Empire), to the appointed *chef de canton* and *chef de village*, whose authority depended not upon his standing in the local political system but upon his efficiency as a tax collector. Orders thus went down the line of command and there was little feedback, or room for initiative, through political channels to which villagers had access.

This dichotomy, however, is rather neater than the reality. Although there are exceptions – and Northern Nigeria in the 1930s is probably the most remarkable – the idea that officials merely advised the chief and interfered no further in the politics of the chiefdom is a fiction. In systems of so-called indirect rule, there was actually plenty of direct involvement and the chiefs soon came to realise that their freedom of action was sharply curtailed. Since much of Africa did not have ready-made chiefly hierarchies through which to operate, the imperial authorities had to create chiefs and establish a traditional political system which was not traditional at all. In short, the exigencies of the time dictated a much more pragmatic policy than the ideal theory allowed. The great observer of imperial matters, Lord Hailey, noted this forty years ago. 'The use of these terms', he wrote in 1942, 'conveys the erroneous impression that there are two opposing systems of rule. This is not the case . . . All African administrations are dependent to a greater or lesser extent on the use of native authorities as agencies of local rule' (Hailey [1942] 1979, p. 13).

In those parts of Africa where there were no distinctly political authorities through which to operate, the imperial powers had to create them from scratch. In some cases, they merely appointed men they knew, interpreters or policemen, who had no traditional status in the communities they were called to represent and administer; in others, as Sir Donald Cameron's autobiography shows, they took great care to select men who were respected for one reason or another in the locality (Cameron, 1939, pp. 33–6, 75–118). Nevertheless, the chiefs so created owed their power and often their status to their imperial masters and became, in effect, paid civil servants.

Their authority among the villagers subordinate to them rested not on any traditional legitimacy, for there had been no chief before, but on the support and power of the European rulers.

In those states where there were chiefly hierarchies, the traditional legitimacy of the chiefs' instruction also became called in question. The imperial concern for law and order soon gave way to an interest in agricultural development, in labour recruiting and collection of taxes. The simple indirect rule model assumed that the chiefs would instruct their people to co-operate and there would then be co-operation. But chiefs virtually everywhere owed their position to their ability to represent a consensus among their people. Their position, therefore, as both spokesmen for their people and administrators for the imperial authorities, bred acute tensions (Fallers, 1955). A classic instance of this occurred in Southern Rhodesia in the 1950s (Holleman, 1969). The Native Land Husbandry Act had been promulgated to affect fundamentally the pattern of rural agriculture, by rationalising land holdings, establishing standards of land use and increasing the productivity of the peasant farming areas. It was bitterly resented by the peasants themselves. Chief Mangwende, as was required of a Shona chief, conveyed the views of his people to the government and refused to implement the Act; the district commissioner performed his duty as a civil servant and insisted that Mangwende should do his duties as a public servant. In the deadlock, naked power prevailed; Mangwende was deposed by the Southern Rhodesian government and another man, more malleable, was installed in his place. The subsequent histories of the men involved are interesting. The district commissioner rose to be chief native commissioner, adviser to the Smith administration in its negotiations with Britain after 1965, a member of the commission which drew up the racially exclusive Constitution of 1969, and ultimately a senator in the years preceding Zimbabwe's independence. The deposed chief Mangwende entered nationalist politics. Chief Mangwende's replacement was appointed by Smith to the Council of Chiefs and was made a junior minister, only to be swept away when majority rule came to the country. Whether indirect rule or direct rule dominated the philosophy of the administration, problems of divided loyalty and conflicting rules could, and increasingly did, occur.

For all the talk of preserving local structures and operating through traditional organisations, major decisions were indisputably taken at the centre. This is a matter of scale. Inevitably, traditional authorities retained jurisdiction over only a part of the territory so that, if there were to be any colony-wide uniformity of policy, they had to accept the 'advice' of the district commissioner or be deposed. After the Second World War, the tensions increased as 'the second colonial occupation' (to use Low and Lonsdale's words) sought to develop actively the economies of the European powers' possessions and thus demanded more and more regulations affecting an ever-widening range of peasant activities (Low and Lonsdale, 1976). The Colonial Development and Welfare Acts of 1945 and 1949, and similar initiatives in France, provided the legislative framework for redressing some of the neglect from which most of the imperial possessions had suffered economically. But this positive imperialism put an impossible strain on administrative structures. The difficulty inherent in the whole philosophy of indirect rule is well caught by an official in Uganda who observed that the right way to proceed was 'by the Administration strengthening the authority of the king with his people while at the same time acquiring, by political conduct on the part of its representative, a controlling influence over the king' (Low, 1964, p. 242). It is doubtful whether, in the long run, squaring this particular circle was ever feasible.

The territorial reach of the imperial power was very uneven. Some areas came under quite close supervision, experienced wage labour in the first decade of the century, had early contact with missionaries and education. Others, however, were barely touched by imperial rule. According to Andrew Cohen, a distinguished Colonial Office civil servant and Governor of Uganda, the Colonial Office of the 1930s still insisted more on 'safeguarding African society than on helping Africans to develop and stimulating the inertia which tended to prevail among the people in many parts of Africa' (Cohen, 1959, p. 18). This concern, dubbed by its critics the 'woad' policy, had many important adherents. The full impact of imperial rule in most of the non-settler territories thus came comparatively late and affected the indigenous way of life most obviously in the 1940s and 1950s. This goes a long way to explain why imperial rule was largely accepted between the two world wars; its impact was slight. It also helps to explain why the nationalist movements gained momentum and popularity after the Second World War, when the peasantry became acutely aware of their subject status.

The policy of indirect rule, with its tendency to emphasise district administration and district identity, not only hindered the growth of national loyalties; it positively enhanced and, in some cases, created a local and often linguistically distinct identity. By establishing political boundaries and local government units to coincide as far as possible with linguistic units, the British in fact fostered that sense of cultural unity which lies at the root of tribalism. The very incorporation of many independent societies into a new and vastly enlarged state created a more self-conscious realisation of differences and thus encouraged a heightened sense of local community, even to the extent of developing tribal solidarities where there had been little before. This process of self-conscious differentiation occurred in French possessions as well for the same reason. But in the British territories the awareness of cultural specificity was exaggerated by the stress laid on the local, and culturally homogeneous, unit.

The steady erosion of traditional legitimacy, either through the clarification of the contradiction inherent in the whole philosophy of indirect rule or through the realisation that appointed chiefs were essentially agents of the imperial government, demanded of the territorial authorities political innovations. The progressive introduction of councils with elected elements altered further the basic institutions of government, so that at independence there was no tradition of settled administration for the successor governments to continue. Here Africa stands in stark contrast to India. The uninterrupted constitutional and administrative heritage of India is as old as that of the United States; the nationalist movement that brought Pandit Nehru to power in 1947 could boast an unbroken history of action stretching back to 1885. Whereas in India the levels of political authority and political decision-making have remained remarkably consistent during all the vicissitudes of the past two centuries, especially in its higher strata, in Africa there has been a constant flux in the size and scope of political units and a consolidation of small units into larger ones (Low, 1973). Thus, when political independence came to Africa, there were no institutions cloaked in the legitimacy of time and with which politicians were familiar.

Administration, however, is not only concerned with local units of government. Certainly, such a focus distorts the picture of power relations in the imperial context considerably. For all the stress laid on local units, real power in the British Empire lay at the centre with the governor and his civil servants, officials of the British Colonial Service. It was these men, and to some extent Whitehall and Westminster, who made the crucial decisions about tax rates, commodity prices, marketing organisations, labour regulations, land policy, and so on. The imperial system was a bureaucratic system, concerned above all with efficient government, free from the partisan argumentation associated with competitive electoral politics in the metropolitan state. It left its mark on the bureaucracies of independent Africa, for civil servants not only inherited the structure, working methods and orientations of their predecessors; they had also themselves experienced and, to some extent, internalised the conditions, traditions and faintly dismissive view of mere politicians held by professional white administrators. The apolitical atmosphere of the bureaucracy was something of a myth, for there were often arguments within the Executive Council (a sort of Cabinet composed of senior civil servants under the chairmanship and ultimate authority of the governor), but such disagreements only impinged on the local units of administration after their resolution. Indirect rule did much to insulate the districts from the centre.

This was, of course, part of the appeal of the philosophy of indirect rule. In the first instance, as Sir Donald Cameron himself put it, it was a 'measure of expediency' (Cameron, 1939, p. 81), for there was no other way in which the imperial power, short of manpower and starved of funds by Treasury parsimony, could actually communicate with the scattered and non-literate peoples of Africa. The famous anthropologist, Evans-Pritchard, saw the pragmatic basis of this rule at first hand in the Sudan and noted then that 'policy tends to be an intellectualisation of a process of development and not the cause of that process' (quoted in Johnson, 1982, p. 241). Yet it would be a mistake completely to ignore the avowed aims of administrators as guides to action; the concept of trusteeship was much abused, but it provided a benchmark against which policy had frequently to be measured and justified (Robinson, 1965). And trusteeship, like indirect rule, belongs to the family of relationships epitomised by guardian and ward; in the British Empire, as a consequence, district commissioners saw their task often as being to insulate 'their' people from the contamination of the wider society and the imported urbanisation.

This separation of locality from the national scene was further enhanced by the romantic aura which was associated with traditional society and which appealed to the British proconsul's mystical attachment to a past somehow nobler and simpler than his own age. Certainly, there is plenty of evidence that imperial civil servants disliked, and even despised, the partly educated Africans and Asians who attempted to imitate the white man's ways. The way ahead, as far as they were concerned, was to strengthen local government before moving on to the next stage of participation in a national government. Those Africans who sought to play a national political role were thus distrusted and were seen as hindering the ordered development from local focus to national focus. Rewards, status and often economic advantage were granted to those who operated the local political system and it was there, at the district level, that loyalties were established and political strength built. At independence, therefore, little nationwide attachment to the new country had been developed and individual politicians drew their political support from the locality rather than the nation at large; a major consequence was that in most countries a number of political barons emerged, each with his localised, often tribally homogeneous, support. The situation in the French possessions, by contrast, developed in a very different way.

One central difference between the French and British philosophies of imperial rule can perhaps be summed up by saying that French policy was designed to create black Frenchmen, while British policy was designed to create Africans with British characteristics. One speaks of the 'assimilationist' policies of France, but there was never any thought of assimilation in the minds of British Cabinet ministers. Education in the French

Empire from primary to university level was free, secular and carried out exclusively in the French language; curricula were identical to those in metropolitan France; civil servants were moved from country to country without concern for local specialisms; in the West Indies and the four communes of Senegal after 1879, and in the rest of the empire after 1946, black people took part in the election of deputies to the French Assembly in Paris; in short, the empire was envisaged as a single entity under the same bureaucratic universalism which organised, some say stifled, provincial initiatives in France itself. This assimilationist policy was in many ways much less conscious of race than British imperial ideas. Blaise Diagne, a black man from Senegal, became a member of the French Assembly in 1914, and an influential one at that; during the Fourth Republic Félix Houphouet-Boigny was a minister without whom, for a while, no government could be formed; during the Fifth Republic, the president of the Senate was the West Indian deputy, Gaston Monnerville. The thought of Nigerians or Kenyans taking their place in the House of Commons or becoming members of a British Cabinet was quite unthinkable. 'Alone among the Western nations', Henri Brunschwig has written, 'the French found it normal to entrust their interests to black lawyers, their health to black doctors, their children to black professors, and their recruits to black officers' (quoted in Symonds, 1966, p. 213).

The reality was somewhat more complex than this. Apologists for the French would point to Felix Eboué, whose rise from poverty in French Guyana to the governorship of French Equatorial Africa and a burial in the Panthéon exemplified the openness of the system, where self-discipline and effort, the Protestant ethic in action, prevailed. But there was another side to the story; Eboué, the Parisian rake with gambling debts, an Italian mistress and illegitimate children, the *commandant de cercle* operating forced labour regulations with a severity that once stood in the way of his promotion, provides a rather different picture. Black men born in the four communes of Senegal may have enjoyed the same rights as their white French counterparts but, once the scramble for Africa was under way, the social Darwinism so prevalent in Europe at the time and the realisation of the practical consequences of extending equal rights to the new subjects in equatorial Africa, persuaded politicians in Paris to treat their wards very much as subjects (M.D. Lewis, 1962 – 3). The educational system was so under-developed – in 1945 only 5 per cent of primary school-aged children were in school, while even in 1957 barely 10 per cent of this group in Guinea attended schools – that very few black men were fully assimilated. Indeed, the élite was smaller in numbers than in the British Empire and much further distanced culturally from their uneducated compatriots; many were lost to Africa to the profit of France. The extent of forced labour was considerable and there was a consequent steady emigration from French territories to British territories throughout the interwar years. In many ways, the French presence was actually harsher and more disruptive than the British.

Both the good and the bad flowed from the assumption in Paris, and among the administrators overseas, that the duty of France was to bring the *civilisation francaise* to its empire and that direct rule was the most efficient way of doing this. General de Gaulle was quite clear about this purpose; the reasons the ex-dependencies received economic aid, he wrote in his memoirs, was 'so that they will speak our language and share our culture' (quoted in W.B. Cohen, 1971, p. 203). His successor as President of France, Georges Pompidou, agreed. He once said:

> Of all countries France is the one that cares most about exporting its language and culture. This characteristic is genuinely specific to us. When a Frenchman travelling abroad meets someone who speaks French, who has read French authors, he feels as if he has found a brother. This is a need of our thought, perhaps of our genius. Our co-operation is undeniably oriented, and ought to be so, towards the expansion of our language and our culture. (Quoted in W.B. Cohen, 1971, p. 204)

The money spent by French governments after the disintegration of the empire on cultural matters abroad is massive by comparison with British expenditure; even in an ex-British colony, like Kenya, it is the French cultural centre in Nairobi which predominates. This mystical attachment among French-speakers is real; even the younger generation of educated Africans in the 1960s retained a close identification with France. Although Léopold Senghor cried from the heart against the necessity to express his deepest emotions in a foreign language, he remained irrevocably French in habits and cast of thought and was elected to the immortals.

The contrast between Britain and France is indeed great, but it is easy to exaggerate it. French direct rule often looked suspiciously like British indirect rule on the g'round. In 1908 a senior French administrator was writing that 'direct adminis-tration is impossible in the colonies . . . Therefore, we must institute a policy of help and collaboration with the native chiefs . . . [but] all the chiefs must be subordinate collaborators, not protected potentates' (Weinstein, 1970, p. 110). And many chiefs were very much more than mere agents or simple subor-dinates and enjoyed an influence of their own; given the vastness of the French Empire, it is not surprising that in some areas the ordinary people often rated the chief as more powerful than the administrator, who was rarely seen and normally stayed in one place for a single year at most. A little later a French governor was issuing a circular to remind his subor-dinates that there were not two authorities in each district, the French authority and the native authority, but only one: 'Only the *commandant de cercle* commands; only he is responsible. The native chief is only an instrument, an auxiliary' (Buell, ed., 1928, Vol.I, p. 997). This has the authentic ring of direct rule. But now read what Lord Lugard, the doyen of indirect rulers, wrote at much the same time. 'There are not two sets of rulers – British and native – but a single Government in which the native chiefs have well defined duties and an acknowledged status equally with British officials – the chief himself must understand that he has no right to place and power unless he renders his proper service to the State' (Low, 1973, p. 24).

The actual practice of politics nearly always depends more on the intransigent factors of reality than on the theories of intel-lectuals. As John Hargreaves has written:

Less evident perhaps [than the differences between French and British administration] are the similarities imposed by the colonial situation itself, by realities unavoidable by Europeans exercising power in West Africa during the early decades of the twentieth century. Both powers were constrained – by the parsimony of the metropolitan parliaments, the scarcity in Africa of money and skilled men, the unsettled conditions of African societies suddenly faced with the onslaught of Europe – to devise systems of government which would concentrate immediate administrative control in the hands of agents on whom they could rely. At the grass roots, both empires were governed by authoritarian paternalism, checked by the sense of responsibility of the man on the spot – the district commissioner or *commandant de cercle*. In neither system was there any doubt about the ultimate authority of the administrative officer. (Hargreaves, 1967, p. 139)

The ideas behind the policies may have been different, but the practice of imperial rule could also be very similar.

Yet there was, none the less, a marked difference between the French and British territories which goes beyond the pavement cafés in Abidjan, the language differences, the styles of dress, or the smell of food in the cities so reminiscent of Paris's Left Bank. They *were* different in the imperial days and their differences have carried over into the post-independence period. In the French Empire, the chief did not head a local government unit with some discretionary power; he was the agent of the central government in the locality. The chief was not necessarily selected according to customary procedures (indeed, in some areas the villagers secretly elected a 'real' chief if they disliked the appointed one too much). The chief did not basically administer justice according to traditional norms; he collected taxes and administered the hated *idigénat*, an arbitrary part of the French legal code. The French administration did not divide their territories into cantons that approximated to pre-colonial political units; they sometimes broke up large chiefdoms into smaller units. They moved their staff around from territory to territory to avoid their becoming too identified with a particular area; the only thing administrators had in common with each other or their articulate subjects was their Frenchness. In their scant respect for local institutions and in their professed, and often practised, philosophy of assimilating Africans into the French culture, the French differed markedly from the British. As is to be expected, therefore, the French heritage showed some similarities and some dissimilarities with the British.

The conscious attempt to weaken pre-colonial units and the emphasis on direct rule at least gave little impetus to a powerful parochialism. The centralised political structures and the assimilated élites moved the centre of political competition to the national level, where the political parties were responses not to local barons but to the need for influence in the French National Assembly. The gulf between the black *evolués* and their poor fellow citizens was wider than that between themselves and their imperial masters, with whom they often enjoyed amicable relations. At independence, several white administrators stayed on in high positions; the Finance Ministers of the Ivory Coast and Senegal and the Minister of Information and Tourism in Chad were all former members of the overseas civil service. In 1964 one-third of the students at the University of Dakar were French, since the educational system in Senegal was still integrated with the French system. This encouraged a considerable number of Frenchmen to move to French West Africa to assist in development work and in 1964 there were more French doctors, teachers and agriculturalists there than had been the case in 1960. Relations between French-speaking leaders and the French metropolitan politicians have been mostly cordial (at one stage de Gaulle's minister responsible for the former African Empire had actually been Houphouet-Boigny's *chef de cabinet*!). Despite the indignities of the imperial relationship, the bonds which keep the former French colonies – even radically rhetorical ones like Congo-Brazzaville or Benin – close to France through some mystical special relationship remain strong (Golan, 1981). The other major inheritances are, first, the gulf that exists between the local bourgeoisie and the peasantry and, secondly, the long tradition of centralisation. These three factors remain central to any understanding of the developments in that part of Africa which once fell under French rule.

The Economic Heritage

The economic consequences of imperialism have provided a source of considerable academic controversy. Since the intensity and form of contact between Europe and Africa show so many variations, this is to be expected. In those areas where genuine colonies were established and settlers acquired a measure of independent power, the African subjects were more immediately and more deeply affected than in those distant lands where the habitat and its resources did not attract whites. It was the mining areas of Africa, disproportionately situated in the southern part of the continent, which most disrupted the traditional societies. Generalising from the history of Zimbabwe or South Africa to the rest of the continent is fraught with problems, for the massive involvement of international capital and the need for a large and cheap labour force to operate the mines was not replicated in the fertile lands surrounding Lake Nyanza, for instance, or the savannah lands of Mali and Chad. Whether, in the light of current popular expectations, it was better to have been deeply involved in the imperial system is debatable; but Joan Robinson makes a telling point when she writes: 'There was only one thing worse than being exploited by colonialism; that was not to be exploited at all' (Robinson, 1964, p. 46). This is not the place to attempt a balance sheet of the imperial years (Perham, 1961; Rodney, 1972; Gann and Duignan, 1969) which, in any case, ends up in an arid argument over the appropriate criteria for judgement, but it is as well to caution against the hysterical writings of some people, both of the left and of the right, who forsake the ambiguities of the data for the easier, and self-indulgent, recourse to polemics.

Just as there is a danger in failing to differentiate between distinct types of economy in tropical Africa, so too there is a danger in imagining that Europeans created an economic system from scratch. Particularly in West Africa, trading was well developed by the last quarter of the nineteenth century and the increased contact with Europe, through an expanding market, provided new opportunities for entrepreneurial activities which were already widespread. Imperial rule, by putting an end to the economically debilitating slave trade and creating an ordered environment for increased production from the land, provided conditions in which local West Africans could themselves innovate; the provision of improved transport facilities and credit also assisted the growth of small capitalists and traders (Hopkins, 1973). The ground-nut industry in Nigeria and the cocoa industry in Ghana owed their growth to an indigenous response to the new environment opened up by the closer administrative control of the imperial powers (Hill, 1963). This increased involvement in the world market had political consequences as well. The commercialisation of peanuts on the Upper Guinea Coast, for example, began along the Gambia River in the early 1830s and spread rapidly through the region as African cultivators and traders responded with remarkable swiftness to the new opportunities. Internally, this established new élites and the basis for later economic different-iation. Externally, the rapidly growing demand for peanuts in France, together with helpful tariffs in France, favoured the French and Senegalese traders, a commercial advantage which was translated towards the end of the century into a territorial advantage (Brooks, 1975).

The involvement in a market economy, which spread over time through the length and breadth of the continent, altered the utilisation of the factors of production on the family hold-ing, adding for the most part burdens on to the women and increasing further the power of men within the family (Mbilinyi, 1972; Kitching, 1980). Power relations changed not only within families; they changed between families and regions. Some people embraced the market system with a reckless enthusiasm, while others reacted to it with careful disdain. The more settled and instrumental societies on fertile land prospered; the more nomadic and consummatory peoples and those on marginal land, if anything, grew poorer. The contrast between the affluence of Buganda and the relative poverty of Lango in Uganda is one case in point; the Ibo dominance in so much of the modern economic sector in much of Nigeria is another. What developed, therefore, was a more stratified society than there had been hitherto as some groups grew richer, investing their small surpluses in further product-ive enterprises like transport or additional land, while other groups stagnated and fell back relative to their more thrusting neighbours. By the time of the Great Depression, the comparative equality of traditional society had been irrevocably destroyed and incipient class divisions were already observable (Berry, 1975; Kitching, 1980; Vaughan, 1981).

There is more to the economic impact of imperial intrusion than the increased opportunities and differential responses already mentioned. Some governments had positive economic aims. In the French Empire, there was a more open commitment to making economic gains from African possessions and a greater readiness to use force to provide labour for infrastructural improvements and plantation agriculture than in the British Empire. The cynical determination to profit from the scramble for Africa reached its zenith in King Leopold's Congo; the king wrote to Baron Solvins in 1877: 'We must lose no chance of winning a share in the magnificent African cake' (quoted in Davidson, 1964, p. 36). Leopold exploited his acquisition with a ruthlessness which has few parallels; fifty years later it was estimated that the population in the Congo had been halved. The British, by contrast, were less direct and more subtle in their approach. Since territorial budgets were expected to balance, the primary concern of their governments was to raise enough revenue to cover running costs; general taxes and import taxes, as well as tariffs on the publicly owned railways were the normal procedure for doing this. Additionally, crops were encouraged, not so much to meet British demands as to find some practical form of revenues. In Kenya, for instance, sisal, coffee and maize made the colony self-supporting; they did not satisfy an existing need of the British economy. Of course, in some countries, especially where minerals were to be found, the dominant factor behind the precise shape of the economy was metropolitan requirements. Whatever the essential purpose of these economic developments, those not already in the money economy were forced to earn cash, usually by working a few months each year in the non-traditional sector. The policy also tended to emphasise what were thought of as growth points, such as the settler farms or plantations, and thus gave governmental backing to one sector over another, increasing the already incipient economic differences in the country.

As the economies grew, so too did the towns. In West Africa, there had always been a number of cities and along the cost of

East Africa, too, small towns had grown up round the ports which managed the trade between Arabia and the African hinterland. Imperial rule in Africa hastened on this process of urbanisation. In settler societies, this was most marked. The need to earn cash to pay taxes, the gradual impoverishment of rural areas in the face of an expanding population and limited land, the demonstration effect of a consumer-oriented society, and the cost of education pushed men off the land into the towns, or on to the mines and farms of the Europeans, in search of wages. There was some forced labour in the early days of the century, but generally economic forces were enough to extrude from the rural areas manpower to meet the needs of an economy based increasingly on wage labour (Arrighi, 1967; van Onselen, 1976). But there was also a pull, as well as a push, towards the urban areas. Many Africans in the 1920s, like their contemporaries in Europe at the time and their grandchildren in the 1980s, were drawn – in small numbers, initially; in larger numbers, later – to the bright lights of the city. As the limited life on a peasant landholding became recognised, perhaps through exposure to education, perhaps through the description of an older relative embroidering the new excitement of urban life, more young girls and boys desired to sample such an experience (McKenzie, 1975 – 6).

The consequences of this process of urbanisation have been many. In economic terms, it further stratified society, producing over time an incipient bourgeoisie, a labour aristocracy, *and* an underprivileged proletariat. Since much of the labour was migrant, it increased the cash available in the rural areas and provided for some people the initial capital on which traders and transporters later built. It also brought to peasant households a new perspective on imperial rule as well as fresh ideas gathered in the bars and workplaces of the towns. The urban areas were the preserve of no single linguistic group but the meeting place of many. The parochialism of rural life could there be contrasted with the wider focus of nationally oriented politicians; yet, at the same time, the strangeness of the urban experience drew each fresh migrant into social relations and organisations dominated by people from his own region or linguistic group. This encouraged a solidary ethnicity which created an identity in an alien environment and provided a vehicle for the articulation and prosecution of individual interests.

The monetarisation of African economies and the effects of this process were essentially continuous and evolutionary. But there were shocks in the economic system which radically hastened, or stalled, developments. The first of these traumatic moments was the Great Depression. It was at this time that the imperial state most obviously introduced regulations and laws which discriminated economically against the African farmers. Broadly speaking, the first quarter of the twentieth century had witnessed, in Central Africa as in East and West Africa, an expansion of economic activity and a growing affluence among peasant producers. The terms of trade were favourable; the markets were open. But from about 1930 the balance of forces changed. Where settlers were present and could bring their influence to bear upon the imperial authorities, laws were passed to protect white farmers from the cold winds of worldwide recession and African competition. The small tobacco farmers of Malawi, the maize producers of Zimbabwe, the growing cash-crop farmers of Kenya, all were sacrificed at this time to the preservation of viable white farms and estates (Leys, 1975; Palmer, 1977; McCracken, 1982 – 3). Even where settlers were not so closely linked to the imperial government, the slowdown in trade reduced the opportunities open to African farmers and in West Africa, too, the well capitalised, expatriate concerns weathered the storm better than the small-scale African traders and emerged in a stronger position at the end of the 1930s.

The second major shock was the Second World War and Britain's parlous economic position after the war. The need for raw materials during the hostilities and the essential requirement to develop the sterling area resources in the late 1940s resulted in what was in the perspective of the time a massive investment in the African continent. Self-interest strode side by side with a more morally directed imperial policy now that the Labour Party had taken office in London. Extension officers, agricultural advisers, educational experts and a whole bevy of expatriate specialists decamped on to the African peasantry to cajole it, push it, threaten it, into more productive activity. Trusteeship may have called for this positive concern to increase the wealth of the imperial possessions; but so, too, did British self-interest. The result was twofold: the African peasantry was drawn, whether it liked it or not, conclusively into the market economy and was made aware, in a way that in much of the continent had never been so obvious before, that the imperial authorities controlled so much of their lives. This increased awareness of imperial overrule was paralleled by an increased differentiation among the peoples of Africa, as those best placed to benefit from the new expansionism acquired wealth and modern skills faster than their neighbours.

Just as periodisation is important to understand the impact of the new economic forces let loose on Africa so, too, it is essential to distinguish between the national and the individual inheritance. Economic policy in Africa provided raw materials for the European factories and shops and markets for European-produced manufactured items. The consequences of this Eurocentric perspective can be seen in Nyasaland (Malawi), where railway development served both a strategic interest and a domestic interest by its use of British steel; the massive debt which the colony thus incurred virtually prevented all development and turned the territory into little more than a labour reserve for the South African mines and Southern Rhodesian farms (Vail, 1975). Because each territory was not conceived of as a separate economic unit aiming at its own self-sufficiency but a cog within a wider empire, there was a tendency towards specialisation and, as a consequence, towards the concentration on one crop or resource which seemed suitable for that particular geographical area. In the early 1970s, as a consequence of this, many African countries were dependent upon only one or two products for their foreign earnings; Zambia's copper brought in 93 per cent of her foreign exchange, Ghana's cocoa 74 per cent, Uganda's coffee and cotton 77 per cent. The lack of diversification meant that the independence governments were at the mercy of fluctuating primary-product markets. Planning was well nigh impossible, when a sharp fall in the price of the major export – and a 30 per cent fall in a single year was by no means uncommon – cut the available foreign exchange by a quarter. What made this dependence on a few crops or minerals even more disastrous was the generally unfavourable terms of trade experienced by primary producers in the 1960s and 1970s. This had not always been the case; earlier in the century, the price of primary products had risen faster than the price of manufactured goods. But in the two decades after independence, except for oil producers and a few good years for coffee growers in particular, the price of raw materials has consistently risen more slowly than the price of those manufactured products which make up the vast bulk of Africa's imports. Between 1958 and 1964 cocoa production in Ghana doubled, but the price virtually halved and foreign currency generated by this massive improvement in productivity increased not at all. In Tanzania, farmers produced on average 8·6 per cent more each year during the first few years of independence but, because population was rising by nearly 3 per cent and import prices were also rising steeply, at the end of the period the country was 1 per cent worse off in real terms. When commodity prices did enjoy a small boom in 1973–4, the even greater rise in oil prices all but obliterated the potential gain. Because local markets had always been small and the conception of a single, mutually interdependent empire so strong, there had been little incentive to establish industries in the African possessions. Some processing, the brewing of beer, the making of shoes, these were about the limits of local industry. Thus, when independence came, the economies of the new states, and thus the revenue available to the governments for their development plans, were circumscribed by the essentially undiversified nature of their economies inherited from the imperial days.

That, then, was one form of dependency. But the dependency was deeper and more limiting than that. The only market available for the products of Africa remained the rich, industrialised nations of Western Europe, North America, Japan and Australasia, what may, for the sake of shorthand, be called the international capitalist system. Tropical African countries, with the exception perhaps of Nigeria, were individually of marginal significance to the industrialised nations and enjoyed a weak bargaining position. They depended heavily upon that international capitalist world for markets, for capital and for technology. If they wanted to improve their transport systems, build modern hospitals and educational establishments, inaugurate a manufacturing sector to process their own raw materials, or engage in large schemes of mineral exploitation or agricultural development (as all the new states' governments did), they could not do it alone. Unsurprisingly, the assistance provided to African countries in the years after independence came largely upon the donors' terms, since their need to invest in or help an individual state was very much less than the state's desire for their involvement. The imbalance in the relationship was exacerbated by the African inability to provide a continental front to the outside world, itself the product both of individual and national pride as well as the imperial heritage of Balkanisation of the continent, and also by the inexperience of African negotiators which allowed them in the early days often to be hoodwinked by unscrupulous foreign entrepreneurs (Schatz, 1969). There is no doubt that outside aid is absolutely essential to all the new states of Africa and without it such improvements in health care and educational facilities as have occurred could not have taken place. At the same time, the dependence on aid has often meant that the priorities of foreigners rather than domestic politicians have prevailed (Hayter, 1971; Arnold, 1979). The exact nature of this dependency is actually extremely complex and will be discussed later. At this stage, what needs stressing is the general point that at the end of imperial rule the nations of tropical Africa were deeply and uncertainly dependent upon the world capitalist system for any major physical improvements upon which they might want to embark. The Eastern bloc, poorer, more self-sufficient, and less interested in basic economic development, has provided only minimal assistance outside the arena of defence and some massive, prestigious projects – such as the building of the Aswan High Dam. Being almost of necessity incorporated into the world capitalist system, Africa is affected by the domestic economies of the rich world, especially the United States. It used to be said that when the United States sneezed Europe caught a cold; in the 1970s, when the United States sneezed and the oil producers flexed their muscles Africa caught pneumonia.

Concentration on the macroeconomic aspects of the economic inheritance should not obscure the effects at the micro-level. Because of the essentially *laissez-faire* economic philosophy of the imperial age, the inequalities for which nature herself and the accidents of history were responsible grew. Access to favourable soils, geographical location and the acquisition of new skills imported from Europe gave some peoples and regions enormous advantages. At independence, no new state inherited an egalitarian society. Those which had been most neglected and despised had a semblance of equality, but it was the equality of poverty. In those where the tentacles of imperial rule had reached furthest, the extent of differentiation was much greater. In Mozambique, where indigenous involvement in the modern economy had been so slight, Samora Machel inherited an impoverished and therefore largely unstratified economy after the exodus of the Portuguese colonialists; in neighbouring Zimbabwe, where indigenous bus operators, businessmen and professional people were thick on the ground, the contrast between the affluence of the black middle classes in the suburbs of Harare and the poverty of the essentially subsistence farmers in the communal areas was overwhelming. Since political activity is closely related to, even if it is not determined by, economic interests, the structure of political divisions was markedly different in the two countries.

The academic controversy over imperialism's economic heritage is not yet stilled. Broadly speaking, analysis has tended to cluster round one of two major approaches, the modernisation and dependency paradigms respectively. In the 1960s, for reasons largely connected with the intellectual and political climate of the United States (D. C. O'Brien, 1972), it was generally held that foreign stimulation was not only beneficial but inevitable, and that the consequences of this involvement would be to draw the African states out of the bonds of traditionalism into the arms of modernity. Sociologists had for a long time been fascinated with the notion of progress; Darwin's theory of evolution, Tonniens's belief in the natural development from *Gemeinschaft* to *Gesellschaft*, or Durkheim's notions of mechanical and organic solidarity, all find echoes in the modernisation literature. Many believed that there were set stages of growth through which peoples inevitably moved as urbanisation, education, technology and secularism had a wider impact (Rustow, 1960). This ethnocentric view, assuming that Africa would tend to grow into a version (if probably a poor one) of the United States, slowly became discredited as the prognostications seemed less and less likely to be fulfilled and its normative assumptions were increasingly challenged.

It was replaced by a rival paradigm which seemed, at first sight, to be saying quite the opposite. The dependency theorists maintained that external influences were malignant, rather than beneficial, because they created and preserved an economic backwardness by chaining those economies at the periphery of the world capitalist system to the centre through the rich world's control of markets, capital and technology (Frank, 1969). The modern sector, far from providing the impetus for development, created bastions of privilege which drained wealth and resources from the countryside and preserved its dominant position through an alliance with the metropolitan bougeoisie. This conceptual framework, too, was ethnocentric with its intellectual roots firmly within the Marxist tradition. But it shared much else with the concept of modernisation which it challenged. It is all-inclusive, applicable to all societies and to all recent history; it is not entirely free of evolutionary assumptions, for it argues that some 'normal' path of development has been disrupted; it, too, posits only two kinds of society, the dependent and the independent rather than the traditional and the modern (Hopkins, 1979).

Of course, the summaries presented here are, as they must be, simplifications of often complex, and all too often inelegant, arguments. But what they both lack is an important place for African initiatives. The economic heritage of the imperial years is unquestionably considerable, but it did not dominate to the exclusion of indigenous choice and it permitted considerable variations. The price of being dragged into modern productive processes and economies of scale has been high, as indeed it was in Britain in the nineteenth century and the Soviet Union more recently. But the resources, both human and physical, consequently released have provided opportunities virtually unimagined at the turn of the century. Few Africans would have it otherwise. The appeal to a less frenetic time, to the rustic simplicity of some imagined but unreal golden age, is a luxury of a European middle class which has already sampled, and often enjoyed, the fruits of industrialised economies. Life in Africa in the nineteenth century was tough and harsh, as indeed in much of the continent it still is. For all the massive changes that have so visibly taken place, there is still a continuity in many of the rural areas. This continuity is not merely a technological and social continuity; it is also to some extent an ideological continuity. Just as so many West Africans adapted to the opportunities of trade in the nineteenth century, so their successors have been ready and quick to exploit new economic opportunities in the last quarter of the twentieth. It may be an exaggeration to say that every peasant is a rural capitalist at heart. But it is extremely doubtful whether all but a small minority of Africans are genuinely committed to a socialist economy, in which private property has no central place; they value their independence too highly. In this respect the economic philosophy of the imperial rulers found fertile soil.

The Cultural Heritage

There is something artificial in distinguishing between the administrative, economic and cultural heritages of imperial rule, for they are intimately interrelated. Administrative forms and economic systems are the expressions of particular ideas; they are also interpreted by those who are involved in them as embodying certain principles. The ideas which the Europeans thought provided the impetus for their organisations were not always congruent with the African perceptions of them, so that the cultural heritage of the imperial years was by no means the inheritance intended by the metropolitan powers. The ability to borrow new forms and ideas from Europe without jettisoning all indigenous practices and values was the central feature of that attempt to transmit to Africa the ideals and philosophies of Europe – what might for brevity's sake be termed 'cultural imperialism'.

The basic principles which underpin the market economy were not entirely new to tropical Africa, but there is little doubt that the spread of economic opportunities and the increased centrality of money radically altered the perspective of many people in the continent. Individualism, the very bedrock of capitalism, became accentuated; private wealth and entrepreneurship became more widely approved; the purchase of consumer goods was increasingly desired. The extent to which the new economic values was embraced differed from region to region as well as within regions, but the overall effect was to see affluence and success as clearly correlated. Most African societies had been conscious of status differences and the appropriate behaviour to be expected of people in different social positions. Many communal values still survived; the extended family, often a drain on capital accumulation, remained a very real social factor; villagers assisted one another in home building, protection against wild animals, raising money for overseas fares, and other community matters. There was, then, change alongside continuity but the attractions of the new economic order became more and more widely accepted. The model to which young people in the villages came increasingly to aspire was the well-dressed, sophisticated, man of the town; and this demanded the earning of money in an economic system built upon private property and private effort. The conceptual models which the educated graduates of economics faced in their British and American universities were essentially those of the rich, industrialised nations in which macroeconomic theory focused on the virtues of an increasing GNP and microeconomic theory on the profitability of the firm. Although some attention was paid to the inequalities and inefficiencies which tend to emerge from a free enterprise system, the prevailing orthodoxy supported the fundamental principles of capitalism. Central critiques of the definition of development or the role of private enterprise in a welfare state were rarely raised. The technological model, too, was drawn from the developed West, which was partly an expression of an African determination not to be seen to be inferior and partly a reflection of what the developed world offered. But it could have unfortunate results; between 1964 and 1970, while Kenya's GDP was increasing by 50 per cent largely through the growth of private industry, employment in that sector, as more sophisticated production techniques were employed, increased by only 10 per cent; the total number of paid employees in 1970 was actually lower than it had been in 1961.

However, there are two important glosses that need to be made to this picture. First, few Africans would probably admit to a preference for capitalism because the concept was so intimately tied in rhetoric, and in reality, to imperialism which the nationalist movements in the 1950s and 1960s opposed so vigorously. Most conceived of the world as being composed of two antagonistic and mutually exclusive types of society, capitalist and socialist. This led them inexorably into protestations of socialist commitment. Yet this was, in reality, more a rejection of imperialism and what it was supposed to represent than a genuine commitment to socialism which, in any case, was rarely recognised as a single elastic term encompassing a range of ideas from Owen's Utopianism to Stalin's *dirigisme*, with many a stopping point in between. Secondly, there has always been a small number of articulate African defenders of alternative economic strategies. Nyerere's developing ideas represent one original mind, borrowing his ideas from many sources and fitting them to a very African context (Glickman, 1967; Nyerere, 1966, 1968). However, most have been content to echo the ideas of European writers of the left. Their number has been steadily increasing, partly in line with a growing radicalism among Africanists in the developed world, partly in response to a realisation that the inherited economies and conventional economic theories had not brought a rapid improvement to the standard of living of the majority of Africans. In those parts of Africa where the struggle for independence was long and violent, the leaders became more aware of the intellectual arguments underpinning a socialist economy and more committed to a socialist strategy in the post-imperial years. But rhetoric, which is too often imprecise as to the meaning being given to socialism, is not always a good guide to action. The Marxist-Leninism espoused by governments of the Congo-Brazzaville permits what in another context would be seen as neocolonial relations with France and international capital. Mboya's claim that Kenya's development strategy was both African and socialist rightfully raised a number of eyebrows (Mohiddin, 1981).

The ideologies of African ruling élites have been essentially eclectic. This was true of the nationalist movements themselves, which borrowed from Mill, Marx and Rousseau with unembarrassed evenhandedness (Hodgkin, 1961). In the post-independence years, the broad tradition of European socialism and the perceived need to assert a socialist philosophy allowed a vast range of policies and priorities to be subsumed under the emotionally satisfying, and extremely capacious, title of African socialism (Friedland and Rosberg, eds, 1964; Mohan, 1966). The concentration on that aspect of the socialist tradition which emphasised state control and national rather than sectional interests has even led some observers to detect a strong fascist streak in some states claiming to be socialist (Gregor, 1967; but see Hughes and Kolinsky, 1976). The ethic of distribution, general welfare and human rights has tended to be much less stressed. The free enterprise assumptions of unequal reward have survived into a political age in which the use of state power is often directed to the advancement of sectional groups, or even personal wealth, rather than to the improved well-being of the people as a whole. So the ideological heritage is confused. Private property remains strongly entrenched, among the peasantry as among the burgeoning bourgeoisie; statism has its roots both in the vanguardist ideas of Lenin and in the centralised reality of imperial rule; notions of growth and plans for economic growth owe more to the liberal economists of the capitalist West than to the command economists of the Soviet bloc; the panoply of oppressive legislation limiting the freedom of speech, association and publication are retained, and sometimes strengthened, after independence; above all, however, is the widespread need to espouse socialism as the antithesis of capitalism and its progenitor, imperialism. Some, such as President Banda of Malawi, feel no such need; others, such as Samora Machel of Mozambique, try genuinely to establish a socialist state. Once more the variety within Africa, as much the consequences of human choices as of economic forces, is striking.

The intellectualising of African leaders would not have taken the form it did unless they had been exposed to the education provided by the imperialists. There had always been a form of education to prepare children for their adult roles in society, as there still is, but the new education was in several ways a revolutionary innovation. And in much of Africa its agency initially was the Christian churches which wanted their potential converts to be able to read and discuss the Bible. As with all other aspects of European involvement in Africa, there is no simple formula to encapsulate their effect. Where there was great rivalry for souls between competing denominations, missionaries sought potential converts with enthusiasm. The gross provision of education gained by the duplication of schools, although the quality often did not, nor did this rivalry necessarily lead to a high level of genuine spiritual conversion. Where territories were effectively zoned between denominations, quality rather than quantity was more likely to be espoused. In Uganda, for instance, the competition between Catholics and Protestants resulted in primary schools being established in most villages and political factionalism later grew up along religious lines. Different missionaries, even from within the same denomination, responded to traditional African practices and mores in varied ways. Some conducted a direct onslaught against what they took to be barbaric and indefensible behaviour and primitive notions of the Almighty; others attempted to adapt traditional religion and spirituality to their version of the Christian faith. Most came to be seen as outriders of the imperial power, for they rarely challenged the administrations' attempts to alter the lifestyles of the African peasantry and often interpreted for their African charges the regulations promulgated by the imperial government.

Despite the association with the imperial powers the mission churches gained many adherents, some of whom died for their new faith and were honoured as martyrs. It may be that the earliest converts were individuals who had fallen foul of their own societies and found comfort in the white man's religion. In time, more and more people came to the missionaries, and not always for spiritual purposes. In British Africa, in particular, it was the church which provided education and the politically aware soon realised that the skills to be acquired in the classroom were essential both for advancement within the country and for confrontation against the state. Many chiefs ensured that some of their sons were exposed to this novel experience and they thus managed to retain leadership within the family, transferring the right to lead from inherited position to modern skills. It is no accident that in Western Nigeria, for instance, the major political figures in the nationalist movement and in the political struggles after independence were chiefs, such as Chief Anthony Enahoro and Chief Obafemi Awolowo. There is, therefore, a close correlation between the educated and those exposed to Christian teaching, and the morality of the New Testament is never far below the surface even among those with the most radical rhetoric. The association with the white rulers, however, added a tension to the relationship between missionaries and their flock; in much of Africa, especially where the church leaders were clearly perceived as supporting the imperial authorities on an issue which divided the races, many Africans left the established churches and set up their own independent churches and schools, synthesising parts of the new with parts of the old. In central Kenya in the 1920s, where the Protestant missions gave religious sanction to the government's attempts to eradicate the traditional Kikuyu practice of clitoridectomy, this splintering was especially evident (Rosberg and Nottingham, 1966). In the Portuguese colonies, too, the Catholic Church became an arm of the state and did much to blunt potential opposition by stressing upon the small educated élite the paramount obligation to be loyal to the church and to the state which supported it. The recent Latin American growth of radical priests espousing a Christian Marxism never permeated Africa; there were some great liberals who were perpetually seen as thorns in the imperial governments' flesh, but their liberalism was concerned more with civil and economic rights and human dignity than with radical social and political change.

The education which the church, and later the imperial civil services, brought was essentially a literary education, designed to produce clerks, book-keepers, catechists and elementary teachers. Although there were attempts to introduce more technical training, this approach was strongly resisted by educated Africans and their friends in Europe as an attempt to hold back the intellectual training of Africans and therefore extend the white dominance in administrative tasks. The Ashley Report on Nigerian education found in 1960 that 'the literary tradition and the University degree have become indelible symbols of prestige in Nigeria; by contrast, technology, agriculture, and other practical subjects . . . have not won esteem' (quoted in Symonds, 1966, p. 133). First in West Africa, later in East Africa and finally in Zimbabwe, paper qualifications, rather than experience or technical expertise, provided the major entrée to the lucrative and powerful positions in the bureaucracy and parastatal sectors. Africa suffered from the diploma disease (Dore, 1976). Although some countries tried hard to re-emphasise practical, essentially agricultural skills along the lines that district commissioners had advised unsuccessfully a generation or two earlier, the pressures from the rural areas and the accumulated expectations from the past almost invariably strengthened the hands of those who favoured formal, literary education. On the credit side, the emphasis forced educated Africans to become proficient in the single language of the imperial masters, which helped to provide some unifying force across the divisions of tribe and language and introduced them into a worldwide intellectual tradition which local languages would have denied them. Communication throughout a territory and between peoples of several territories became possible and nationalist ideas spread much more easily from radicals in Europe and North America through the Asian continent to Africa itself. Without literary skills, the petitions and appeals which early nationalists used to stir the consciences of liberals in the metropolitan countries and to provoke responses from the imperial agents closer to home would not have been possible. The French-speakers and the English-speakers, already divided geographically by imperial systems whose purpose was to integrate overseas possessions into the metropolitan powers rather than provide links between neighbouring territories, were thus kept even further apart. There was also a marked stylistic difference between the two educational systems. French intellectuals were more metaphysical and Marxist in their approach to the study of society; British intellectuals were more pragmatic and pluralist. Although the language and the ideas of French-speaking and English-speaking nationalists in Africa were different, they both used those languages and their literatures to challenge imperial overrule.

While it is true that access to European education was a significant catalyst in the conflict between rulers and subjects, it did not provoke hostility to imperial rule in the majority of the villages. For education remained very much a minority experience. In 1960, as the first surge of countries in Africa achieved their independence, only a pitiably small number of children between the ages of 15 and 19 were at school; 8·8 per cent of that age group were enrolled in Western Nigeria, 3·9 per cent in Kenya, 3·0 per cent in what is now Zaire, 1·9 per cent in Senegal, and only 0·3 per cent in Northern Nigeria (Hunter, 1962, p. 245). A UNESCO survey of 1950, when the nationalist movement was beginning to gain some mass support, estimated that the percentage of those over 15 who were illiterate was 95 – 99 per cent in French West Africa, 90 – 95 per cent in Tanganyika and the Sudan, 75 – 80 per cent in Ghana, and 60 – 65 per cent in Zaire (UNESCO, 1957). For the majority of Africans, then, this education had no meaning because it did not touch them. Absolute figures tell the story even more starkly than percentages. After forty years of British administration in Tanganyika, only 318 pupils were enrolled in the top class of the secondary school system and only 245 school certificates, providing the qualification for further study, were achieved. The situation was better in West Africa, worse in the Portuguese colonies. There was also a distinction between the British tradition of trying to educate comparatively large numbers a little and the French tradition of trying to educate a much narrower band of people more deeply, as the figures clearly demonstrate. The Belgians, whose imperial presence was exploitative, produced a more literate population than any other metropolitan power; but few chances were given to the educated to take on responsible positions.

The crude literacy figures draw attention to the patchy, and often very shallow, impact of the European occupation of tropical Africa. For very large numbers of rural inhabitants, women more than men, the cultural impact of Europe was slight. Untouched by literacy and the visions it might conjure up, hardly marked by the teachings of the Christian gospels, aware only peripherally of the overarching authority of the district commissioner and caught up but slightly in the monied economy, they came to independence with their cultural roots still largely intact. At the other end of the scale were many, more men than women, who were graduates of universities in the developed world, committed Christians, fully cognisant of their subordinate position within a European-dominated empire and deeply involved in, and marked by, their contact with the monied economy. The experience of most Africans lay somewhere between these two extremes; but the tensions that existed between these two worlds were very real (Okot p'Bitek, 1966).

This ambivalent heritage is well illustrated by a brief look at elections. On the one hand, Europeans would easily recognise the mass parties which grew up in the 1950s and 1960s, the well-dressed and articulate leaders, the campaign speakers, the posters, the meet-the-people tours. On the other hand, the illiterate voters needed help in the polling booth to place their crosses in the appropriate place for they could not read the names of the candidates. To help them, the parties or candidates used symbols to establish a visible identification. Tom Mboya once chose an aeroplane as his symbol and on election day hired an aeroplane to fly over Nairobi to remind the electorate of that symbol; in Eastern Nigeria selection by the National Council of Nigerian Citizens (NCNC) was colloquially referred to as having been 'given the cock'; in Tanzania each candidate was, and still is, allocated either the house or the hoe as his symbol. These symbols do more than help identification; they often provide a framework within which candidates structure their appeals and a powerful assistance to a party's success. In India the Congress Party's assumption of the holy cow as its symbol helped to give it a special status in the eyes of many of the overwhelmingly Hindu electorate. In Zimbabwe ZANU(PF), the Zimbabwe African National Union (Patriotic Front), used the cock – a symbol which was acquired almost by accident – to great effect in the 1980 election; supporters crowed and waved their arms like the wings of a cock, while in discos dancers strutted like cocks. So side by side with the trappings of Western formal democracy are practices unknown to contemporary Europe; in February 1982 a Nairobi city councillor was found guilty of practising witchcraft during the 1979 municipal elections.

The whole question of the applicability of liberal democracy to Africa revolves around the extent of the European impact on the continent. It should be remembered at the outset that liberal democracy in Europe had its own unique history (Macpherson, 1966). The liberal state preceded the extension of the franchise so that the nineteenth century saw both a democratisation of the state and a liberalisation of democracy. Liberalism is the ideological bedrock of free, competitive elections. It accepts the basic frailty of man, but it also upholds his essential goodness. It therefore insists on freedom to speak and publish new ideas, to associate with likeminded people, to organise for political ends; it does this because it accepts that rulers may be imperfect and that a free interchange of ideas, like the perfect market in economic theory, is most likely to produce the 'right' answer. This free political market, however, could only flourish in a particular economic climate. In Europe industrialisation, with its appalling toll on the lives of ordinary workers but with its ability to create unimagined wealth, pre-dated the extension of the franchise; the exploited had no political voice until there were sufficient surplus resources to meet some of their demands. In Africa democracy has preceded industrialisation; governments are thus faced with the impossible task of revolutionising the society and the economy while being electorally dependent upon the uprooted (Lofchie, 1971; Wallerstein, 1971).

Not only does liberal democracy have special historical roots; it is also a system of power designed to uphold specific values. The liberal's ideological agnosticism and preference for a free economic market have not been internalised by many African leaders. The need to transform their countries radically after the imperial years of comparative neglect and the inegalitarian consequences of an economic philosophy which largely supported a free market has produced a belief in a confident use of state power for development, what the French call *dirigisme*, the antithesis of the pure liberal-democratic model (though even the liberal democracies are becoming less liberal and more *dirigiste*). Liberal democracy is a fragile plant, functioning successfully only in special, sheltered conditions. In a sense it is a luxury enjoyed by peoples with a relatively high level of national cohesion and wealth, conditions hardly ever encountered in Africa. The Northern Ireland experience reminds us that, when a threat to the integrity of the state is perceived, elements of illiberalism and a disruption of the free market of political ideas take place.

This foray into aspects of liberal democracy nicely illustrates the ambivalence of the imperial powers' cultural heritage. On the one hand, it introduced new ideas and new assumptions which percolated unevenly through African society. These innovations were adopted in some instances, rejected in others and frequently altered to fit with existing ideas and assumptions.

The African response was essentially syncretic. On the other hand, ideas do not exist in a vacuum but become relevant and powerful only when they are apposite for a people's needs. There is a symbiotic relationship between the interests of various social categories in a society and the dominant ideas of those categories; each feeds on the other. Thus, the imperial powers were never able to impose their own dominant values upon their African subjects; there were in any case counter-values in the marketplace of ideas and the African peoples employed what was offered essentially to support their own varied interests.

Conclusion

Although it is difficult to evaluate with certainty and accuracy the precise heritage the European powers left to Africa after their years of imperial rule, it is certain that this heritage cannot be ignored. The structure of the administration, the nature of the national economy, the relationships with the rest of the world, the range of values, the lines of cleavage, all these owed a great deal to the policies of the metropolitan parliaments and their imperial agents. That cannot be doubted. But the conclusion should not be drawn that the subsequent history of tropical Africa can be explained, even explained away, only in terms of that heritage. That would be far too mechanistic a way of looking at things and would unduly undervalue the contribution of African politicians themselves. But it would also be a distorting perspective for two further reasons.

First, the imperial powers did not enjoy a monopoly on the outside world's impact on Africa. Islam, for instance, which in much of tropical Africa pre-dated the European arrival by several centuries, contained a religious and moral order which survived the buffeting of European Christianity and, indeed, continued to expand its influence. In some parts of Africa, especially in West Africa, one line of political cleavage was definitely the Islamic – Christian divide. The politics of Senegal are deeply marked by the Muslim brotherhoods there. Political policies, too, in places owed their intellectual inspiration to Islamic teaching. And the social and economic development of regions within a single state could be significantly affected by the presence of a strong Islamic tradition. For instance, in Northern Nigeria in 1934 only 10,000 children from the region's total population of about 11 million were in school; in Southern Nigeria there were twenty times as many children from a population one-fifth smaller. In the Ilorin and Kabba provinces, which had been animist and where the missionaries had established schools, 40 per cent of the children aged between 6 and 13 were enrolled in schools in 1962; in the Islamic provinces of Kano and Katsina, from which the missionaries had long been excluded, the proportion was only 5 per cent (Symonds, 1966, p. 145). The European control over information did effectively prevent other models from being seriously considered, but the coming of independence broke this virtual monopoly. Alongside the Marxist notions some educated Africans had imbibed, in Paris more deeply than in London, the People's Republic of China and Cuba came to provide for African leaders alternative ideas which seemed more relevant to their needs. At independence, however, the weight of the European precedents was overpowering.

Secondly, the peoples of tropical Africa were not supine recipients of what the European powers thought fit to take to Africa; there remained an authentic autonomy which endured. For all the impact of the monetarised economy, peasants were not entirely captured by the economic system but retained an element of independence from that system (Hyden, 1980). Africans were eclectic in the way that some practices and values were absorbed, while others were discarded. And beneath the surface of sophisticated modernity there were always local forces, locally impelled and expressed in local forms, which could erupt and destroy the outward and visible signs of the European world (Naipaul, 1979). Indeed, it has been argued that, for all the effort expended by imperialists and their successors to force Africa into a mould decreed by the metropolitan powers' interests, the continent has resolutely refused to be coralled but has retained its own autonomy to redefine or ignore much of what was thought to have been the imperial heritage (Marnham, 1980). Striking the correct balance between the autonomy of the indigenous Africans and the constraints imposed upon them by their imperial heritage is no easy exercise.

3 The Transfer of Power

One of the primary characteristics of the tropical African states is their newness. Only Ethiopia, with a long history of expansion and consolidation, and Liberia, the American-supported country dominated until 1980 by emancipated slaves, did not gain their independence after the Second World War. The acquisition of political freedom is thus a recent development whose architects are, in many cases, still alive and exercising power and the recollection of which is part of many people's real experience rather than the stuff of national folklore.

This newness has two important contemporary significances. In the first place, the ideas and organisations through which independence was achieved remain acutely relevant, just as the precise response of the various imperial powers has coloured the political practices and economic possibilities of the new states. The esteem in which the nationalist politicians and their political parties were held has in most countries survived the vicissitudes of the first years of independence. They provided some of the first national heroes and certainly the first modern organisations to which large numbers of people became emotionally attached. In much of eastern Africa the same parties, and indeed the same individuals, provide the governments twenty years after independence; in those parts of Africa where the military has swept the civilian rulers from power, the old organisations and leaders have not been forgotten. Many of the personnel and structures of support for the Convention People's Party in Ghana, or the various regional parties in Nigeria survived years of military rule. At the same time, the conditions on which power was transferred from metropolitan rule to local rule have coloured the performances of the post-independence governments. Constitutions may have been amended or radically restructured, but that should not hide the essential enduring legacy of the departing powers; the contrast between French-speaking Africa, apart perhaps from Guinea, and Portuguese-speaking Africa is dramatic and due, in large part, to the readiness of France to grant independence to its empire in 1960 and the determination of Portugal to hold on to its empire well into the 1970s. At a more obvious level, the technical competence of the successor states depended very much upon the degree of preparation in which their imperial masters had indulged. Since governing is not, in fact, a simple operation and African expectations of the consequences of independence were high, the basic skills which Western powers take for granted — the ability to deliver educational and health requirements, to monitor governmental expenditures, to ensure transport facilities, power and water to their people — were not only in high demand; they were in dangerously short supply.

If the first significance of newness is a certain continuity, the second significance is paradoxically the search for change. The constitutions which were inherited were often merely the fruit of bargaining between nationalists and metropolitan powers and were always, except in those states where independence was wrested by force, the creations of the metropolitan powers. They were not in English-speaking Africa autochthonous and they did not grow out of an evolutionary process unique to each particular country which would grant them a nationwide legitimacy. They were largely imposed; and they often advantaged one sector of society over another to a degree unacceptable to powerful forces in the new states. The extraordinarily complex Ugandan Constitution, for example, involved provinces with a fully federal relationship, a quasi-federal relationship and a non-federal relationship to the central government; in Zimbabwe there were a number of preferential arrangements for whites entrenched in the constitution. In neither country did the most popular party accept these constitutional arrangements as appropriate to their countries' needs. In the aftermath of independence, therefore, there has inevitably been intense political activity designed both to create a genuinely autochthonous set of political institutions and to represent more accurately the true balance of forces in the country. What has been lacking everywhere have been institutions which are very widely seen as legitimate and appropriate. This is partly a matter of the imperial provenance of so many independence constitutions; but it is also a matter of time. Attachment to institutions such that power can be transferred from one set of individuals to another in an accepted and peaceful transition only develops over a period of time. It took many years for the Constitution of the United States of America to achieve legitimacy and to provide the unquestioned rules in which the struggle for power could be played out peacefully (Lipset, 1964). And, even there, a bloody civil war was needed to establish the exact nature of its federalism. In a handful of African countries, the regularity of elections and a peaceful succession have, perhaps, laid the foundations for a legitimisation of the current rules of the political game; but, in most, there remains a more naked competition for power in which might is frequently victorious. Parallels with the Europe of the Middle Ages can too easily be drawn; yet there is no denying that the process of establishing state loyalties and political ground rules which receive widespread popular support is still going on. The newness of the states of tropical Africa thus encompasses both strong links to the former imperial powers which granted them independence and a lively search for an institutional form which wins the acceptance of a country's people.

African Nationalism

Criticism of imperial rule had been expressed in words and action by many individuals throughout the first half of the twentieth century. For the most part, however, in British Africa objections derived from personal experiences of discrimination and were aimed at opening up the imperial system to all talents; they were, therefore, essentially reformist and sought not the overthrow of the system, which appeared so secure and permanent, but its liberalisation. Qualified and educated Africans wanted primarily to hold down jobs commensurate with their skills and wanted greater access to the decision-making process, at first in local government and later at the national level. The French *evolués*, fewer in number but more highly educated, did not feel the same constraints so much for there were more avenues of advancement, including the opportunity at the highest level of membership of the National Assembly in Paris and even, for the very few, ministerial office (Mortimer, 1969). The Pan African movement, originated largely by West Indians and black Americans, provided a forum and an impetus for those articulate Africans who began to challenge the very system of imperial rule (Legum, 1962). By the time of the Manchester Conference in 1945 there were a number of potential political leaders, almost entirely English-speaking, who were committed to what was then the radical demand for self-determination and national independence.

The third phase of the relationship between the metropolitan powers and their African dependencies had its roots in the years between the world wars, but it blossomed in the immediate aftermath of Hitler's war. There were many factors that contributed to this development. The idea of the invincibility of white power had been shattered by Japanese victories in South-East Asia; the ideological justification of the war itself had been the rejection of racial superiority and the assertion of national independence; the emergence of the Indian subcontinent to full political independence provided a model of emancipation which Africans could see as applicable to their own experience; the opportunities to communicate, both with liberal anti-colonialists in the West and with fellow Africans, provided moral and intellectual support for the new leaders (Rathbone, 1981). There thus arose a plethora of parties throughout British Africa which called for political change and ultimately independence from the European powers. Many of their primary demands were economic and social, but Kwame Nkrumah's injunction 'Seek ye first the political kingdom' became widely accepted as the appropriate tactic. Starting in West Africa and spreading through East Africa to Central Africa, the demand for independence became stronger, more strident and ultimately victorious.

This continent-wide movement is normally referred to as African nationalism. A close inspection of its philosophical and social base is essential for any understanding of the early years of independence which its vigour and activities hastened. It was, to start with, a nationalism of a very special kind. Classical

European nationalism, both in its philosophy and in its practice, was different. Like virtually all 'isms', nationalism was both a set of ideals and a movement to translate those ideals into reality. At the level of ideals, the philosophy held that the proper territorial boundaries for the state were those which encompassed a single nation, or people, normally defined by its linguistic distinctiveness. The nationalist movements have sought to create new states which met this criterion, in short to make the *pays réel* coterminous with the *pays légal* (Kedourie, 1960). The creation of a unified Germany and unified Italy provides the classic example; but the same forces fuelled Balkan nationalisms after the First World War as they now fuel Basque separatism. African nationalism was different in this one single and fundamental respect: whereas in Europe nationalists began with the concept of a naturally united people seeking to mark out an appropriate political state, in Africa nationalists took state boundaries as given and attempted to wrest its control on behalf of the variety of peoples who had, by chance, been located within those boundaries. There are few exceptions to this general rule, most noticeably among the Somali, whose national flag contains a five-pointed star representing the five areas of Somali occupation deemed the basis of a true Somali state. Since 1960 Italian and British Somaliland have been united, Djibouti has been coveted, incursions have been made into the North-East Province of Kenya, and a bloody war was fought in the Ogaden in an ultimately unsuccessful attempt to wrest that Somali-occupied part of Ethiopia for a greater Somali Republic. Such 'classical' nationalism, however, is extremely rare.

Not all organised opposition to imperial rule was nationalist. Those movements which corresponded to the classical nationalist movements of the European experience were attacked by most Africans for being too narrowly focused and for assisting in the Balkanisation and fragmentation of Africa. In Uganda the Ganda people sought a special status within the country and on more than one occasion threatened to secede, a threat which was carried out verbally in 1961. In Nigeria a secessionist movement aiming to create an essentially independent Ibo state precipitated the Biafran civil war. These movements were classically nationalist; but they were not African nationalist: nor was that revolt in Kenya in the 1950s which is known as 'Mau Mau', for its leaders, although they espoused the notion of freedom from colonial rule, were drawn from only one section of Kenya, the Kikuyu. African nationalism is broader than any of these movements, for it consciously embraces all the peoples within a given state just as it seeks self-determination for the whole, rather than a part, of its black population.

At first sight, the nationalist movements in Africa were élitist in form and conservative in ideology. The leaders were almost exclusively men, and on rare occasions women, who had often been educated abroad and enjoyed a certain status as teachers or lawyers in their own countries. Their ideas were a complex *mélange* of John Stuart Mills's liberalism, the anti-colonialism of Lenin, a dash of Marxian class analysis, and a touching belief in the existence of Rousseau's general will (Hodgkin, 1961). In so far as the various individuals who called for the termination of imperial rule shared a common perspective, they joined together in rejecting the dominance of white rule and called for genuine local self-determination. What fuelled the leaders was not an economic and social vision of a new society so much as the immediate need to redress the political injustices of the past. The rich, the foreign and the white controlled the state; the nationalists identified with the poor, the indigenous and the black. As Ali Mazrui has so accurately but inelegantly expressed it, African nationalists were united by their common search for 'pigmentational self-determination' (Mazrui, 1967b). The importance of race, of an Africa for the Africans, had its profoundly conservative side; for many activists sought only to inherit the colonial state and to enjoy the powers and privileges which had been denied to them on account of their race. Frantz Fanon, the West Indian psychoanalyst who fought alongside the FLN in Algeria, had foreseen this; what he feared would happen, black faces appearing in white masks, generally did so (Fanon, 1965, Fanon, 1968). Nkrumah later came to accept this perspective when he wrote: 'In many cases, all they were concerned with was taking the places of the former colonial occupiers of their jobs and making the same money as these did in the same social and economic pattern' (Nkrumah, 1968, p. 65).

It would be wrong, however, to assume that all nationalist leaders were bourgeois in terms of occupation and ideology. Inevitably, given the low level of general literacy, the articulate spokesmen for national independence tended to be lawyers, teachers, or local government officials, for these were the only sorts of jobs open to the educated class. In French West Africa the leading politicians who formed the Rassemblement Démocratique Africaine (RDA) for a while flirted with the Communists; but the reason for this was not ideological fellow-feeling so much as the need for allies in the search for local autonomy. In the Portuguese colonies and in Zimbabwe, where independence was only gained after a protracted armed struggle, the leaders were more radical and less homogeneous socially. Guerrilla war threw up both intellectual leaders, such as Edouard Mondlane, Agostinho Neto and Amilcar Cabral in the Portuguese territories or Robert Mugabe in Zimbabwe, and also largely uneducated guerrilla commanders. The struggle also sharpened the ideological commitment of many, particularly when training took place in communist bloc countries. Even in those territories which moved smoothly along the constitutional and largely peaceful road to independence, there were some whose anti-colonialism embraced also a radical view of the post-independence society. But they were few, and many, like Oginga Odinga in Kenya or some progressive leaders in the Nigerian labour movement, were squeezed out by the more consensus-minded who bargained as intermediaries with the imperial powers.

Just as it is too easy to assume that all the leaders of the nationalist movement were members of a bourgeois élite for whom independence was essentially a transference of formal power from white guardians to black nationals, so it would be wrong to ignore the role of the ordinary people in the nationalist movement (Mohan, 1968). The crowds that turned out in their tens of thousands to listen to and applaud the well-known leaders were genuine adherents of the movement; the workers who challenged the imperial power in strikes, from Takoradi on the west coast to Mombasa on the east, were expressing their profound antagonism to the continuation of their subject status; the women who acted as couriers for the Mau Mau fighters or for the Zimbabwe liberation armies, or who organised and encouraged the mass meetings which imperial authorities could not ignore, were determined to achieve their own independence. The support of the masses was essential for the success of the African nationalists, for the imperial rulers tended initially to assume, with some justification in the early days, that the people's spokesmen were a dissatisfied and self-seeking minority in a majoritarian sea of acquiescence. The legitimacy of the leaders as national spokesmen depended upon their being seen to have mass following. That was the democratic necessity without which no British government, at least, could consider the transfer of power. Leaders therefore sought followers; they went into the country districts to drum up support for their demands for freedom. It was the meeting of the educated leadership with the mass base which made the nationalist movements ultimately almost irresistible.

But, by and large, the mass of Africans joined willingly. There was, of course, considerable pressure exercised by activists, as there is everywhere, to swell the crowds and contribute to party funds, but the pressure was more social than physical, except where the movement itself was deeply split by factionalism, as was the case in Southern Rhodesia in the early 1960s. What happened in the 1930s, and even more in the 1940s, was a steady, but perceptible, increase in the intensity of imperial penetration. The positive colonialism of the postwar years build upon a foundation in which the peasantry was already subject to many rules and regulations. Good agricultural practice necessitated coercion: contours had to be dug, diseased plants had to be burned, drought-resistant crops had to be planted, cattle had to be culled, and so on. The years of benign neglect gave way to the new interventionism and generated considerable resentment, especially as more and more Africans came into contact with the racially discriminatory norms of so much of the imperial world. Thus, peasants began to seek spokesmen from their own people to intercede on their behalf with the authorities and to act as a buffer between themselves and the alien experts, admittedly with many local assistants, who were creating so many problems. The mass of Africans, peasants, migrant workers and urban proletariat alike, were pushing for change and the overthrow of imperial rule; the educated élite became their spokesmen.

The position, however, was more complex than this. The notion of a united country, *evolué* and peasant, working together in a single organisation for independence, is largely an illusion. Nearly every country in Africa was divided in the years immediately preceding independence. In some countries important segments consciously attempted to put a brake on the process for they feared that their interests might be ignored in the independent state. In Northern Nigeria the party dominated by the indigenous religious and landed élite attempted to slow down the movement towards independence for they feared that the Southerners, with their better education and more modern skills, would dominate the economy and bureaucracy of an independent Nigeria to the Northerners' disadvantage. In Uganda the Ganda had long enjoyed a privileged position under imperial overrule and saw independence as necessarily reducing their existing autonomy under the tide of democratic equality which the nationalists preached. And throughout much of Africa some strata in African society had vested interests in the continuation of imperial rule, as their status and privileges depended upon their special relationships with it. But they also had less self-interested reasons; chiefs, in particular, often voiced a deeply felt hostility to the nationalists whose claim to lead was in no way traditional, and they garnered support from many of their elder and more conservative fellows who found it hard to accept the younger and more modern political activists as legitimate spokesmen for their people. Even amongst those who shared the same vision of a liberated Africa there were often bitter divisions. Only a handful of states (Tanganyika, Malawi, Guinea spring to mind as examples) obtained independence through a single nationalist party. In most of Africa there were rival parties, divided for the most part not by differing ideologies but by differing sources of support. In some, regional particularism predominated; in others, personal rivalries divided the mass of electors. On occasions, as in Southern Rhodesia in the early 1960s, more energy was expended on attacking competing nationalist parties, physically as well as verbally, than on challenging the alien rulers themselves.

The heritage of African nationalism is therefore an ambivalent one. Its adherents often had multiple aims. They were united on a single platform: independence and the end of

imperial rule. When that was achieved, the divisions which this
general aim had largely hidden began to surface and the
imagined unity, itself belied by rival organisations seeking to
inherit the imperial state, was shown up to be the illusion it
really was. Regionalism, personal rivalries, class conflicts, ideological disagreements, all now surfaced, their myriad problems
to be resolved by the group which inherited the colonial state,
itself scarcely altered in its economic form by the transference
of power. Since the ideological and social centre of gravity of
the victorious nationalist parties differed considerably, the
policies of the new governments differed too. The radicalised
leadership of FRELIMO in Mozambique was bound to
introduce a programme very different from the bourgeois-
dominated parties of Nigeria; the Convention People's Party
of Kwame Nkrumah in Ghana owed its strength to the
'new men', clerks and workers, rather than to the more established élite composed of teachers, businessmen and lawyers,
and its programme was accordingly more radical than most
West African governments. Despite the overwhelming desire
for independence, therefore, the lack of ideological cohesion
and the very different aims of participants in the nationalist
movements meant that the new states of Africa were
bequeathed a set of conflicts which proved difficult to manage.

The Imperial Response

The end of the formal European empires, which took place in
Africa mainly in the 1960s, seems in retrospect to have been an
inevitable process; but that is to enjoy the benefit of hindsight.
When the Second World War ended neither the French nor the
Portuguese governments had any intention of granting universal franchises to their African possessions as independent
entities. The British, although committed to the granting of
independence in the long run, certainly did not envisage so
rapid a transfer of power. Although the vast majority of the
continent did achieve its independence as a result of peaceful
negotiations, parts had to resort to armed uprisings to persuade
their alien rulers to relinquish power. In Portuguese Guinea,
Angola and Mozambique wars of liberation continued for more
than a decade; in Southern Rhodesia, too, it needed several

years of guerrilla war before an internationally accepted independence settlement could be achieved. These, however, were the exceptions; for the most part, the imperial powers voluntarily gave up their sovereignty.

At least Britain had some experience in granting independence to its overseas possessions. As Clement Attlee observed to Sir Stafford Cripps before he went to Delhi in 1942: 'There is a precedent for such an action. Lord Durham saved Canada for the British Empire. We need a man to do in India what Durham did in Canada' (quoted in Austin, 1980, p. 26). The granting of independence to India, Pakistan and Ceylon (Sri Lanka) in the years immediately after the Second World War was of great significance for Africa. There had, broadly speaking, been two traditions in imperial relations: the first, applicable to the white empire and reluctantly accepted after the American colonies had fought successfully for their independence, assumed that settlers had the British right to control their own destinies, while the second, applicable to the non-white empire and modelled on India, assumed that there would be a long period of training, tutelage and oversight before the inhabitants could exercise those rights so readily allowed to white Canadians and Australians. The Indian subcontinent ended its years of trusteeship in 1947; how much longer would Africa have?

The granting of independence to India represented a new consensus in establishment circles. The hastening of the process owed much to Gandhi and Indian nationalism; but it owed as much to a new intellectual and moral climate among policymakers. The confidence to which Nehru had once alluded had dramatically waned; the fall of Singapore, the strain and stress of war, the shabbiness and shortages of the 1940s, all served to puncture most delusions of imperial grandeur and invincibility. It suddenly seemed highly likely that the sun might set on the British Empire after all. Furthermore, the ideological climate had altered significantly. Defeating Nazism implied a detestation of philosophies based upon notions of racial superiority and a commitment to the concept of national self-determination. The United Nations enshrined these new moral imperatives. The currency of debate in international affairs, too, had shifted. Notions of *Realpolitik*, the overriding force of the national interest, and the right of strong states to employ

that strength at the expense of weaker states, were called into
question. Now a new emphasis was placed upon the rights of
small states. In the decade which followed the end of the war,
what may be called the new morality gradually came to dominate official thinking in Britain. A new generation of civil
servants and a Labour government, amongst whose deep
patriotism lay a strong anti-colonial streak, encouraged this
change; but the Conservative Party, too, was not immune to
these changes of emphasis.

A change in the ideological climate did not cause the
increased pace of decolonisation, although it clearly assisted it.
In a sense, British governments were compelled forward while
travelling in the same direction. Yet it was not always a smooth
ride. The Suez invasion of 1956 looked back to the former days
of imperial glory and gunboat diplomacy; its failure marked not
only the altered, and suddenly significant, attitudes of both the
international community and much domestic opinion on
imperial issues, but also the limited resources of the British
government in the face, especially, of American displeasure.
For there was another force which encouraged the movement in
favour of early decolonisation and that was an awareness of the
increasing practical difficulties of control. The ending of
National Service, the comparatively weak economic position of
Britain, and the domestic political repercussions of putting
down insurgencies in the empire made any long-term commitment to containing nationalism in Africa seem very expensive.
It could be done; the Mau Mau uprising in Kenya in the early
1950s was contained, as was a much less serious breakdown of
law and order in Nyasaland soon afterwards. But the essential
pragmatism of most British politicians led towards a broad
consensus that the time had come to transfer the empire into the
Commonwealth.

There were a number of dissenting voices, especially in the
Conservative Party, but the dissension was as nothing compared to the argument over imperial policy in France. There,
the response to the end of the war had been somewhat different
and the intellectual tradition of French imperialism, with its
emphasis on assimilation and an integrated empire, predis-
posed French politicians to devise means of retaining overseas
possessions within the empire. A bloody, and ultimately unsuc-

cessful, war was fought for this very purpose in Indo-China while in Algeria the French Army was deeply involved, both physically and emotionally, in keeping *Algérie française*. The position was spelt out with clarity at the 1944 Brazzaville Conference called to consider the future of the French African possessions. 'The objectives of the work of civilisation accomplished by France in the colonies exclude any idea of autonomy, any possibility of evolution outside the French imperial bloc; the constitution of "self-governments" [sic] in the colonies even in the distant future, is to be excluded' (Mortimer, 1969, p. 51) The contrast with British public policy could hardly be clearer.

In time, however, the impossibility of this philosophy was realised. But it took a series of severe shocks for that realisation to be fully accepted. The defeat of France in 1940, the defeat at Dien Bien Phu in 1954 and the failure of the Suez expedition in 1956 had made the defence of African possessions a matter of military honour and national pride. It needed the revolution of 1958 which brought General de Gaulle to power to defuse the Algerian crisis; in the process of educating French people to the realities of Africans' determination to achieve self-government in Algeria, he sought to devise a Commonwealth-like arrangement by which the empire could remain closely tied to France. The notion of a Community did not last long; but it provided the crucial step between an organic empire and the special relationship which currently marks relations between France and her African possessions.

In Portugal there was another domestic environment in which yet a different policy was rooted. There was no tradition of democracy in Portugal, certainly not in the days of the Salazar government, and thus no conceivable backing for democracy for the colonies among leading politicians. Furthermore, the whole concept of the Portuguese Empire was organic. This was not merely a political perspective; it was an economic fact. Portugal was itself essentially a poor and largely underdeveloped country whose economy depended heavily on the preferential links with its African possessions and whose peasantry saw the colonies as an escape from the rural impoverishment at home. Ideas of self-determination had even less support in Lisbon than they did in Paris. However, it was precisely these two factors – dictatorship and economic backwardness at home – which led to decolonisation, for they were the root causes of the military coup in April 1974 which swept the successors to Salazar from office. Within a very short space of time Mozambique and Guinea-Bissau had been granted their independences, since in each country one political party dominated the nationalist movement. In Angola, however, where three rival parties vied for power, the new Portuguese government tried, with the help of the Organisation of African Unity, to create a coalition government, but the rivalries between the parties were too great. Ideological differences and personality clashes could not be resolved. The Portuguese then named a date for independence and left; it took a civil war, marked by Cuban, Soviet and South African intervention, before the Popular Movement for the Liberation of Angola prevailed. As had happened in the Belgian Congo at the beginning of the 1960s, the imperial power had made no plans by which power was transferred smoothly from Europe to Africa.

Portugal and Belgium thus left Africa in a hurry and did little either to prepare their possessions for self-government or to develop new relationships with them. By contrast, France and, to some extent, Britain tried to ensure that the loss of empire was mitigated by strong ties with their former empires. Macmillan and Macleod in London had become acutely aware that the 'winds of change' blowing through Africa in the late 1950s could not be indefinitely contained; the public interest in decolonisation exemplified in the Soviet Union's moral and sometimes physical support for anti-colonial movements in the Cold War era, and the newly aroused and widespread desire for autonomy among the peoples of Africa could not be gainsaid. They therefore sought to bend to the wind and to guide its direction. Bending and guiding are two interconnected responses. British negotiators thus attempted to retain the good will of the African leaders by conceding the principle of self-determination while leaving their mark on the formal institutions of the new government. In this way, the least amount of disruption to the economic and cultural ties between metropolitan power and African possession could be achieved.

Three consequences flowed from this pragmatic policy. First, the actual conditions on which independence was granted were by no means always the most suitable for the individual territories. In a sense, decolonisation was a game; nationalist leaders asked for institutions and political rights which they felt Britain could not in all conscience refuse because they were valued so highly in Britain, while Britain offered imitations of her own institutions because she felt anything less would be demeaning and unacceptable to the nationalists. There is little evidence that both sides sat down to devise a form of government specifically for the conditions of each, or any, country moving towards independence. Instead, there was a bewildering kaleidoscope of constitutions, each new one following before its predecessor had had time to be fully understood or gain legitimacy; some, indeed, were frighteningly complicated and clearly temporary. In the end, the leaders of the new states in English-speaking Africa, in particular, inherited constitutions which often gave exaggerated power to minorities – such as the Senate in Kenya or the white seats in Zimbabwe – and which frequently failed to reflect the reality of power within the new state. Much energy was thus spent after independence in redressing what were seen as the imperfections in the very written rules of political action.

Secondly, with the exception of the Portuguese colonies and Southern Rhodesia (where the effective rulers did not readily cede their formal powers), the process of decolonisation was mostly devoid of rancorous friction. Even those who had done a stint in prison or restriction forgave their former masters astonishingly quickly. Indeed, Jomo Kenyatta, the very man whom a governor of Kenya had called a 'leader to darkness and death', became its first Prime Minister and President and a staunch friend of the West and its capitalist economy; Dr Banda, in Malawi, was similarly transformed from an outspoken and unremitting opponent of the British-instituted Central African Federation into one of the most conservative leaders of all Africa. The French experience, though different in kind, produced remarkably similar consequences. The ties of personal friendship and shared politics which the leaders of French-speaking Africa enjoyed with the metropolitan power continued after independence. And French governments took good care to foster them. However, where the offer of independence was not accepted on the French terms, the Paris government could be ruthless. When Sékou Touré chose independence outside the proposed French Community, the French withdrew entirely from Guinea – typewriters, files, experts and all. The effective quarantine of Touré's regime inevitably directed his lines of friendship towards the Eastern bloc, yet the ties with France could not be entirely ignored or forgotten. Twenty years after the traumatic break, the links were being repaired and the remarkable, almost metaphysical, power of Francophonie reasserted. It is the generation that grew up in the years following independence, nurtured on a new diet of nationalist history and cultural assertiveness, who have become more virulently anti-colonial than their parents who actually lived under imperial rule.

Thirdly, the generally smooth transition to self-government was accompanied by the continuation, and often strengthening, of economic and cultural links between the former African possessions and their imperial overlords. This was particularly so in the French case. Language, élite culture, friendships, experience of French accounting, bureaucratic and legal procedures were always likely to make this so. The continuing need for experts and advisers in the new states inevitably drove their leaders to France whose governments enthusiastically financed the continuation of technical assistance. Again, not surprisingly, the manufacturers suggested, the products approved, the technicians hired, the finance houses employed, were overwhelmingly French. The establishment of a currency embracing virtually all French-speaking Africa, the CFA franc, which was freely convertible, the tariff-free entrée to the French market for exports from the former empire, and the rule that 75 per cent of all foreign currency reserves be kept in Paris, where the French franc backed the international value of the CFA franc, all contributed to the very close relations which mark the links between France and most of her former colonies. The situation in English-speaking Africa was similar, yet sufficiently different to provide a genuine contrast. The British never showed quite the same mystic attachment to Africa as the French. Economic, educational, financial, business and cultural ties continued. The smooth transition meant that existing practices and links were continued; Africans understood and had experience of British banking and insurance procedures and continued with them. But the English language was less exclusive than the French language and the British government, as fitted its tradition of keeping the empire at arm's length, did little formally to integrate the economies of its former possessions into its own. A much higher proportion of French-speaking Africa's trade is carried on with France than is English-speaking Africa's with Britain. Nevertheless, however economic ties are calculated, there is little doubt that the granting of political independence to tropical Africa was not accompanied by economic independence.

It is, then, essential to see the imperial response to African nationalism as an important factor in moulding the new states' economies and political forms. The imperial powers remained the dominant actors in this terminal phase of political control; they did not have a free hand, but they could, and did, ensure that special consideration was given to certain sectors of a country's population and provide the fundamentals of the new constitutional order (Wasserman, 1976). They also saw this phase not as the end of the road, but as a beginning of a new relationship in which economic factors remained important. This peaceful transfer of power has sometimes been called the neo-colonial solution, in that the imperial powers' economic interests were largely preserved and their political interests little impaired, given the economic and cultural dependence bequeathed to the new governments. Yet it should not be thought that independence was no more than the lowering of one flag and the raising of another. It symbolised the transfer of political power from outsiders to the indigenous Africans of the country. And the African leaders, constrained as they unquestionably were, have nevertheless been their own men; they have operated within inherited structures to alter the priorities and policies of their countries.

Preparations for Independence

Governing any country requires a range of skills. There are the technical skills needed to run the various services provided by the state; there are the bureaucratic skills needed to administer and monitor the government's programmes and finances; and there are the political skills needed to build up support for the government and defuse the differences within the country. Some of these skills can be taught; some must be learned; a few are simply possessed. The appropriate skills will differ from country to country as the conflicts within countries and the institutions which structure the resolution of conflicts also differ. In Africa independence was not the culmination of a long process of careful preparation in which the end was long known and the means carefully developed; it arrived in a hurry, before either the departing imperial powers or the local inheritors were fully prepared. In the British and French possessions some attempt was made to bequeath a minimum of necessary skills to the successor states; in the Belgian and Portuguese cases there was an unseemly abdication.

Although social and economic forces are significant factors in delineating the contours of a political system, the formal institutions are also central. The British, in particular, spent much time and effort devising constitutions for the new states (de Smith, 1964). The basic model was the Westminster model; but there was a wide range of variations, in which American-style federalism and second chambers appeared as well as bills of rights unfamiliar to the British citizens. The French model was essentially the President-centred form introduced in 1958 to cater for General Charles de Gaulle. Although there were differences of some substance between the two basic models, there were two ways in which they left a similar heritage.

In the first place, they were both potentially authoritarian. The electoral systems exaggerated the representation of the larger parties; the majoritarian principle on which governments were formed strengthened further the power of the larger party. In the United Kingdom it is self-restraint which limits the extent to which a victorious party at the polls translates its preferences into laws; a disciplined party, parliamentary rules and the lack of entrenched minority rights provide, in theory at least, the ideal conditions for party dominance. In Africa that sense of self-restraint and consideration for minorities, as well as the fear of future elections and incipient divisions within the ruling party which check the untrammelled use of political power in Britain, is largely absent. Party leaders use the available power to the full; and the available power in both English-speaking and French-speaking Africa was considerable. There was little preparation in British Africa for the consultative and incremental principles on which a system of parliamentary supremacy depends for its efficient working.

In the second place, in the territories of the British Empire the constitutions were often seen as continuing signs of the old imperial relationship. They were, after all, acts of the European state; they were, moreover, often the consequences of bargaining between nationalist leaders and imperial politicians. Like the Irish before them, many African leaders emerging from British overrule resented their constitution and sought something more autochthonous and more firmly rooted in their own sense of priorities (Wheare, 1960; Robinson, 1961). In the terminal phase of imperial rule, the fact of independence was more important than its form; in any case, leaders differed on the shape of the future when they agreed on the primacy of political self-determination. Consequently, the years after independence frequently witnessed a restructuring of the very principles of the political system as the victorious party and its leaders attempted to establish a form of government that met their requirements. Preparation, such as took place, had often been directed at a set of institutions, and the unwritten conventions associated with them, which was soon replaced.

At one level, the political level, there had been little appropriate preparation. Imperial rule, the only model experienced in English-speaking Africa, was centralised, authoritarian in essence and bureaucratic; the institutions bequeathed professed the importance of devolved power, of negotiation and compromise just as they also had to operate in a truly political environment marked by competing groups seeking political advantage for themselves. The nationalists had made their reputations in agitational politics and in opposition, where simultaneous attacks on government from several angles can be effective tactics; in office, the need to settle on a single policy and defend the government against dissent fitted ill their earlier experience. Their followers, too, expected that power would be translated into action and suspected that the compromises on which liberal democratic politics depend were betrayals of the nationalist cause. In part of French-speaking West Africa the experience of individual leaders, like Houphouet-Boigny and

Senghor, was a better preparation for the politics of coalition building; but they, too, had to pay attention to their lieutenants whose concern to benefit from the acquisition of political power often hindered reconciliation between rival factions.

At other levels, the technical and bureaucratic, the preparation had been more directly concerned with the needs of a new state. The very notion of preparation had been employed, by British politicians in particular, to postpone the day of independence; in the 1940s, it was widely accepted, there were minimum conditions for the granting of independence of which size, economic strength and administrative skills were some. These were wonderfully flexible because they had no fixed measurement. A colony was prepared when the British government decided it was prepared; and that was very much a political judgement (Schaffer, 1965 – 6). Attempts were made to localise the civil services; in West Africa in the 1940s and early 1950s, in East and Central Africa somewhat later. And much progress in terms of numbers had been made by independence in Nigeria, Ghana and Sierra Leone; in terms of experience the record was less good. In the Eastern Region of Nigeria, one of the more widely educated parts of the African Empire, only thirteen officers in the entire administration had been in government in 1960 for as long as ten years. In East Africa the situation was worse. In 1960, 70 per cent of the senior administrative posts in Western Nigeria and 84·8 per cent in Ghana had been localised, while in Kenya and Tanganyika the figures were 9·6 per cent and 10·6 per cent respectively.

Technical skills were perhaps even less developed. The education system, as has already been noted, was essentially designed to produce literate clerks. There was thus a dearth of accountants, electrical engineers, public health officials, and so on; for many jobs, which were sensitive either because they were visible or because they retained discretionary power, white expatriates had to be employed. At the time of Zambia's independence in 1964, for instance, the country possessed less than 100 graduates and under 1,000 secondary-school graduates. By 1966 the dependence on expatriate skilled manpower remained high; all but 4 per cent of high-level manpower with degrees and all but 12 per cent with school certificates were non-Africans (Jolly, 1971). Rapid growth in educational provisions has taken place, but dependence upon foreign teachers – many of whom do not themselves speak English very fluently – and the sheer pace of expansion has not been able to resolve the problem satisfactorily. A minimal accounting qualification is not sufficient to provide a sophisticated response to the often labyrinthine financial complexities of deals between government and sometimes unscrupulous foreign businesses; the new states have often lost out, therefore, due to their own lack of modern skills (Schatz, 1969).

In French-speaking Africa the position was hardly better. Although at the very highest level there was probably a greater number of experienced bureaucrats, the universalist values inculcated during their years of service for the French state often conflicted with the nationalist priorities of the politicians. Here, too, there was a paucity of experience and an imbalance between bureaucrats and technicians. France encouraged a continuing dependency by providing from her technical assistance budget the salaries of expatriates. Two-thirds of the technical assistance personnel in Senegal in the mid-1960s saw no difference between their jobs there and the equivalent jobs in France. Administering and directing were their prime functions in both countries; advising came a poor third (R.C. O'Brien, 1972). The existence of many *petits blancs*, lower-class whites, and the inability to train on the job limited further the skills that Africans could acquire. And the efficiency of the state apparatus, certainly so far as the ordinary citizen is concerned, depends very largely on the skills of comparative humble functionaries, like overseers, local tax inspectors, road engineers, and so on. Producing a balance sheet between the French heritage, with its élitist emphasis on a few, highly qualified men and women, and the British heritage, with its wider but less specialised focus, is a game of endless possibilities. No satisfactory criteria can be agreed upon. Both countries provided some training; neither provided enough (Smith, 1978).

Conclusion

Independence was no accident; but it was a kind of happenstance. It may be of academic interest only to consider whether it was achieved by the force of nationalist pressure alone or was engineered by shrewd imperial rulers seeking to minimise their losses. The consequences for the new states of the precise method by which power was transferred and of the precise forms in which independence was gained have been real enough.

The instability which has been such a marked aspect of West Africa has actually been labelled 'inevitable' by one scholar because the inheritance of the governments at independence has been so unfavourable (O'Connell, 1967). Constitutions which are merely bargains between a nationalist élite and a departing imperial power provided inappropriate frameworks for the real political battle which ensued; the inexperience of politicians in the arts of governance added to the problems; the economic and social environment in which politics take place contribute further, and perhaps irreconcilable, pressures on governments. The argument is beguiling; but it is too mechanistic and hardly allows for those states, of which there are a good number, who have experienced twenty years of stable government. Even if instability is not inevitable, there is little doubt that the new states of tropical Africa gained their independence without the sort of preparation which is taken for granted in the developed world. Preparation is not enough of itself; as the next chapter suggests, there are significant factors in the political environment which pose additional challenges to the politicians' skills.

4 The Political Environment

Politics is a universal activity. In all states there is a process by which mutually exclusive demands on that state are mediated and regulations made which are binding upon its inhabitants. Who gets what, when, and how, in Harold Lasswell's famous phrase, remains a central question for all students of politics; in every state there is an 'authoritative allocation of values', to use David Easton's unlovely but instructive definition of politics (Easton, 1956–7). There is, therefore, much in common between the developed, industrialised and long-established states, on the one hand, and the less-developed, agriculturally dominated and new states of Africa on the other.

But there are also fundamental differences. Many of these stem from the very different political environment in which government operates. The general poverty of tropical Africa and its paucity of resources, whether human or material, is one significant factor; the survival to some extent of a system of social differentiation based upon linguistic particularism is another; a political culture which stresses the instrumental purposes of political action is a third. These are not unique to Africa. Indeed, the United States for at least the first third of the twentieth century was much affected, too, by areas of poverty, ethnicity and instrumentation. Whether the contrast between Africa and, say, Western Europe is merely a quantitative matter or is genuinely qualitative is immaterial; politicians in tropical Africa have to operate in an environment so manifestly different from that enjoyed by European politicians that it is essential to spell out those differences at the outset.

The Crisis of Resources

The practical possibilities open to any government are closely related to the resources available to that government. The unhappy truth for virtually all of tropical Africa is that it is poor, both absolutely and relatively to the Americas, Europe, the Middle East, Australasia and parts of Asia. Only the Ivory Coast, Nigeria and Gabon had per capita incomes in 1977 of more than $US500; Canada, France and Sweden, for instance, all enjoyed per capita incomes of over $US5,000. On virtually any index of affluence – doctors per 1,000 inhabitants, length of tarmacked roads, access to electricity, proportion of teenagers in education – the tropical African countries fall a long, long way behind the states of Western Europe (Kidron and Segal, 1981). For the most part the soils are infertile; there are few waterways to carry commerce or ideas; the rainfall is erratic. The non-agricultural resources of the continent are unequally distributed and are disproportionately located in the southern tip, apart from oil which has become a significant factor in the economics of several states along the West African littoral. As far as minerals are concerned, there is bauxite in Guinea ($13 \cdot 9$ per cent of world production), chrome in Zimbabwe ($7 \cdot 56$ per cent), copper in Zaire and Zambia ($16 \cdot 16$ per cent), industrial diamonds in Ghana and Zaire (27 per cent), iron ore in Liberia ($5 \cdot 3$ per cent), manganese in Gabon ($11 \cdot 11$ per cent), and uranium in Niger ($6 \cdot 54$ per cent). In comparison to the great mineral giants such as the Soviet Union, Canada, Australia, the United States and the Republic of South Africa, tropical African countries are pygmies. They rely overwhelmingly on their agriculture to generate wealth and on peasant producers to grow the crops for home consumption and export sales.

The plight of most Africans is well known. Its political relevance is less often spelt out. There is, to start with, a shortage of skilled administrators, technicians and professionals. This is largely due to the limited degree of education provided by the imperial powers and by the reluctance to permit Africans to take up responsible positions (Symonds, 1966). There is no alternative to experience; and African officials are generally short of experience. Hence, the capacity to administer the state, to oversee the nationalised industries and parastatal organisations which so dominate the national economies, and to mediate between competing claims for government assistance is limited. Running a country is not an easy task and an arts degree, while a useful starting point, does not of itself make its holder an efficient bureaucrat and financially aware administrator. Crash courses in Institutes of Public Administration can assist to some extent, but it is the truly exceptional person who does not need several years to learn the techniques and procedures necessary for good government. A dearth of accountants adds to the difficulties. In short, therefore, on top of a basically low level of available resources was a governmental structure whose personnel in the initial years of independence, through no fault of their own, lacked the sophisticated skills necessary to make the best use of what few economic resources were available.

Financial and technical aid from outside Africa has been seen in some quarters as a partial answer to the essential poverty of the continent (Brandt, 1980). As will be indicated in Chapter 7, there are good reasons to examine this contention closely. But a necessary condition for any effective use of foreign aid is the ability to absorb it. In too many countries, it has been shown that the transport facilities and local administrations were ill suited to the projects financed from overseas. This is very visibly the case when large amounts of famine assistance in the form of foodstuffs are concerned; the local expertise and facilities are simply often inadequate. But it is true also in other areas; the requirements of donor countries are often complex and call for considerable documentation, costing and project appraisals. These are not always forthcoming. The experience of the European Community's Directorate 8, which deals with aid to Africa, has demonstrated that those countries with comparatively developed and sophisticated planning ministries tend to use their allocation of funds more than the less well-organised countries; and this merely increases the already powerful tendency towards cumulative inequality in the continent.

Human resources are not all skilled. One of the fundamental problems facing the new states of Africa is the age structure of their populations and the speed at which they are growing. Half the population is not yet 16. This puts a tremendous burden on the educational services, which have grown considerably since independence, and on those who are economically active and have to provide financially for this youthful population. Many children, of course, are economically productive and make a valuable contribution to the family economy but, generally speaking, the extent to which governments in Africa have to provide for the non-productive members of the country is high. What is more, the numbers of young people coming on to the labour market each year, now that in many countries there is a shortage of land, are presenting increasing problems. Unemployment and underemployment, fertile ground for agitational politics, are likely to grow.

Meagre natural resources, an underdeveloped industrial structure, a limited pool of administrative expertise, a burgeoning population and high level of dependence contribute to a state of poverty. There are two general responses to such a situation. The evidence from rich, industrialised nations of the world indicates that the poorest sector of the community participates least in political activity; the less-educated, low-income earners are significantly less likely even to vote, let alone instigate contact with political authorities, than are their more educated and affluent fellow citizens. Partly this is a sign of alienation, partly an indication of the apathy of failure, and partly the consequence of an all-consuming struggle for survival which allows no time for political activity. In some ways, this non-participation is conducive to political stability for a failure on the part of the most disadvantaged to express their resentment enables the advantaged, provided they are not themselves deeply divided, to preserve the control over the apparatus of political power. Whether such political stability should be valued highly is, of course, another matter.

But there is a second and more immediately significant response since it generates considerable political activity and conflict. In countries marked by poverty even the smallest advantage is to be sought with vigour and preserved with effort. In the developed world there has been a general expectation that the national wealth was growing sufficiently fast for all to benefit, although the exact amount of benefit was unlikely to be equal. At least, one person's gain would not be another's loss. In tropical Africa, however, there is a much more widely held assumption that politics is a zero-sum game in which the available pool of resources is strictly limited. The extreme importance of small benefits – the siting of a water pump in a village to save the women perhaps three or four hours' walking to collect only limited supplies of water is a case in point – and the belief that advantages must be fought for, lest another village or group gain them, leads to a singularly intense view of politics. In much of Africa politics are of paramount importance; in extreme cases it *is* a life-and-death matter whether the district administration allocates its meagre development moneys to one village rather than to another. Political action is essential for economic advance and sometimes economic survival itself. There are few crumbs for the vanquished; the store cupboard of resources is generally too bare for that. Victory is thus paramount and the fear of defeat a potent source of pre-emptive action. So poverty has an ambiguous effect on the politics of tropical Africa; in some cases, it depoliticises; in others, it overemphasises the paramountcy of politics.

Yet poverty is not equally distributed and statistics measuring the average monetary income of Africa's peoples can be misleading. Until the 1970s, when wars, revolutions, mismanagement and drought contributed to a massive upheaval of peoples, hunger was not one of the continent's most pressing problems. The number of new refugees in Africa in the 1970s, however, was enormous. In 1964 there had only been 400,000; in 1967 there were about 735,000; by the end of the 1970s the figure had risen to 4 million (Adepoju, 1982). These are in themselves some of the most poverty-stricken people on earth and they create a drain on their host country's resources and, frequently, a source of disorder and tensions. Although much attention is rightly given to their plight, it should not obscure another perspective, that the vast majority of the African peasantry continues to cultivate its fields and feed its families as its parents did before. Calculating the value of production grown and consumed at home is not a simple statistical exercise, but the figures also underplay some of the less tangible aspects of life. Warmth, friendship, a sense of community, religious satisfaction, all contribute to an individual's evaluation of the quality of life. So, too, does a person's experience of the past and expectations for the future. Governments operate in a surprisingly congenial climate because peasants' experience of the past and knowledge of the present has not led them to expect a great deal more than they already have; they may have high hopes, but they have a shrewd expectation of what is likely (Oberschall, 1969 – 70). The objective condition of the peasantry may well be bad; but its destabilising potential is less than is often imagined.

Peasants have good reason to feel that they are carrying a disproportionate burden of Africa's development efforts. Nearly all governments, whether avowedly socialist or unashamedly conservative, are forced to exploit the peasant producers. There is not yet a sufficiently developed monetary sector for a government to raise its needed revenue through some progressive scheme of income tax. The agricultural basis of most economies means that government revenue must largely come from paying the small producers less than the open-market price and pocketing the difference. If 90 per cent of the families in a country depend for their livelihood essentially on their farms, governments must turn to them for revenue purposes. As Nyerere has rightly observed, it is the peasantry that earns the foreign currency which pays for the modern sector of the economy from which the peasantry derives little immediate benefit (Nyerere, 1968).

Parts of Africa are manifestly not poor. Here, too, the statistics of average per capita income can be misleading. Any casual visitor to Abidjan or Nairobi – indeed, to almost any capital in tropical Africa – will immediately see signs of affluence. Fine shops, good restaurants, large cars and smart clothes are all to be seen. There is a stratum in nearly all countries which eats well, lives well, drinks well and has money to spend. The contrast between the confident bureaucrats in their dark suits gathered on the terrace of the United Kenya Club in Nairobi and the shanty-town dwellers of the Mathare Valley a few miles away is striking; much the same could be said of almost every African country, where the contrast between the male élite of the capital city and the labouring women on the peasant farms is enormous. It is little wonder, therefore, that men and women who have achieved well-paid and prestigious jobs in the capital cities use every political device to retain them; nor is it surprising that others attempt to employ any political resources they may have to raise themselves into the small, but advantaged, white-collar class.

The crisis of resources which has been sketched out so briefly here thus has several dimensions. There are absolute shortages, of trained and experienced manpower, of infrastructural development upon which economic growth depends, of natural exploitable resources in high international demand, and of sources of taxation for development-minded governments. But there are also relative imbalances, often masked by the statisticians who tend to trade in mean or average figures. The inequality between Africa and Europe hardly needs mentioning; the inequalities within Africa, both between states and inside individual states, need stressing for the politics of these new states help to establish these inequalities just as they respond to attempts to redress them.

The Extractive View of Politics

Governing a state that is short of resources is always a difficult task. If there are institutionalised competitive politics as well the problems are greater as rival groups struggle for a limited supply of rewards. Politics in Africa are not entirely a zero-sum game, although they are often practised as if this were the case; but there is little doubt of the central importance of access to government. The state dominates the job market, is deeply involved in most economic activities and commands control over an extremely wide range of goods and services, as well as badges of status. The lack of a developed indigenous private sector, of entrenched pressure groups and of secondary organisations results in the 'monopolistic' state (Aron 1966 – 7). Countervailing sources of power tend to be found only in the transnational businesses and foreign-aid agencies. Whereas in the United States the friction between groups could be eased by the abundance of wealth available for distribution and by the multiplicity of social organisations in which individuals could earn status and power, Africa lacked both (Potter, 1954; Kornhauser, 1971). Politics has thus become an activity of extreme importance in which failure could be economically disastrous and success economically rewarding.

Politicians in Africa have tended to use control of the governmental machinery to preserve their positions of power at all costs. The election in Western Nigeria in 1965 is an extreme case in point. Here the incumbent party resorted to every imaginable ruse. Returning officers suddenly left for Europe as the opposition candidate came to present his nominating papers; nomination papers, when accepted, were sometimes mysteriously proven out of order; government money was used to encourage certain opposition candidates to stand down; promises of office or threats of violence were also employed. Since the incumbent party controlled the administration and the police force, a person had to be resourceful and brave just to get his name on to the ballot paper. The tactic of eliminating a rival party by administrative means has also been used on the other side of the continent. In 1968, for example, the returning officers for the Kenyan local elections, being part of the administration, obeyed their political masters in finding every nomination paper presented by members of the opposition Kenyan People's Union to be improperly completed, while every nomination paper presented by members of the ruling Kenyan African National Union was in order. One official, however, was so efficient that he had already accepted a candidate's papers before the government instruction reached him, but a reinspection showed that it had, after all, been incorrectly filled in. More often, opposition leaders and parties have been banned outright so that the danger of defeat at the polls is eliminated. The emergency legislation bequeathed by the imperial powers and the readiness with which they had incarcerated inconveniently critical black politicians before independence together made the harassment of opposition politicians after independence a simple and familiar act of government.

Political leaders everywhere seek to retain power; only a few countries place an absolute limit on the period a politician may hold office. But in the Western, industrialised world the loss of office is followed more often by offers of lucrative and highly regarded jobs than by the ignominy of enforced unemployment. Because of the lack of alternative positions in most of Africa the fear of losing power is very real. In some countries, such as Kenya where a thriving indigenous capitalist sector exists alongside a tradition of re-employing in parastatal organisations major politicians defeated at the polls, this fear is much reduced and competition for office is enthusiastically joined. As the psalmist once sung, 'the King's wrath is as a roaring lion', but he went on to say that 'his favour is as dew upon the grass'. There are, indeed, positive advantages to be gained by winning power just as real disadvantages are feared if power is lost. This aspect of politics has clearly caught the imagination of many African novelists who have written emotional denunciations of the way some politicians have used their political power to advance their own economic self-interest. Bank loans and licences, foreign-exchange allocations and preferential access to land can all follow from the very fact of being a minister. 'To us', Sembene writes in *God's Bits of Wood*, 'their mandate is simply a licence to profiteer' (Sembene, 1970, p. 277). More common in West than East Africa, this tendency to plunder the governmental machine to accumulate riches is widespread, although not universal. The enormous wealth of Zaire's President Mobutu, the acquisition of farms by the Kenyatta family in Kenya, or the burgeoning Swiss bank accounts of some Nigerian politicians cannot be ignored. Without political power these people would not have so enriched themselves.

Yet to have the opportunity to behave in this way does not entail taking that opportunity. What makes the use of political power for private ends so common can be explained, in part, by reference to an important strand in almost all contemporary African political cultures. This can be called 'the extractive view of politics'. The dominant assumptions underpinning political actions are instrumental rather than programmatic. They are not unique to Africa; indeed, the politics of the United States can largely be characterised in the same way. Contributions to candidates or political parties, intercessions with legislators, calculations on voting behaviour in the Congress are all closely related to the concrete, and personal, interests of the participants. Companies used to 'invest' in politicians directly, before alterations in the Campaign Finance Laws made such direct contributions impossible, but they still expend a great deal of money in attempts to secure the election of a candidate agreeable to them; local groups remind their legislators that the duty of the representative is to fight for the sectional interests of those they represent. The style and emphasis of British politics is very different. Ideology, party loyalty and historical hangovers all tend to weaken the open, and unashamed, connection between self-interest and political behaviour.

Using politics is not merely an élite activity. It is followed also by the majority of African citizens. 'The dominant concern of the vast majority of participants in politics at all levels', it has been said of Nigeria in the 1960s, 'was the receipt of the largest possible share of benefits in the shortest period of time' (Post and Vickers, 1973, pp. 46 – 7). In Chinua Achebe's novel, *A Man of the People*, the minister is challenged by a young, idealistic intellectual who inveighs against what he sees as the minister's corrupt and indefensible behaviour; but it is the minister who wins the election for he has access to governmental jobs and funds which can be extracted for the benefit of the local community (Achebe, 1966). In Ghana, too, the same perception of politics is to be found. Maxwell Owusu, for example, has argued that participation in politics is instrumental to the achievement of social status through the acquisition of wealth for 'political relations are considered extensions or primary dimensions of economic relations' (Owusu, 1970, p. 5). A less stridently economist interpretation of Ghanaian small-town politics nevertheless stresses the instrumental assumptions of most political actors (Dunn and Robertson, 1973). The development of patron-client networks, through which so much political activity in the continent is structured, was based on reciprocity; the peasant farmer trading wanted votes for access to government. In choosing candidates, local activists have tended to prefer people who were likely to have the skills and contacts to impress the central government and abstract resources, however meagre, from them.

The task of the ordinary politician, therefore, came increasingly to be seen as an entrepreneurial one, as a broker between the 'masses' and the government. In those legislatures whose members still needed to win popular endorsement at regular intervals, representatives saw their role as being essentially spokesmen for local interests. This was the case in Tanzania, as it was also in the rest of eastern Africa for the most part (R. F. Hopkins, 1971; Hodder-Williams, 1979). A few individuals in Kenya and Zambia did attempt a more ideological or principled approach and found expressions of support; but the likes of J. M. Kariuki were the exceptions. When it came to election time, parochialism prevailed and voters evaluated rival candidates on their record as actual or potential garnerers of resources (Hyden and Leys, 1972). The immediacy of needs, the ubiquitous presence of government and the emphasis of majority rule over minority rights have all strengthened the tendencies towards an extractive view of politics and its corollary, the single-party state.

But there are two factors from the past which also assist. Imperial rule was distant and bureaucratic. Individuals approached the government not as an institution whose form and politics they had taken some small part in affecting but as a source of rewards and punishments. No commitment was owed to it; no sense of its own problems of ordering priorities was considered. The government was there to be used, to be manipulated or hoodwinked, so that advantage might accrue to the supplicant. In the second place, the rights and obligations of the extended family did not end with a man's election to a position of authority. On the contrary, they were felt all the more keenly. Those who gained office often found themselves besieged by relations and friends of relations expecting benefits for, just as blood links helped to cushion adversity, they would also be expected to confer advantages. To have a family member in local government or in a ministry was seen as a benefit; it is little wonder, therefore, that the poorest families in the Third World have often had the largest number of children since the odds on producing one who might achieve influence are thus improved.

While the extractive view of politics is understandable and widespread, it is not universal. There are many selfless men and women working hard for pitifully small rewards, taking decisions in a fairminded and responsible way and resisting the importunities of friends and relations. There are activists whose ideological commitments force them to adopt unpopular positions and to stand on principle; their access to the wielders of power is usually slight. There are too many pressures which make it difficult to ignore an extractive view of politics. There are few men who are in politics out of a sense of duty — whether crowning a career in the trade union movement or living out the image of the squirearchy. They are in politics for a purpose; and purposes are not achieved without having direct access to the seat of power.

Tribalism

It is difficult to discuss contemporary Africa, in university common rooms as much as in private houses, without alluding to the problems of tribalism. The term itself has become a subject of debate. Some would ban it altogether from the discourse of social scientists because it is assumed to have derogatory connotations and to imply an element of primitivism. Certainly, there are few people who use it as a praise word; but that of itself is insufficient reason to ban it altogether from the analyst's vocabulary. In any case, Africans themselves use the term prolifically; politicians inveigh against tribalism, journalists uncover examples of tribalism, academics bemoan the existence of tribalism. Indeed, in Gideon Were's inaugural lecture as Professor of History at the University of Nairobi he asserted, as late as 1980, that it was 'important for historians to analyse the twin problems of corruption and tribalism' (Were, 1981, p. 5).

However, it is essential to be careful about the precise meaning of the term. A first distinction, which clearly reflects the concern about its normative content, is the distinction made by Tom Mboya between positive and negative tribalism (Mboya, 1963). There he differentiated sharply between the traditional cultural and social practices of a particular tribe, which he saw as positively virtuous and necessary in Africa's search for an authentic culture of its own, and the political practices of those who categorised all people according to their tribe and evaluated them, usually negatively, exclusively in terms of tribe. Tribal loyalty became the primary political virtue and political reality, so that in all conflictual situations a person's behaviour was dictated by considerations of tribal unity. It is in this negative sense (for Mboya believed such motivation was in the interests of neither the individual nor the nation as a whole) that the term is commonly used.

There are, however, still difficulties with its use. The word 'tribe' has been used in at least two distinct ways. Its earliest use by anthropologists was confined to the largely independent political divisions of a population sharing a common culture. As with the tribes of Israel, writers could speak of the Ibo tribes, subdivisions of a wider grouping which, although the members shared a language and a mythology, nevertheless competed against each other in antagonistic conflict for land and other desired resources. Its later, and ultimately dominant, meaning referred to the wider population itself so that the Ibo-speaking people of Eastern Nigeria became regarded as a single tribe. It is not a word that is much used in European studies (to refer, for instance, to the Basques or the Walloons) and is thus seen by many as yet another example of Europeans' demeaning attitude towards Africa. Many scholars, therefore, sought another term, more neutral in connotation and more universal in application, and preferred to speak of ethnic groups although this phrase, too, had a specific history which has largely been forgotten. The term's application to Africa – it had been common currency in the analysis of American politics for some time – originated when sociologists wanted to distinguish the social networks and behaviour established in urban environments by individuals sharing a common language from the social networks and behaviour established by the same people in the rural areas. Whether ethnic groups or tribes are used as the units for analysis, they now refer to the same phenomena.

Using the terms tends to imply that there are real entities called tribes, or ethnic groups, which have a life and dynamic of their own stretching back into the pre-imperial past. This is not necessarily true. The role played by tribe is not that of some primordial, and internalised, sense of group loyalty that directs political action. For one thing, many contemporary tribes are the creations of imperial rule and not natural social organisations (Mafeje, 1971). The enlargement of scale represented by the establishment of colonial states brought the peoples of Africa into contact with a much wider range of outsiders than had been the case before, a development which necessitated for all peoples a heightened sense of personal identity. The situation among the Ibo has been well described in this way. Tribal identification emerged primarily in a town when men encountered people with different languages, customs and beliefs. To deal with other groups, social categories or labels were utilised. Ibo was actually a word originating in the New World as a classification covering slaves who spoke any of the various Ibo dialects. Iboland itself was divided into independent village groups whose inhabitants only became conscious of their shared 'Iboness' when they came into contact with non-Ibo. 'Thus', Bohannan and Curtin have written, 'within a century between 1850 and 1950, an identity first imposed from the outside as a cultural classification became a reality and ended as a major force in Nigerian politics' (Bohannan and Curtin, 1971, p. 348). What was true for the Ibo was true for many others, including immigrants from the Indian subcontinent who became lumped together in Kenya, despite their religious and linguistic differences, as the Wahindi. Although migration and intermarriage throughout the continent have manifestly reduced the number of 'pure' members of a tribe, there is no escaping the fact that the vast majority of Africans are able not only to identify their own tribe but also to allocate fellow nationals to *their* tribes with an uncanny accuracy. In this sense, tribes are inescapably part of the contemporary reality.

To identify oneself or others as members of a tribe is not to make this identification the primary, let alone the natural, motive for political action. Abdul Nasser once wrote that every individual is involved in several 'circles of identity' – African, Arab, socialist, colonist, father, politician, and so forth – which are not all relevant to every situation (Nasser, 1955). It is the specific characteristics of each individual situation that determines which 'circle of identity' predominates. Most behaviour in tropical Africa is thus not tribally determined at all. In the Zambian copper mines or in the Nigerian ports, for example, political behaviour was dependent at different times on the saliency of different identities; thus, workers exemplified a degree of class consciousness in their dealings with management but were influenced by tribal factors in their selection of workers' representatives (Epstein, 1958; Melson and Wolpe, 1970). In other words, the exact context of each political situation must be examined before assumptions about tribalism can possibly be made. As Nelson Kasfir has written, 'the creation of social solidarity in response to a situation turns the members of an ethnic *category* into an ethnic *group*' (Kasfir, 1978 – 9, p. 373). What becomes imperative, therefore, is to examine the situations when this group solidarity is seen as specifically relevant.

Tribe only becomes a relevant differentiating category when there is a situation of competition. For much of political life, therefore, it is supremely irrelevant since a great deal of activity occurs wholly within tribally homogeneous localities. In choosing local councillors or representatives for the national legislature rural Africans seek effective brokers, or intermediaries, between themselves and the government which allocates desired resources. Admittedly, outsiders are usually excluded; Benedicto Kiwanuka, for instance, although Prime Minister of Uganda, could find no seat to contest in 1962 because he had been rejected by his own Ganda people for ideological heresies and rejected by other peoples for being an outsider. Within rural communities, however, two factors are important. First are class loyalties. Often the critical point is a subdivision within the tribe, as is to be expected in linguistically homogeneous constituencies where some badge of differentiation is needed to structure competition. Second are more instrumental calculations of efficacy. Ordinary peasants then behave as though they are clients of a local patron, trading support for resources; the patron survives as the preferred intermediary so long as he satisfies the expectations of his clientele (Powell, 1970; Lemarchand, 1972; Clapham, ed., 1982). In dealing with government, for the most part peasants wisely choose for their brokers men, and occasionally women, who have a proven record as successful intermediaries or who are thought to have the experience and qualifications to become successful intermediaries. In deciding the geographical allocation of development projects within a locality – the siting of roads, primary schools, health clinics, bore holes, and the like – the significance of clan is much greater. In neither case is tribalism a factor.

In towns, however, the situation is different. It was in the culturally heterogeneous milieu of the urban areas, after all, that some tribes came into existence. The earliest voluntary associations assisted in the integration of migrants into the strange world of the towns, preserved a semblance of village culture with their distinctive dances and other social practices, and provided welfare support at times of crisis, particularly death, when the importance of proper procedures was especially keenly felt. These associations were also places where men and women learned the skills of leadership and organisation and became the focal point and organisational centre for political action. They were not the only organisations through which people expressed their political aspirations but they provided a ready-made base for a political machine, offering a range of benefits to their members and votes for their leaders. Later, when Africans took on executive jobs with a degree of discretion in the exercise of their responsibilities, one criterion used in deciding who was eligible for municipal housing and who was not, for instance, was a person's tribe. Such non-bureaucratic behaviour follows from points that have already been made; the extractive view of politics persuades individuals to seek personal advantage from the government machinery just as its agents accept the propriety of such action; the survival of familial obligations, by definition tribe specific, puts great pressure on those with discretionary authority to exercise that discretion in the interests of their family members. Such behaviour is thus sanctioned by political culture and social expectations.

If the focus is now moved still further from the village level to the political leaders themselves, tribe again often becomes a relevant category. The parochialism emphasised particularly by the British through their policy of indirect rule and the growth of various tribal welfare organisations in the towns meant that nation-wide political parties tended to be agglomerations of many local political machines. Kenya is the classic example of parties being knitted together as coalitions of regional political barons (Bennett, 1969). But in West Africa, too, parties and then governments were created by bloc-building, by providing an umbrella under which a range of people whose power was very locally based could shelter. What was originally necessary soon became convention; the need for 'balance' between members of different tribes in the government developed into normal practice. Furthermore, in states where class divisions are not yet well developed or where religious differences are not deeply felt, tribe becomes, in effect, the residual category necessary for distinguishing rival groups in the search for limited power and limited resources. Political leaders have thus tended to use tribalism ideologically, since appeals to tribal loyalty against others not only touches on a consciousness which exists but also builds up the impression of an individual's significance in the politics of the state. In countries where elective politics cannot measure the relative popularity of rival politicians or parties, it is still necessary for the aspiring leader to be associated with a numerous, and preferably significant, sector of the whole population to carry weight in the councils of state.

Appeals to tribal loyalty or assumptions about the centrality of tribal support can only be effective if there is a widespread feeling that tribe *is* a category significant for the allocation of desired resources. The fear of tribalism is probably more potent than tribalism itself. Certainly, there is virtually no instigation from the rural areas for tribally chauvinistic parties; in other words, there is no innate feeling of tribal exclusivity which transcends all other divisions and which impels the peasantry to act as tribes. At one level, people naturally gather together into organisations where a shared consciousness exists; it is not surprising, therefore, that the football teams in the Kenyan premier league are drawn either from large companies, where the workplace provides the common denominator, or from people sharing the same language. When tribal names for the football clubs were banned the recruitment policy did not change. Abaluhyia may have been renamed F. C. Leopards; its players remained overwhelmingly Baluhyia and its scouts picked out the best of the young players in the Luhyia-speaking districts of Western Kenya. At another, when choices have to be made between individuals with similar qualifications, the differentiating criterion not unnaturally becomes tribe. And when a position is not gained, or a promotion not made, the reasons are frequently taken to be tribal favouritism on the part of the employers rather than the candidate's lack of merit.

The possibility that tribal loyalties become the basis for movements which threaten the stability of the state is a real fear. The countries of tropical Africa are, for the most part, so heterogeneous that the establishment of a deep-seated national loyalty is difficult to build. It has to be worked at. Although the issue of nation-building has faded from the centre of stage among Africanist scholars, it remains an issue about which few political leaders are not concerned. War, verbal attacks on neighbours, invection against neo-colonialists or internal bogeymen, such as foreign workers or Asian immigrants, have all been used to create an enemy precisely to foster a national consensus. There are, however, few examples of tribally exclusive movements seeking to secede from a state or to gain domination of the state; support for tribal movements is more likely a visible tactic for advancing self-interest, just as the bitter attacks on tribalism, whether real or imagined, are mostly the reactions of political leaders who fear a diminution of their political dominance. The search for, and retention of, power is at the root of most conflicts; and tribalism is one appeal which happens to unite large numbers of people and thus grants to its spokesmen the potential for exercising power.

Tribe is more than just a residual category, but its significance is enhanced by the lack of other, more significant lines of division. The more the focus moves to local politics, the more important other factors become. The rich peasants tend to monopolise the local party structures and the co-operative organisations and their class interests predominate over the poorer, less-articulate peasants. In the cities, too, class is becoming a much more significant dividing line and politicians in Nigeria and Kenya have attempted to build their reputations and power on their associations with a working class composed of members of many tribes. They have not, on the whole, been very successful in electoral terms. But they have certainly alarmed political leaders whose middle-class lifestyle is threatened by a radicalism aimed at a redistribution of wealth and status. Thus, any simple notion that African politics is merely the politics of tribalism is naïve and misleading. There are times and places where a person's tribe is of great significance; but there are many times and places, too, where it is entirely irrelevant.

Corruption

If the problems of Africa are often blamed on tribalism, corruption is not far behind as a scapegoat. Yet there is little thought given to what actually constitutes corrupt behaviour, why it takes place, or what its consequences really are. There is no universal definition of corruption; what is thought of as corrupt behaviour in one society may be condoned in another, just as what was once deemed to be legitimate behaviour is later called corrupt. The subjective, and culturally specific, nature of the concept can be seen in the common definition that an action is corrupt when an individual uses a public position for private, usually pecuniary, gain in a manner deemed unacceptable in that particular country's political culture (see Leys, 1965). A business which had contributed $50,000 to the Republican Party's candidate for the Kansas Senate seat would have expected some favourable act from the senator in return; a Member of the British Parliament who used his influence to benefit a major contributor to party funds would be roundly attacked for improper behaviour. In India, it has been said, bribing officials is permissible so long as nobody is excluded from offering a bribe; in Nigeria, individuals are expected to flaunt a certain amount of wealth if in a position of authority and to use that position for personal and family benefit provided this is not excessive (Achebe, 1966; Werlin, 1972). Precisely what is deemed to be excessive shifts over time, as indeed it has done in the United States as well.

Yet it is unsatisfactory to be entirely relativistic, for the general existence of what might be thought to be corrupt behaviour would then cease to be corrupt by the very fact of its generality. The extractive view of politics is one factor which enhances the likelihood of individuals using public office for private gain. In Ghana, for instance, a kickback of from 5 to 10 per cent was expected in return for getting government contracts or an import licence from the Ministry of Trade, while the Convention People's Party used the state-run Cocoa Purchasing Company to provide loans and other favours for party supporters. In Nigeria, too, members of parastatal organisations were appointed 'as a matter of political party patronage' and tended 'to place politics before the interests of the corporations they served' (Adedeji, ed., 1968, p. 97). What is observed here are two different types of behaviour which violate the Western bureaucratic norms that officials' decisions should be governed by fixed rules or by the interests of the organisation, rather than by personal whim and party wishes. Such behaviour is sometimes not regarded as misuse of the office, and hence corrupt, so long as the prevalent expectations of how the office should be discharged have not been violated; an extractive view of politics makes it easier for officials to behave in this way for it is widely expected, and indeed encouraged, to happen.

Working in the opposite direction is the still strong tradition of bureaucratic impartiality and the philosophy of service. Africans see this sort of behaviour about them and they know it is corrupt and to be deplored. Virtually every military coup includes among its public reasons the need to eliminate corruption. This may sometimes be a smokescreen and few military regimes have not themselves been later accused of just that corruption against which they earlier inveighed. Ordinary Africans are not blind; they see the great advantages politicians and public servants derive from their positions. In the early 1960s in Tanzania, the élite were categorised by observant nationals as the Wabenzi, a new 'tribe' defined by its access to a Mercedes-Benz. And in Uganda, at the same time, Milton Obote, who had just issued a document called the Common Man's Charter, was once greeted as he stepped from his chauffeur-driven Mercedes-Benz with the cry, 'Here comes the Common Man in his common car'. Christopher Mulei summed up a common perception in the Kenyan *Daily Nation* in this way (5 February 1982):

> The basic reason for wanting leaders to account for their riches is very simple: as these people are in a position to enrich themselves by virtue of office, it becomes necessary to institute checks and balances so that we have an honest administration . . . One must really be blind, and dishonest at that, to insist that all the wealth we see displayed on the road (flashy big cars) and at parties (shiny watches and Savile Row suits) is the result of hard work . . . If we really want to make politics an honest calling (which is different from making it a commercial enterprise as seems to be the position today) then we must set some standard ethics comprising a coherent leadership code which will ensure that leaders do not poke their mercenary fingers in any activity.

Some countries have introduced a leadership code, expressly designed to prevent government and party figures from exploiting their privileged access to funds and loans. In Tanzania the family of each politician or party leader (which is widely defined) is entitled to only one source of income so that politicians, who might have used their status to borrow money for investment in rent-creating blocks of flats or in cash-producing commercial farms, were forced to disinvest. In Zambia, too, the same idea has been promulgated. But the effectiveness of such codes depends upon a readiness to enforce them. In Tanzania a parliamentary committee report on the sugar industry late in 1981 accused Joseph Mungai, the Minister of Agriculture, of employing relatives, entering into unfavourable contracts, mis-appropriating funds and using scholarship funds to send himself to Harvard. Within a fortnight he had been dismissed. In Zambia, by contrast, the leadership code appears to have been honoured more in the breach than in the observance. In a few countries – Malawi would be one – the bureaucratic norms of the imperial rulers have survived longer, mainly because some of the imperial rulers themselves continued to hold office after independence and because the President publicly punishes those who he feels are acting improperly. But even here, and increasingly in Tanzania, small-scale corruption occurs; the poverty of much of the urban dwellers leads them to use their positions and discretionary powers to increase their meagre take-home pay. A combination of poverty, venal leaders, poor accounting practices and a readiness to pay for advantage provide a climate peculiarly conducive to what most Western observers would think is improper public conduct. The opportunity cost of small-scale corruption is, frankly, small.

Africans know their governments are often riven by corrupt practices; yet those practices continue. Why? There are a number of reasons besides the extractive view of politics to which reference has already been made. Some people have argued that social norms are largely responsible. 'Nepotism', noted David Apter, 'is considered a grave offence in western bureaucratic practice, yet in African practice providing jobs for the members of one's family is socially compulsory' (Apter, 1963, p. 6). Certainly, the pressures on individuals from relatives is very great and it is extremely hurtful for most Africans to ignore that sense of mutual obligation which seems one of the few uniquely African characteristics worthy of cherishing in an environment overwhelmingly dominated by Western values. There is little doubt that the basic assumptions of the indus-trialised world's bureaucracies – professionalism, impartiality, rationality – are not widely internalised in the Third World. The syncretic nature of adaptation to involvement in the world system permeates administrations as all other facets of political life (Riggs, 1964). But traditional practices have also been abused. The respect for authority expressed by bringing a chief some gift is a very different matter from the necessary payment of a fee to a bureaucrat to perform a job he is paid to do in any case. A distinction must, then, be drawn between two sets of behaviour, each of which has been defended in terms of traditional values, but both of which are economically irrational. Nepotism distorts a meritocratic system but, at the same time, it serves an important social function; the demand for bribes to perform tasks also distorts a bureaucratic system, but it serves only a personal and selfish interest.

There is no escaping from the fact that many of Africa's élite are venal. The Swish bank accounts, the golden beds, the vulgar parades of personal wealth, the unscrupulous use of public position for private gain are all well catalogued. They are neither accidental nor universal. A survey in Kenya's Rift Province in early 1982 found that in that province alone the Ministry of Education was paying the salaries of 1,900 bogus teachers. This was not a matter of incompetence but of a deliberate and co-ordinated attempt by several officials to defraud the state. There are unquestionably a large number of 'kleptocrats' in Africa (Andreski, 1968). Once the practice has become widespread it is extremely difficult to eradicate. Lord Acton's famous aphorism that power tends to corrupt has an essential truth in it; sometimes the power is exercised in a bullying and overbearing manner to limit people's freedoms and ensure the survival of political leaders, while at other times it is employed in far less brutal ways to feather a leader's nest. Africa is not unique. Britain, although not without its corrupt aspects, took a long time to establish the current ground rules on the use of power and privilege (Wraith and Simpkins, 1963). In the last analysis, only a sense of self-restraint and a wide acceptance of the proper role for bureaucrats and politicians throughout the political community can eliminate the practice of private individuals using public positions and public funds for the selfish interests of themselves or their kin.

This is not just a phenomenon of English-speaking Africa. In Senegal corruption had emerged over the years as the country's 'national political style' (D. C. O'Brien, 1975, p. 187), although its actual form differed from social category to social category. And throughout West Africa the French-speaking states can provide similar examples to those readily gleaned from Ghana, Nigeria, or Sierra Leone. The conditions for its flourishing are as prevalent there as elsewhere. A monopolistic state, great inequalities of wealth, little tradition of political service, an extractive view of politics, the intense pressure from family and clan and technical failings on the accounting side are all prevalent. It is in such circumstances that corruption can thrive.

Yet there may be benefits as well as costs (Nye, 1967). Unconfident junior bureaucrats can snarl up important developments which may be expedited by a judicious application of cash to a higher official; the counter-productive populism of the African antagonism towards Indians can be offset by special arrangements forged between African politician and Asian trader; the shortage of party funds can be ameliorated by a careful use of patronage and a readiness to accept tenders other than the lowest; potentially dangerous political rivals can be neutralised by the careful distribution of financial or political rewards. Yet these advantages – and they are, in many instances, genuine advantages – derive from fundamental failings in the political system itself. What is more, as such practices become institutionalised they cease to serve their primary function and come to be no more than sources of ancillary earnings for individuals who are normally already privileged members of society.

Shrewd apologists can argue the theoretical case that corruption can play an important part in assisting economic growth or a more egalitarian distribution of wealth; but the facts suggest that, in reality, the opposite is the case. Once the transition has been made from symbolic payments and small rewards to large and necessary pre-payments for action which should, in any case, be the official's duty and to large and expected contributions to personal bank accounts, then a cancer has set in which is hard to eradicate and which is dysfunctional to the political and economic system. But it is not surprising that it can take root so strongly. As Yossarian (in *Catch 22*) so cogently explained to his commanding officer when asked what would happen if *everybody* refused to fly sorties, he would be a damned fool to do anything else!

Conclusion

The developed world is not without its instrumental political actors, ethnic loyalties, or corrupt politicians. What distinguishes the politics of most of tropical Africa is the saliency of these factors rather than their unique characteristics. Their combination creates a political environment in which government leaders and officials have to operate which is markedly different from that familiar to their British equivalents, for instance. These factors work themselves out in the institutional arrangements establishing the form and processes of national governments and, to a large extent, explain the difficulties the new states have had in establishing enduring political structures which also appear legitimate to the people of Africa.

It is important, however, not to be carried away into imagining an Africa which is no more than a battleground for competing individuals, whose extractive instincts and primordial ties destroy the possibility of principled and accepted politics. Tendencies, not absolutes, are to be observed. What needs to be remembered is the difficulties facing those who have chosen to guide their respective nations; not only are the resources available to them limited in quantity and subject to external forces, but the internal forces and tensions which fuel political action are peculiarly hard to manage. What I now want to consider are the institutional forms which have been adopted – and indeed adapted – by political leaders in these circumstances.

5 The Search for Appropriate Structures

Independence constitutions were largely modelled on those of the imperial powers and were not designed for the special requirements of the African states. They reflected two assumptions – that the African nationalists would accept nothing less than an approximation to the constitutions of their imperial rulers and that the imperial rulers would not be prepared to offer constitutions markedly different from their own. For English-speaking Africa a variant of the Westminster model was bequeathed, with many of the conventions and informal limitations on government spelt out in words (de Smith, 1964). Some African leaders, and this was true of Nkrumah in particular, were conscious that their constitutions were not autochthonous, or homegrown, but the product of the British Colonial Office and Parliament. This seemed to detract from the reality of independence and Nkrumah, like the Irish before him, sought to produce a wholly Ghanaian Constitution that did not owe its legality to any imperial power (Robinson, 1961). Others used the existing mechanism for constitutional amendment to alter the rules of the political game and bring them more into line with what the government felt was appropriate (Okoth-Ogendo, 1972). Behind both these responses was a single reality: the cultural values and historical legacy shared by most people in Britain, which underpinned the operation of the Westminster model, was largely absent in Africa. Within a short time, it became clear that the ostensible manifestations of the European systems of politics – competitive parties representing conflicting interests and competing for political power, an active and influential legislature and an executive negotiating between pluralist forces – were absent in Africa.

What grew up was something much more centralised and much less pluralist. The first manifestation of this trend was the decline of multi-partyism and the rise of the single-party state (W. A. Lewis, 1965). The second trend was the replacement of single-party rule by the military through coups d'état. By the 1980s there seemed to be a slight retreat from the centralising and authoritarian tendencies associated with the first two decades of independence as three of the tyrannical rulers of Africa – Amin in Uganda, Bokassa in the Central African Republic and Nguema in Equatorial Guinea – were removed from office, military governments in Nigeria, Ghana, Mali and Upper Volta handed power back to civilians (although Ghana, Nigeria and Upper Volta have since returned to military rule), and single-party states such as Senegal and the Ivory Coast opened up their political processes to a wider population (Chazan, 1981–2). Central to all political systems, whatever their outward form, remained a dimension largely unimportant in the politics of the industrialised nations, the pre-eminent role played by individuals. In contrast to the liberal democracies, where there is a broad congruence between people's expectation of how a political role should be performed and how an incumbent actually performs that role, in African politics it is often the person rather than the role that determines political practice. Personal rule, with its own often unpredictable conventions, could be seen as a central characteristic of almost all African states' politics.

Single-Party States

The most common organisational form of the new states of Africa has been the single-party state. Few countries in Africa actually achieved their independence with only a single nationalist party. Within a few years of independence there was scarcely a country in tropical Africa which retained a political system of competing parties. Gambia and Botswana, with their tiny populations, were the prime exceptions (Wiseman, 1977; Stevens and Speed, 1977). In the late 1970s and early 1980s there were indications of the resurgence of multi-partyism and a relaxation in the central control of some dominant single parties. Nigeria provides the most dramatic example of this resurgence in the first elections following the years of military rule and, at the time of writing, there is every indication that the multi-partyism so evident then survived through the 1983 elections which, although they were not perhaps entirely 'free and fair' by British standards, were certainly competitive. In Senegal, opposition parties were permitted to participate in the 1983 elections and won some seats; in Malawi, on the other side of the continent, the examples of Kenya and Tanzania were, to some extent, followed in opening up the process of electing representatives to the National Assembly. In none of these countries, however, did the dominant party institute a system which Western observers would have described as free and fair.

In no African country has the central government ceded power because of defeat at the polls. Only in Sierra Leone in 1967 has an election resulted in the opposition replacing the government; and even there it needed two interventions from the military before this occurred. The general rule throughout the continent, in Sierra Leone as in most other countries, has been the consolidation of party power, the establishment of a single-party state and, in about half the countries, the subsequent intervention of the military.

Most leaders have felt it necessary to justify this tendency towards the single-party state and to explain why the exclusion of opposition parties was both essential and democratic. The importance attached to the appearance of being democratic is comparatively new. One of its earliest international expressions was in the Treaty of Versailles in 1919. Presented to the defeated German people by the victorious allies as a *fait accompli*, the treaty explicitly mentioned 'the right to self-determination'. The Russian Revolution had taken place two years before Woodrow Wilson tried to persuade Lloyd George and Clemenceau, the prime ministers of the two largest empires on earth, to spread the democratic principles for which the United States so prided herself to the furthest corners of those empires. Instead of rule by a hereditary few, so many thought and hoped, would be the desires and aspirations of the ordinary people. The advance of democracy as an ideal has never looked back from that day. Yet its meaning is not clear. Rule by the people sounds simple enough, but different traditions have emphasised different interpretations of the meaning of 'the people' (Mcpherson, 1966). Even within Africa, justifications for the single party have taken many forms.

First, it is argued that the popular unity represented by the nationalist movement's opposition to imperial rule was continued into the post-independence period as a united national party determined to develop the resources of the country in the interest of all its people. This argument is deeply flawed. Only in a handful of countries was there actually one single organisation which, to the virtual exclusion of all others, dominated the agitation for independence. For most of Africa at least two rival parties competed for the spoils of victory during the terminal phase of imperial rule. Besides, African nationalism represented a temporary unity of a territory's people whose cohesion depended upon the existence of a common enemy; but independence removed that enemy and the personal, ideological and economic conflicts which had hitherto been largely, but never entirely, masked came into the open. Furthermore, the very notion of a single, common national interest defied historical experience and became less and less plausible the more differentiation grew in African countries. The continuing economic and social changes in Africa produced new classes, new vested interests, sharper lines of cleavage. The function of politics is to mediate between the rival claims of competing groups; a single party may, in certain circumstances, be able to perform this function but the reason for this is, by definition, not a unanimity within the country.

The second argument in defence of the single-party state is a direct refutation of the notion of natural unity. Here it was argued that there *should* be at least the illusion of a single popular will. Indeed, the nationalist movement was seen by some as so all-inclusive an organisation that the very term 'party' with its sectional implications was inappropriate. It was Félix Houphouet-Boigny who once observed that 'our disaffiliation from the French Communist Party was forced upon us; the RDA (Rassemblement Démocratique Africaine) is a movement and not a political party'. Most of the new states were artificial creations, deeply divided internally and united only in the desire to end imperial rule. With the enemy gone, the danger of Pandora's box revealing the ethnic, regional, class and religious divisions was deeply disturbing. 'The most important problem for the countries of Africa', according to Modibo Kéita, 'arises out of our aspirations for unity' (W. A.

Lewis, 1965, p. 26). Whether unity is such a paramount need or whether the only way to achieve this aim is through the elimination of rival parties is, of course, a matter of dispute.

The need for unity has been closely related to politicians' perception of the role of the state. It is fighting a war, against poverty, disease, ignorance and inertia, and a war effort cannot afford constant criticisms which weaken its direction and sabotage its purposes. Economic progress can only come through hard work, sacrifice, wage controls and other tough policies which are manna to an opposition irresponsibly preaching a Utopia round the corner. It was Nyerere who observed that African states needed accelerators powerful enough to overcome the inertia bred of poverty. The same assumption lies behind the widespread antagonism to the federal elements in independence constitutions, to the blocking mechanism of second chambers and to those independent commissions which were responsible for the selection of people to public office. Although much of the criticism was no more than the expression of frustration at fettered power, much was genuinely based on the belief that governments knew the best path for development and that the urgency for that development necessitated the minimum of hindrances.

The very role of the post-colonial state was envisaged in a different light from that normally held in the developed liberal democracies. The state in these latter countries was often perceived, almost certainly incorrectly, as indifferent to moral systems and ideals; it provided the confines in which the pluralistic battle between ideas was fought and the struggle for the 'authoritative allocation of values' took place. The post-colonial state was perceived by its political leaders more often as a bearer of ideals, the incarnation of a set of beliefs. As the Ghanaian slogan ran, 'Ghana is the CPP [Convention People's Party] and the CPP is Ghana'. Although there has been a considerable debate about the class basis of the forces which determined the exact ideals of which the state was alleged to be the bearer, in few countries have leaders acted as though the state was neutral. This necessarily reduces the legitimacy of opposition for criticism of the government or ruling party can easily be equated with anti-state behaviour.

If everyone had agreed upon the priorities and methods of

achieving the desirable goals of affluence, health and mutual understanding, the single party might have been a suitable vehicle for their achievement. But neither the detailed ends nor the means were universally accepted. The vanguardist assumptions, part of the heritage of the nationalist movements themselves, assumed a breath-taking confidence in the party's monopoly of wisdom. Most political leaders were not only *dirigiste* by inclination, they were also Leninist in their notions of the leadership role. There were excellent reasons for such a position. The societies over which they now ruled had been largely neglected by the imperial rulers and remained attached to a way of life which seemed incompatible with the kind of modern society which provided the model for development in the eyes of the new leaders (Ajayi, 1982). In the initial period of independence, the reaction against the monopolising role of European models and the search for more autochthonous institutions and practices had yet to begin. Consequently, even essentially liberal politicians felt it legitimate to *lead* their people along the paths of righteousness and to constrain those who obstructed this process. Furthermore, some leaders argued that the human resources available to a government at independence were so limited as a result of the niggardly educational policies of the imperial powers that it was a cruel waste to have able men and women outside the government machinery. Underlying this second broad defence was a mixture of a fear that dissent would divide a country along uncontrollable lines of ethnic or ideological cleavage and a desire to harness all the human resources of the country behind a single determined, and undeviating, path towards development. Behind these beliefs was both an unreadiness to accept the functional consequences of conflict and an unawareness that the very different paths to development espoused by parties through the continent suggested that faith in a single correct path was a delusion.

The third defence of the single-party state is more sophisticated and less absolutist for it acknowledges the reality of divergent views. Julius Nyerere was the most articulate exponent of this viewpoint (Nyerere, 1966). He argued that there were fundamental weaknesses both in the Anglo-Saxon two-party system and also in the monolithic single-party systems of the communist bloc. A plausible parody of the British system described it as 'football politics', in which two teams opposed one another for no reason other than the belief that there should be an opposition. Either the issues divided people too deeply for any peaceful reconciliation or they were too insignificant to warrant the energy and time devoted to sharpening minor disagreements over them. Certainly, the need for an institutionalised opposition was questioned. This was a view shared on the other side of the continent; Sir Abubakar Tafawa Balewa, like Nyerere deeply affected by the British obsession for games, likened the British system to cricket where each side must be given an innings in turn. For Nyerere, a single party could embrace the range of nuances that surrounded a basic consensus on goals and within that party all members could contribute to the discussions from which agreed policies emerged; nobody need be excluded; nobody need be branded as anti-government merely for voicing doubts and criticisms about the route to the accepted goals. Factionalism within the party was deemed preferable to structured antagonism between separate parties vying for power. It was a pleasing picture, with that combination of Utopianism and pragmatism that appeals to liberals. But radicals felt that it lacked the necessary role for a strong and committed vanguard, while realists came to see that it ignored the very stuff of politics in which new forces emerge to challenge a consensus. Nyerere himself found that the open party he wrote about was impossible in Tanzania and, indeed, unsuitable for the country's needs.

The fourth defence comes in two different guises. The monopoly of a single party, it is said, is natural to Africa. This harks back to simplified notions of traditional society in which policies were supposed to emerge from a general moot and be accepted by all the polity. But this vision of a golden age of harmony, as has already been argued, was not the norm. In any case, the enlargement of scale whereby a very large number of previously independent units, themselves mostly culturally homogeneous, became incorporated into the varied mosaic of the colonial state destroyed one of the fundamental underpinnings of traditional society, its assumed bond of blood ties, and one of its safety valves, the right to nomadic self-determination. Values and institutions have a symbiotic relationship with historical events, each affecting the other in a complex process of reciprocity. Too much has changed, especially economically, for the values of the 1890s to be recreated in the 1980s.

More interesting, however, is the second guise in which the argument appears. This posits the hard-headed view that the logic of contemporary African politics inexorably leads to the single-party state. Maurice Duverger once argued, by contrast, that the two-party system was 'natural' (Duverger, 1954). But divisions rarely replicate themselves along the same lines of cleavage on each issue, so that the multi-partyism of the European states is a more natural expression of a pluralist society whose different interests are represented by parties. From the standpoint of the individual, however, the single party must be preferred because one is always the victor and never the vanquished. This is especially important in Africa where the power of the state is so far-reaching and the price of defeat so high. A competitive party system can only survive if two conditions are met: opposition to the national government must be accepted as legitimate and there must be channels for acquiring wealth and status outside the patronage of government. The identification of party and state made legitimate opposition difficult to sustain, while the paucity of opportunities outside the state apparatus made loss of office a matter of extreme seriousness. The opportunity cost of challenging an incumbent government was uncomfortably high. All political leaders, it is true, seek to retain power; but African political leaders have a greater incentive than their counterparts in the developed, industrialised states of the West.

In some African countries the single-party state evolved without compulsion. In Senegal, to take one example, the opposition party fused with Léopold Senghor's dominant Union des Partis Socialistes (UPS) after six years of powerlessness. The reluctance to give jobs to non-UPS people, a certain amount of electoral manipulation and the 'single national list' system which granted all Assembly seats to that one party which gained the most votes made opposition a fruitless exercise. After the merger, opposition could be expressed within the single, more broadly based party (D. C. O'Brien, 1966 – 7). Much the same occurred in Kenya where Ronald Ngala dissolved his Kenyan African Democratic Union in order to amalgamate with the ruling Kenyan African

National Union; fourteen years later his deputy, Daniel arap Moi, succeeded Jomo Kenyatta as the country's President and head of government. Behind this merger was the realisation that government patronage was too important to be forgone and the knowledge that governments rewarded their friends and punished their enemies. This truth was often made explicit. The Secretary-General of the Ghanaian TUC once enunciated it in its extreme form when he said: 'We shall analyse the votes ward by ward and we shall know where the people have refused to go and vote for the CPP and they can be sure we will take the necessary action against those traitors of our cause.' When Dr Okpara was campaigning in Eastern Nigeria in 1961 he told his audience: 'I will give you all the amenities you require but you must vote for me. Booty of war is always shared after the war' (Mackintosh, 1962, p. 203).

It was not only ambitious politicians who realised the necessity of being associated with the government of the day. The electorate itself was aware also of this fact. The history of the NCNC in Eastern Nigeria provides a perfect instance of the consequences of this realisation (Vickers, 1970). At whatever level the important allocative decisions were taken, a process took place at which the NCNC consolidated its monopoly of power by attracting independents and minority parties to its fold. By the time of independence, and beyond, part of the identity of an adult easterner was support for the NCNC. 'They say we will vote for the NCNC', one elector said in 1959, expressing well the assumption of community loyalty (Post, 1963, p. 317). In rural Uganda, too, the same realisation of where self-interest lay was evident, as Democratic Party supporters in Acholi urged their representatives to cross the floor of the House of Assembly and join the government benches (Leys, 1967). One of the clearest developments of the first years of independence is the steady attrition of opposition party representation and the continuous trickle of parliamentarians across the floor. Self-interest lay behind this; but it was also a self-interest fostered by the pressures from their constituents. In this way, opposition parties withered away and the party which formed the government at independence came to monopolise power more and more. Pressure for the single-party system can thus be seen to emanate both from the leading politicians themselves who can intellectualise a defence for their monopoly of power, and from the rulers' subjects whose extractive view of politics leads them inexorably into demands to be linked formally to that dominant party whose control of the state apparatus dominates the allocation of resources.

Given the different explanations for a single-party state, it is not surprising that different forms have arisen. These, it was once thought, could be conveniently categorised along two dimensions: the type of organisation and the type of ideology (Coleman and Rosberg, 1964). Some parties were tightly controlled from the top, as the classic communist model depicts, and the degree of popular participation was limited. Membership of the party was a privilege rather than a right; it granted to its members obligations rather than opportunities to contribute ideas. Others were more open, permitted a wider membership and, to some extent, responded to demands and pressures originating from the branches. Whereas in those approximating to the centralised model most secondary organisations were subject to party control, in the pluralistic parties such organisations as co-operatives and trade unions enjoyed, in theory, an autonomous existence even if, in reality, their freedom of action was often constrained. The second dimension contrasted those parties whose ideology was pragmatic with those which were revolutionary in their articulate concern to change the fundamental distribution of power and rewards in the society. Coleman and Rosberg (1964) thus suggested two ideal types, the revolutionary-centralising party, such as might be found in Guinea or Mozambique, and the pragmatic-pluralist, such as might be found in Kenya. Such a typology, like most typologies, draws attention to significant variations between parties, but it fails to provide clear criteria by which all parties can be confidently allocated to one category or another. The single party in Tanzania, for example, has changed its nature over time, becoming more centralised, vanguardist and revolutionary. Yet it remains far more participatory than the Convention People's Party in Ghana ever was.

As the 1960s progressed, categorising single parties presented increasing problems. As the opposition withered away and the need to revitalise local party organisations for elections diminished, the function of the party became unclear. In the 1950s it had been a recruiter of candidates, a machine to get out the votes, an instrument for the communication of anti-government propaganda, a vehicle to ensure victory in a competitive election. After independence it turned more into a hortatory arm of the government, concerned with relaying central government's policy rather than articulating and aggregating the interests of constituents. As the leaders became more immersed in the business of governing and started to grapple with the immensely difficult task of overseeing development in their countries, they came to place greater reliance on their educated civil service than on the rumbustious, vote-catching enthusiasts who dominated the local parties. As the country became more bureaucratised in response to the need to implement complex development plans and penetrate into the most distant village, the party often began to atrophy. The era of the no-party state arrived where administration became paramount and where, in some instances, the party and the state became the same. The excitement of the terminal phase of imperial rule which had brought large numbers of nationals into the arena of public politics gave way to the less glamorous process of advertising government policy and organising local people to welcome national leaders when they came to the regions. Funds dried up; volunteers melted away into more lucrative positions within the expanded administration; the urgency of politics was gone.

Different parties responded to this continent-wide development in different ways. In Ghana the party remained a very visible entity, the strong arm of the government in the locality, the ears and eyes of the central committee; it seemed strong and enduring but it had little substance and the reports it sent back to the capital, on which policy was often based, were frequently wishful thinking tailored to the desires of senior figures in the administration. The party was largely hollow; it lacked the local support to be a genuine mobiliser and it was too sycophantic to be a communication channel of opinion from the rural areas to the capital city (Austin, 1976; Bretton, 1973). Certainly, it was not the two-way, all-weather road which Nyerere once asserted the single party could, and should, be. In Kenya, by contrast, the government virtually ignored the party machine whose financial position deteriorated so much that the telephones at head office were once cut off and whose factionalism was so great that elections for its officers were constantly postponed. It was the administration, the same hierarchy of provincial commissioners and district commissioners through whom the imperial government had worked, that Kenyatta used as his agents in the district. Yet there was an important difference between Kenya and Ghana; in one country, Kenya, there was a chance for the ordinary citizenry to participate in the selection of its representatives while in the other there was none.

The single-party states of eastern Africa set the pace for the establishment of participatory single-party systems. It was Tanzania which led the way. Nyerere became conscious that the countrywide support for his party, the Tanganyika Africa National Union (TANU), meant that all by-elections became uncontested elections. The party officials nominated its candidate; no party bothered to put up rival candidates; the electorate was effectively disenfranchised. But it was clear that the voters were not everywhere satisfied with their representatives because independent TANU candidates began to stand and to win elections. Nyerere, whose commitment to the fundamental importance of an active national party is clear from his decision soon after independence to resign the premiership in order to rebuild the party, set up a commission to consider how, within the framework of the single party, democratic participation could be ensured. The solution was this. Qualification for TANU membership should be minimal; nearly anybody could stand. Potential candidates would be screened by the regional party and placed in an order of preference before the National Executive. This body would normally endorse the top two candidates and they would then compete on equal terms, under the eye of an out-of-district umpire, for the electors' votes. Choice was thus reintroduced and members of the legislature were forced to return to their constituents every five years for judgement on their stewardship.

Kenya, to the north of Tanzania, has followed a somewhat similar practice. The *de facto* one-party state which existed between the banning of the Kenya People's Union in 1969 and the establishment of a *de jure* one-party system in 1982 held primary elections every five years to decide who would represent the Kenyan African National Union in each electoral district. (Because no other parties presented candidates, these primaries were effectively a general election.) Once again, the qualifications were not onerous; but in Kenya there were no limitations on the number of candidates who could stand so that in some constituencies voters were presented with a wide range of individuals. In both Kenya and Tanzania the government used its power to exclude a handful of individuals from standing; in both countries the issues were not national policy ones so much as local ones; indeed, Edmund Burke would have felt proud of the way the local electorates considered the virtues of the hopeful candidates as intermediaries and judged their performances after every five years. That judgement was unfavourable more often than not and each fresh legislature was composed of more new members than old ones. Turnouts increased in the first two or three elections of this kind and politicians began to take seriously the necessity of appealing to their constituents and providing for them some of the resources they craved (Cliffe, ed., 1967; University of Dar es Salaam, 1974; Hyden and Leys, 1972). The system of limited choice spread to Zambia and, to a very limited degree, to Malawi; in the early 1980s it spread across the continent to West Africa. But the dominant method of electing politicians there has remained the model established by their imperial masters.

Focusing only on the existence, or otherwise, of national elections hides two significant aspects of African politics. In the first place, it assumes that these elections affect in an important way the composition of governments and the direction of national policies. Legislatures, however, play a peripheral part in the politics of most African states and the obsession with elections shown by some commentators in the Western media ignores their essentially supportive role in the governmental structure. In the second place, there is a great deal more to political activity than that perceived when the capital is the centre of observations. Indeed, in most countries it is proper to think in terms of a dual polity or a political system with two distinct political arenas (O'Connor, 1973; Bailey, 1959, discusses arenas in an Indian context). At the national level, the major questions of macroeconomic policy are taken, the relations with foreign states and multi-national corporations are negotiated, and the monitoring and control of marketing for overseas markets and provision for developments in the regions are taken. It is at this level that the dispute between socialist and capitalist roads to development might be on the agenda. At the local level, however, the agenda is very different. Essentially, the disputes at this level revolve around the precise distribution of consumption goods already allocated within general guidelines by the central government, over the siting of wells and schools, over the provision of agricultural advisers, over the social mores of the community and over status within that community. The two arenas are linked by either party officials or legislators (and sometimes by both) who act as brokers between the rural area and the centre, sometimes being buffers to ward off unwelcome intrusions, more frequently as supplicants for further resources. It is in this last role, as counsel for the community, that legislators are most active and are judged at elections (R. F. Hopkins, 1971; Hyden and Leys, 1972; Barkan, 1979). Participation at the local level can be intense and, to those who do participate, of great significance. The issues that are raised are often the issues that lie high on the rural dwellers' agenda, even if they are low on the central government's agenda. The factional fighting for posts in one local Kenyan African National Union's branch, although objectively of little intrinsic power, was intense (Lamb, 1974). This meaningful activity at the local arena has an important consequence for the stability of the political system as a whole. Although at first sight a system may be authoritarian and permit little opportunity for the ordinary citizen to participate in the making of national policy, as is the case in Banda's Malawi, the existence of an arena in which vibrant politics can take place and in which decisions have genuine meaning for the local people creates a sense of attachment to the system in the eyes of the ordinary people (Hodder-Williams, 1979).

It would be wrong, however, to wax too lyrical about the participatory single-party systems of eastern Africa. In the long run, stability almost certainly requires that there should be at least the prospect of a new dawn; yet in Tanzania, for all the participation that is allowed in party and national elections, the fundamental question of the principles on which Tanzania's policies should be based is not permitted to be discussed. The issue of socialism is closed. The right to self-determination was the basis for the overthrow of imperial rule, but it also implies the right to determine a new direction of national policy. Although in the rural areas there may be sufficient opportunities to take part in decisions that are valued, among those with a less parochial focus there is little chance to challenge the fundamental principles of government policy without suffering dearly. In Kenya some criticism of government has been the norm; but, when the leading figures in the government take it into their heads to define certain comments or positions as going over the line of what is permissible, there is a very real threat of arrest and detention for nonconformists. To argue that an accelerator is needed rather than a brake, or that all the scarce manpower available should be at the government's command, or that the social fragility of the state obviates the institutionalisation of dissent are not sufficient reasons to send to prison people who organise themselves into an opposition. Carew Hunt once wrote:

> It is probably true to say that in the West there has been a tendency to stress the political aspect of democracy rather than its economic aspect; and, although at times this may have been carried too far, the fault is on the right side, seeing that a people which surrenders its political rights in return for promises of economic security may soon discover that it has made a bad bargain, as it is helpless if the promises are not kept. (Hunt, 1963)

Although this was written of the communist states of Europe, the logic holds for Africa. Yet it misses one crucial point; the people may be helpless to remove a government that has failed them, but the military is not.

Military Government

At independence the national armies of the new states of Africa were generally quite small. Their function up to the transfer of power had been twofold: first, they were expected to assist the imperial power to preserve internal order and were thus used, on occasions, to put down small uprisings or break strikes. Secondly, they were used to assist the imperial power in its military activities elsewhere in the world. This was particularly true of the two great wars and many Africans first became politicised as a result of their experiences on these occasions. By the 1950s, however, few such men remained in the army. In consequence, at independence African armies, which were largely recruited from the more 'backward' peoples of a country and still officered by expatriates, were not prestigious institutions in the eyes of the new nationalist leadership nor, indeed, of their general mass following (see, generally, Lee, 1969). In few states were the black military in evidence in the social and political life of the country (Lloyd, 1966).

In the first few years after independence, African armies grew and developed in significant ways. Due partly to the new governments' feeling that independent states should have armies of which they could be proud, partly to genuine problems on their borders which required military action, and partly to outside powers' enthusiasm to establish ties of loyalty through the provision of military aid, they expanded markedly in numbers and became much more sophisticated in their weaponry. They also became more obviously national institutions as the officer corps changed from expatriate dominance to local dominance. The mutinies which swept East Africa in 1964 were not fundamental challenges to the governmental systems so much as demands for improved pay and conditions and, above all, the Africanisation of the officer corps (Bienen, ed., 1968). Within a few years of the imperial powers leaving, therefore, the status, capability and composition of most armies had changed markedly.

It is as dangerous to generalise about African armies as about most other things African. The Sudan Army had a comparatively long history of Sudanese officers and enjoyed a high status at independence; in a few countries an army was shunned altogether or expatriate commanders were retained for many years. Even among the vast majority of armies that fall into neither of these categories, there is an important distinction to be made between those countries, such as Uganda, in which the officers rose through the ranks and those, such as Ghana, in which officers were selected and trained in the exclusive academies of their former imperial masters. This last group, which dominated the armies of French-speaking Africa and much of the old British territories, became part of that small élite which dominated the national institutions of the new states. They were well educated, articulate and politically aware; they took pride both in their military units, many of which had actually seen active service, and in their country whose unofficial ambassadors they had been on overseas courses. Such men shared many of the values and ideals of the political class. Potentially revolutionary were those who had risen through the ranks, such as Amin, or those who were still non-commissioned officers, such as Rawlings and Doe. The time soon came when black nationals, with direct access to troops and armaments, had the means to overthrow governments. The question was whether they would have the will to do so.

The new African armies were also politicised in a number of ways. They had, in many instances, acted as the coercive arm of the state, sometimes against external enemies, sometimes against internal dissidents. They were very conscious, therefore, of the political divisions within their own countries and also of their indispensability to the government of the day. Nowhere was this clearer than in Uganda. When Milton Obote decided in 1966 that the dispute between himself and the kabaka of Buganda could only be resolved by force he called upon the army, whose officers and men were politically unsympathetic to the exclusivity of the Baganda people, to settle the matter by force. But the pacification of Buganda required the continuous vigilance and activity of the army, on whose loyalty Obote came increasingly to depend. Most armies were politicised, too, to the degree that their officers were part of the wider society involved in the discussion of political matters. Some of them knew politicians well; all had relations of whose grievances they would be aware; they were conscious of the judgement of outsiders on their own country; they minded about political matters, talked politics in the mess and watched their country's politics with committed interest.

They were associated closely with politics in a third way. An army career came to be widely valued for it provided good pay, clothes, accommodation, status and training, resources which were generally in scarce supply. Hence, the recruitment to armies and the choice of men for officer training and promotion were intensely political matters, as decisions in these areas provided opportunities for national politicians to reward loyal individuals or loyal areas generally. The imperial powers had been careful in choosing the regions from which police and soldiers were recruited; so, too, were their successor regimes. In addition, as the ability of armies to overthrow governments became more plain, leaders naturally looked carefully at the political stance of prospective senior figures in the army and at the political loyalties of the rank and file. Tribal tensions could not be excluded from the military; members of particular tribes were conscious of that membership and were reminded of it by relatives and politicians alike, who took care to promote members of those tribes who provided the basis of their national political support (Enloe, 1980). The ethnic tensions of Nigeria, for instance, were reflected in the competition for promotion, the interpretation of postings, and the allocation of resources and duties within the army.

The ideal of a homogeneous, unified, professionalised and hierarchical institution was a myth. On the contrary, its members were as conscious of their heterogeneity as their common loyalties, were sometimes nepotistic in their decision-making and, on occasions, unprepared to accept the orders of a senior officer. Ideological debates, too, made their mark on some armies. The radical ideas of young intellectuals provided powerful critiques of many government leaders' conservatism, self-seeking capitalism and links with foreign powers. This made an impression on several young officers, such as Flight-Lieutenant Rawlings in Ghana and Master-Sergeant Doe in Liberia. In Ethiopia the direction of Mengistu's regime was very largely dictated by the ideas and advice of one radical faction to whose analysis of the contemporary situation he became converted after the revolution. In few African societies has there yet grown up a norm of professional public service detached from any judgement on the regime of the day. Although in one sense the French and British officers who taught so many of the military leaders in Africa were intensely political, they tried to inculcate in their students the tradition of impartiality and apolitical support for the government of the day. But this spirit of self-restraint was rarely internalised by their students; African norms were too strong. Even Colonel Afrifa, who imbibed and uncritically absorbed so many of the British Army's folkways, ultimately did not feel bound by the principle of self-restraint on which the civilian governments of the industrialised West depend (Afrifa, 1967).

The fact of widespread military intervention in Africa is indisputable. There have been well over forty successful coups d'état since January 1963 when the Togolese President, Sylvanus Olympio, was assassinated by soldiers; and more than twenty countries have experienced coups. Why? Explanations are almost as numerous as the coups themselves. A starting point is to follow Finer in observing that armies are, potentially, immeasurably more powerful than any other organisation in a modern state (Finer, 1962). They are unquestionably the most powerful pressure group. And it is far from difficult to carry out a successful coup d'état in a small, underdeveloped African country. A presidential palace, the single radio station, the international airport and, perhaps, a few arrests are all that is required to displace an existing government. Those who have direct control over manpower, whether army recruits or policemen, are in the most effective position to organise a successful coup. They can, as Afrifa did, march their men out on a spurious exercise and calmly appear in the capital city. Brigadiers lack this muscle so that, unlike most South American examples, the perpetrators of coups in Africa have been majors and lieutenant-colonels for the most part. Only in the late 1970s were lower-ranking officers able to command the manpower necessary for the overthrow of the government; now the general's baton is potentially in the knapsack of even NCOs.

The larger the country, the more problematic a coup becomes; the second Nigerian coup of 1966 was only partially successful for it did not succeed in the Eastern Region which had its own barracks, its own radio station, its own political system and its own means for running a government independently of the centre. One consequence of this was the Nigerian civil war which was fought to bring the region back into the ambit of the national state. The ease with which governments can be toppled undoubtedly leads some politicians to over-react when there are signs of dissent; it also encourages dissidents to think of direct action as a means of achieving their political aims; but it also means that only a few people, and a small geographical area, are usually affected directly by a coup d'état.

The bloodless coup in Africa is the norm; for the vast majority of urban inhabitants and rural dwellers there is little immediately to indicate that their government has been swept from power by force.

Although popular support is probably not necessary for the successful completion of a coup, it helps; and it is certainly needed if the successor government wants to institute changes. The role of public opinion, however, plays its part in establishing a climate for action. In most African countries the cumulative inequality, which is the logical consequence of the uneven impact of imperial rule and the extractive view of politics espoused by most African politicians, creates groups of dissatisfied citizens. This national disquiet extends into the army whose officers are not monks insulated from the political gossip of the day; and the increasing authoritarianism associated with many regimes, as they try to stamp out opposition to their policies, produces resentment in many quarters; as the single party slowly strangulates the paths by which dissenting views can be expressed, frustration rises. At some stage, it has been argued, the accumulated weight of popular dissatisfaction must express itself in the military's determination to intervene. This scenario is inadequate as an explanation of action for it fails to indicate at what level of dissatisfaction (even if that could possibly be measured) and through what processes the military will act. What it does do is underline the very simple point that the military will have a greater propensity to intervene if the reputation and economic success of a government is low. A happy affluence is poor soil for the unconstitutional overthrow of a government.

In the third place, the disposition of the military itself must be considered. Logically, a deep and internalised attachment to civilian rule is likely to restrain the military from action. In those countries with a low level of political culture, to use Finer's terminology, there is more likely to be involvement (Finer, 1962). But this is essentially a tautological statement since a central characteristic of low levels of political culture is a low level of deference to the civilian authorities. Yet it clearly calls attention to a central feature of African politics, a feature which is noticeably different from the traditions now dominant in the democracies of the industrialised world. As yet, few institutions have earned that degree of legitimacy which virtually excludes thought of revolution and few soldiers have internalised that commitment to political self-restraint which, with few and slight exceptions, dominates the culture of Western armies. In short, African officers less regularly feel that the personalities who occupy the positions of authority in their states are legitimately owed subordination and that it may be proper, as John Locke taught and the American revolutionaries practised, to overthrow an unjust regime.

To say that African armies have the means, could have the motive and may have the will to overthrow civilian rule is not really to say very much. These are indeed the necessary preconditions, but not sufficient ones, for intervention. Many African states have suffered from economic malaise, differentiation between regions, ethnic groups, or classes, and widespread corruption without experiencing military coups (Goldsworthy, 1981). Perhaps their time will come. Certainly, the attempted coup by members of the Kenyan airforce in July 1982 was a reminder that even in those countries where, by African standards, a comparatively successful economy, a comparatively open factional political system and a comparatively civilianised military existed, no government can be totally immune from intervention. Ultimately, explanations have to be reduced to examinations of specific events, to the precipitants which finally persuade the military to take action (Eckstein, 1965).

If the reasons for intervention provided by coup leaders are taken as more than merely rationalisations or calculated explanations designed for outside consumption to hide exclusively selfish motives, a few recurring themes do emerge (Kirk-Greene, 1981). Few do not claim to be saving their country from a deteriorating and unacceptable decline, to be entering reluctantly into the political arena only after long provocation, to be a temporary bridge between the excesses of the overthrown regime and a future democratic dawn, to cleanse the state from the iniquities of corruption, mismanagement, nepotism, extravagance and incompetence, or to rid the country of a whole political class assumed by its very nature to be irredeemably venal. Symbolically, after the January 1972 coup in Ghana, Colonel Acheampong called his government the National Redemption Council. If the dawn broadcast is often a long excoriation of the old government, it is usually short on a blueprint for the future. This is basically because the underlying objectives of coup action are usually to redress past actions and to express rejection of existing policies. Frequently, the precipitant is something distinctly military; it might be dented pride at the usurpation of their role by the establishment of a presidential guard, or disquiet at the creation of a rival internal security force, or disgust at the low level of funding for basic equipment and armaments. There is a strong strand of self-interest running through the unpublicised motives of interventionists; certainly, the tendency to raise salaries for the military and to increase the proportion of the GNP spent on the military is an indication that involvement is not entirely altruistic.

For a time it was thought that Africa's salvation might lie in military rule (D. C. O'Brien, 1972). The acute problems facing civilian regimes were being appreciated; they were short of skills, expertise and funds; they operated in an inhospitable international climate and they suffered both from the debilitating effort to balance competing internal forces and also the understandable tendency to distort rational revenue allocation in order to satisfy political constituencies. Depoliticisation and the discipline of military rule might be necessary, it was argued; democracy, after all, could only flourish in a society of ordered affluence. For some people, the army in Africa was assumed to be cohesive, non-tribal and the modernising agency *par excellence*. But these assumptions were false. Although initially a military government tends to enjoy the honeymoon granted to virtually all new governments, it is the newness not the military aspect which is the cause. Within a few weeks, the intrinsic difficulties facing any government in an African state begin to re-emerge.

The performance of the military has been varied, both in the policies attempted and in the degree of success in achieving them. This is hardly surprising. Three main variables account for this unsurprising variety. In the first place, the different motives which have impelled intervention have also resulted in different consequences. Some coups were essentially negative retorts aimed at preventing specific events from occurring. Amin's intervention in January 1971 is a classic illustration of this; its consequence was a regime lacking policy aims, concerned ultimately only with its own survival. Those coups with positive aims can be both conservative and radical; certainly, the notion that soldiers are essentially conservative must be treated with caution. The aims of Mengistu in Ethiopia, Rawlings in Ghana, or Doe in Liberia, like their North African precursors Nasser and Qaddafi, were radical, even revolutionary. In Mali and in Ghana in 1966, by contrast, the aims of the military were to reverse the alleged socialist policies of the governments of the day.

A second variable is the range of resources available. This starts with the skills and technical abilities of the military itself. Taking power is not the same thing as exercising it; and running a country, even an underdeveloped one, is a very different and more complex operation than running a battalion. Training in straightforward, hierarchical administrative procedures is not the best preparation for co-operation with the civil service in the handling of complex national economic problems which do not consist of clear-cut choices between obvious alternatives. Soldiers can build bridges; they can control crowds; they can relay messages; they can give symbolic expression to national pride and strength. Those brought up to the detachment and privileges of an officer's life in the armed services, however, are unlikely to have a realistic perception of the complexity of the national society and economy or the skill to resolve conflicting demands to the satisfaction of all parties. Either they fall into authoritarian ways as they impose solutions on their subjects, in the same manner as they ordered their subordinates about before the coup, or they increasingly rely on civil servants and former politicians to create and administer policy. The British Army in Germany after the Second World War found itself ill-suited to the political tasks of reconstruction; its training and experience were too apolitical. There are notable exceptions to this generalisation. Some officers, perhaps because of the politicisation needed to commit themselves to the coup, are able politicians, but they still need many non-military personnel if they are to be responsible for the wide range of services demanded of contemporary governments in Africa. Educational policy, social policy, economic policy and foreign policy are simple titles for extremely complicated and interrelated sets of decisions, and they affect large numbers of people whose tacit support, at the very least, is needed for their success.

A second resource, therefore, is the support of significant groups within the country. In the initial stages, the backing of the military can usually be assumed although, as the months pass, the divisions within the military hierarchy, whether ideological or ethnic, begin to produce strains and tensions which the new leaders ignore at their peril. Bureaucracies have normally been the military's greatest assets. They shared the military's implicit dislike of the political factors which distorted their own rational plans for administration; and they soon realised that their knowledge and experience were indispensable to the new rulers. The instability which a recurrence of military intervention suggests has mostly been gainsaid by the stability of the civil servants. This is not to agree entirely with Ruth First's comment that the 'coup as a method of change that changes little has become endemic to Africa's politics' (First, 1970, p. 112). The people of Uganda would dispute that instantly. But there is a continuity which goes some way, in the short run, to compensate for the military's lack of political skill. Normally, too, they can count on the support of those ethnic groups and social forces, such as trade unions or co-operative societies, who had been most keenly affected by the previous regime. But this support is often short-lived for it stems more from hope than commitment.

Hardly less important is the support provided by outside bodies. Coups normally occur at moments of economic crisis; even when this is not the case, African economies are so dependent upon the readiness of overseas banking institutions to lend money, overseas corporations to invest and overseas commodity markets to fix the price of their exports that the freedom remaining to governments in making economic policy decisions is constrained by the requirements of the international community. Luck, too, plays its part. The austerity measures which Busia's civilian government felt obliged to impose upon Ghana were one of the reasons for Colonel Acheampong's coup; almost immediately afterwards, the price paid for Ghana's raw materials rose rapidly and the popularity of Acheampong's government was much assisted by this fortuitous burst to

Ghana's economy. It could well have been the other way round. Although the evidence for external involvement in coups remains minimal, there is no doubt that some of the great powers have used their financial and military strength to bolster those governments and individuals they favour. The French, with direct military presences in many West African states, have not hesitated to use that resource to defend unpopular leaders or to engineer the downfall of those they no longer favoured. French troops, for example, rescued Léon M'Ba of Gabon from an attempted coup in 1964, just as they participated in the overthrow of Jean-Bedel Bokassa fifteen years later. And there is little doubt that Mobutu's continued survival as Zaire's President owes a great deal to American money and personnel. Yet there is no difference here between military and many civilian rulers; they all rely upon outsiders.

A third variable is the form that military governments take. Indeed, it is sometimes difficult to know precisely how to categorise an individual government. In most countries where army officers depose the existing leadership and install themselves in the seat of power, it is simple in the first few months of the new regime to list the soldiers who run the government. There is a junta which is manifestly in control of the formal decision-making apparatus of the state; to prove the point, it issues and enforces decrees. But almost as soon as this occurs the leaders cease to perform military duties, cease to play the role of the colonel or the major and begin to be politicians. They chair national policy-making committees; they bargain between competing interest groups; they represent their country abroad at international gatherings; they draft ordinances and check that their civil servants have carried them out; they replace the uniform and the medals, except for special occasions, with the sober suit and the tie. Not only that, they also create organisations, sometimes actually called parties, which act as a machine to link themselves with the people of their country. This 'personal transition', as Welch has called it, is common (Welch, 1974). In Togo Eyadema consciously attempted to establish a popular legitimacy through the creation of a political party; the same has occurred in Zaire where Mobutu heads what looks suspiciously like a single-party state. In other countries the military remains quite visibly a junta, working alongside the bureaucracy, consulting political spokesmen for various interests but eschewing the establishment of political parties. The politicisation of the army has not meant the militarisation of the state. There may be road blocks manned by soldiers rather than police, and officers may be involved in regional government or in the nationalised industries as well as in the central councils of state, but there is no military tradition such as is to be found in South America, no feeling of superiority by virtue of being part of the military. Deeply infused by the cultural norms and followings of the ordinary people, from whom they have never severed connections, most military rulers are civilians in uniform.

It is the exceptional case when a form of personal autocracy develops in which the military leader brooks no objections to his policies, takes scant consideration of the demands of interest groups or the advice of bureaucrats, and treats the state as a personal fiefdom. Such men can survive for several years, often to the surprise of outside observers. Amin provides one of the most notable examples. For all the wanton violence and lack of human rights that marred Uganda's life from 1971, Amin did not lack support. In the initial stages he garnered it not only from those who had opposed his predecessor, but also from a wider constituency through a series of essentially symbolic acts that stressed his Africanness and his strength; he expelled most of the Asian traders whose wealth and exclusiveness had made them few friends among the black inhabitants of Uganda; he cocked a snook at the great powers and got away with it, the British Foreign Secretary having to plead with him for the life of a British subject. He lost some outside friends but gained others, as the Soviet Union provided him with military hardware and Arab countries assisted him with funds. He eliminated potential alternatives to his rule and made possible rivals dependent upon his survival, as his army became less and less Ugandan; in the last analysis, he cowed those who might have thought of organising some form of assassination plot through the instrument of fear. It necessitated outside force, as was also the case with Bokassa, to remove him. Western notions that economic collapse and policies of brutality would inevitably lead to his downfall ignored the central point about a military government, that it can only be removed by its own volition or the exercise of countervailing force.

But several military governments have chosen to go. Most had asserted at the time of the coup that their purpose was transitory, but many of those have found either that the pleasures of power are too great to be given up, or that the very vices they acted to end cannot be removed as soon as they hoped. But there is a residual category which has consciously civilianised. The coups in Sierra Leone, which ensured that power should be transferred to that party which had won the elections, were perhaps the first of this kind (Fisher, 1969). In Ghana Flight-Lieutenant Jerry Rawlings's dramatic intervention did not prevent the civilianisation promised by Acheampong so much as redirect its course (Hansen and Collins, 1980). Most obvious of all has been the Nigerian process in which Obasanjo, with great care, turned Nigeria from a military government to a civilian government and where genuine competitive elections took place (Joseph, 1981–2). The norm, however, has been to retain power or to be overthrown by another faction within the military, whose interests have been ignored.

The variety among military rulers is thus enormous. Apart from the handful of peculiarly unattractive tyrants who have commanded a disproportionate amount of media space, military rulers usually intervene in politics for worthy reasons and with little intention of turning themselves into perpetual rulers. Indeed, their readiness to relinquish office is distinctly greater than that of their civilian compatriots. Some, it is true to say, become snared by the attraction of power itself, corrupted by the never previously experienced authority to command people hither and yon, and forget the reasons they trumpeted at the time of the initial coup. Some are too naïve to manage the vibrant world of African politics, or to come to terms with the bargaining of domestic policy or the international complexities of foreign policy. Some, however, are born politicians, skilful at manipulating political forces at home and adept at coping with external relations. A few engineer that delicate transition from military to civilian rule, careful always to ensure that the prospective victors of the ensuing election broadly share their ideological orientations and represent the forces with which they themselves identify.

Personal Rule

Whether the state apparatus is controlled by a dominant party or by a military junta, a central feature of post-independence Africa has been the centralisation and personalisation of power. Admittedly, imperial rule was more devolved in theory than in practice, but its successors have rested explicitly on the pre-eminence of the executive, usually represented by the state bureaucracy, sometimes by the party organisation. The superiority of the executive over legislature and judiciary is now well attested (Selassie, 1974). Presidentialism, whether civilian or military, has come to reflect the formal shift of power from the legislature to the chief executive (Nwabueze, 1975). Although this correctly represents the constitutional position, it says little about how the new balance of forces operates. The difficulty lies in the simple fact that in no country has there yet developed an accepted understanding of the role of president, encompassing both its limitations and its powers, separate from the practice of the president. The lack of an institutionalised, and widely understood, system has meant that in most African states the political game is not yet governed by regulations that prevent the unsanctioned use of coercion and violence. Personal rule prevails. Although at first sight it might appear that the very notion of personal rule must connote an unpredictable individuality, it has been argued that it is 'a distinctive type of political *system* with operative principles and practices which can be apprehended by the political scientist' (Jackson and Rosberg, 1982, p. 4).

The idea that personal rule has become the single most typical feature of contemporary African politics should not surprise those who saw in the nationalist leaders examples of charismatic authority. Although the notion of charisma has been overworked, there can be little doubt that many individuals did enjoy a very special, emotional link with the ordinary people which transcended ideological, class and tribal differences. Nkrumah, like Kenyatta, did arouse passions and attachments which created a very special bond between them and many of their people. It is no accident that one speaks casually of Nkrumah's Convention People's Party, or Banda's Malawi Congress Party, or Houphouet-Boigny's Parti Démocratique du Côte d'Ivoire.

Leader and party, later leader and state, were closely identified. This followed from the way in which the mass of Africans perceived their relationship with the state and its representatives. Like peasants throughout the world, 'identification moves from largely familial and village authorities to national figures and institutions without attendant awareness of and moderate attachment to the agencies that are supposed to mediate between the local and national levels' (Frey, 1968, p. 985). The president thus came to enjoy a pre-eminent position, partly due to his heroic deeds in wresting independence from the imperial rulers and partly due to his symbolic significance as the human embodiment of the new state. Perhaps, too, African political culture is conducive to an exaggerated deference to the great man (Mazrui, 1967a). It is as dangerous to extrapolate values in this area from the 1890s as it is to assume that attachment to socialist and democratic ideals is an intrinsic part of rural Africans' assumptions. The evidence is too slender to generalise with confidence; but there is little doubt that politicians, rich businessmen, or the educated with high status are treated in many rural areas with a show of respect very different from the more egalitarian assumptions of the West where few women still approach men of higher status on bended knee.

In some ways personal rule was integrative for it consolidated diverse forces and gave to one man an authority and, initially, the legitimacy to dominate the policy process. But it could also present problems. Some leaders did not have the qualities of which charismatic leaders are made and needed to create, through conscious effort and manipulation, a bond between themselves and their people. The ubiquitous portrait of presidents throughout public places was one manifestation; a carefully orchestrated attempt to distance the president from other politicians was another; parades, pomp, new rituals, titles, and other public displays of the president's very special status and supposed qualities was a third. Few went as far as Macias Nguema, who appointed himself 'president for life, major general of the army, chief educator of the nation, supreme scientist, master of traditional culture, and chairman of the Parti Unique National des Travailleurs as well as the only miracle that Equatorial Guinea ever produced' (quoted in Sylla,

1982, p. 18). These practices were not only indulged in by those who needed artificially to establish the nexus of faith which characterises charismatic authority; popular leaders attempted to prolong their mystical relationship with the people in this way too. Many leaders have come to believe their own propaganda of indispensability, of wisdom and of popularity. And they have been assisted, as have presidents of the United States, by the unreadiness of sycophantic aides to tell them the truth. In extreme cases, as in Amin's Uganda and Mengistu's Ethiopia for a while, the bearers of bad news were liquidated. While it was possible to bargain where issues divided the people, it is difficult to do so when the dividing line is personal loyalty.

A relationship of this personal kind cannot be manipulated for long. To some extent, the personalisation of loyalty did endure despite the failings of party leaders. In Zimbabwe in the early 1960s party loyalty had become structured along personality lines as Nkomo's supporters and Sithole's supporters fought out their differences in the country's townships; a composite leader comprising Nkomo's body and Sithole's head was never a starter. And in Zambia, too, residual loyalty to Harry Nkumbula survived so long as an opposition was constitutionally permissible. Although the mental political maps of ordinary Africans constituted a kaleidoscope of people rather than of ideologies or institutions they did, in time, become disillusioned with some of their heroes. Charismatic authority, after all, is essentially ephemeral and transitory, more effective in galvanising a social movement into opposition to repression with visions of a new dawn than in building loyalties to a bureaucratic administration. Certainly, popularity sometimes quickly withered and the public could seem fickle as it switched loyalties from one individual to another. It was also adept at concealing its true feelings. As the pent-up frustration with Nkrumah's rule exploded on to the streets of Accra in January 1966, the hollowness of the earlier protestations of support and loyalty was manifest (Goody, 1968). Suddenly, Nkrumah was *not* the people's Messiah.

Personal rule, therefore, has one severe weakness for it is intrinsically unstable and unenduring. The transition from one leader to another is a process beset with difficulties when the role of president cannot be divorced in people's minds from the president himself and when there are no formal institutionalised rules which enjoy widespread legitimacy as the guidelines for succession. In the last analysis, it is naked power itself which prevails. And this is true not only for the process of transition. If a personal ruler chooses to hold on to his position, as they almost invariably do, 'nothing can dislodge him but superior power' (Jackson and Rosberg, 1982, p. 17). This is not to argue for a moment that African presidents remain in office only through the use of coercive means. All governments depend on coercion to some extent; and this is true of Africa as of Europe. But there are quite different styles of personal rule which involve quite different levels of coercion.

Jackson and Rosberg have defined four: prince, autocrat, prophet and tyrant. The prince is a manipulator of forces; he permits factions to exist and supervises their competition for resources within the polity. The autocrat, by contrast, dominates the political system, commanding and managing rather than presiding and bargaining. The prophet is a visionary, committed to reshape society to his own ideologically determined vision. The tyrant feels no moral or institutional constraints on his power, rules through fear and brutality and regards the state as his own fiefdom (Jackson and Rosberg, 1982). These categories are not mutually exclusive for their definitional characteristics are not derived from a single family of concepts; furthermore, individuals may change over time, from prophet to autocrat as Nkrumah did, or from autocrat to prince as Kenyatta did. All attempts to develop 'ideal' types have problems of this kind; that does not detract from their usefulness as a reminder of the variations of personal rule to be encountered in Africa.

But the existence of variations should not obscure the similarities, the regularities of behaviour that permit one to talk of a system of personal rule. A starting point is to present the notion of personal rule as the antithesis of institutionalised rule. Instead of constitutional rules and conventions that effectively limit political power and a set of political positions whose roles are circumscribed and widely understood by incumbents and non-incumbents alike, systems of personal rule are characterised by the degree of discretion permitted the ruler, by a dynamic interplay of personal authority and power, and by a readiness to allow expediency and self-interest to contravene the formal grants of power. In short, there is a Byzantine political system in which individuals seek to acquire power, either through patronage or through tribal links, or through the creation of emotional ties with significant sections of the populace, or through whatever means seem available at the time. One of the doyens of Nigeria's intellectuals has expressed the point this way:

A new political élite . . . less idealistic than the intellectuals emerged . . . In the political process, emphasis was placed not on abstract concepts of freedom, human rights, and the dignity of the black man, but on fashioning a network of patronage and brokerage necessary for accession to office, and for its retention. (Ajayi, 1982, p. 5)

This introduces another aspect of the theme. For the significance of personality is not only central to the politics of the national arena; it provides the glue that links the local arena to that national arena. No understanding of African politics can be complete without an awareness of the centrality of patron-client relations. They have already been alluded to on several occasions. Legislators act as intermediaries or brokers between their clients, the voters, and their patrons, the powerful political barons at the capital; patrons to one group, they are clients to another, acting both as buffer and advocate. The political barons can usually only retain their status and prestige – and thus their influence – if they are seen to have a numerous and significant following (see, generally, Lemarchand, 1972; Sandbrook, 1972; Schmidt *et al.*, 1977).

Patron–client relations exist most naturally in fragmented societies where nationwide institutions binding citizens into a single national framework of relationships do not exist. They are usually characterised by unequal reciprocity. That is to say, they are reciprocal to the extent that patrons need from the clients something (a vote, money, appearance at a rally, higher productivity) just as clients need something from their patron (access to governmental resources, assistance in the face of feared bureaucrats, endorsement for a job); they are unequal in that the patron's need of an individual client is appreciably less than the individual client's need of a patron. Yet it is misleading to conceptualise the relationship entirely in terms of individuals. The tendency in the liberal West to assume that society is essentially composed of sovereign individuals hides the importance of community in structuring the behaviour of Africans. A patron's client, thus, is often a whole village or the collectivity of market vendors who are, on occasions, courted by more than one aspiring patron and can therefore use their popularity to negotiate an advantageous deal. Such a system ensures a certain stability for it builds up loyalties which can, in the short term, survive disappointments and failures precisely because it is personalised.

But it is, nevertheless, essentially unstable. It lacks the deep-rooted attachments associated with party loyalty in the West and the readiness to identify with the role rather than the person filling that role. The readiness with which electors in Kenya and Tanzania have discarded many of their representatives testifies to their instrumental vision of the vote's purpose (and perhaps stresses the democratic nature of that relationship) and not unnaturally persuades the country's leaders to limit the areas in which such choices can be exercised. This is not unique to Africa; there are patron–client networks throughout the world wherever depersonalised bureaucratic norms do not prevail (Clapham, ed., 1982). In the African context the emphasis on personality and personal relationships has an ambivalent heritage. On the one hand, it leads to the cult of the personality at the national level, to the pre-eminence of the individual's struggle for power over a group's shared responsibility for policy-making, and to a diminished role for the formal rules of the political game. On the other hand, it provides comprehensible links whereby rural areas and disadvantaged urban dwellers can be integrated into the national political arena and it encourages political patrons to take cognisance of their clients' needs lest they lose support. The outcome is seldom fair or equitable because access to powerful patrons is unequally available. It is also seldom determined by a coherent philosophical assessment of the consequences of the whole range of allocative decisions; policy becomes the accidental result of many unrelated and particularistic decisions, with a leavening of the personal predelictions of the ruler. On balance, such a system is unlikely to produce a range of policies in the best interests of the country's economic and political development.

Conclusion

The hopes that many people held in the early 1960s that the end of imperial rule would free Africa to develop stable, democratic political systems have been dashed. From the time Kwame Nkrumah was removed from power by a military coup d'état in January 1966, scholars have sought to explain both the failure of liberal democracy and the increase in instability in the continent. For some, the explanation lies in the years of imperial rule which bequeathed inappropriate constitutions, ill prepared politicians for the task of governing and created states which lacked the economic resources to satisfy the demands of an ever more educated and aware electorate (O'Connell, 1967). The fundamental consequence of the nature of imperial rule, according to Claude Ake, was that its underlying principle, a single-minded determination to hold power, became internalised by the first generation of political leaders who therefore invested all in the acquisition and preservation of power. This high propensity to invest in power, accompanied understandably by anxiety that political opponents might wrest that power away, leads to a low attachment to the rules of the political game by all its players. Hence there is a readiness to break those rules, behaviour which is central to any definition of instability (Ake, 1973).

This perspective partly explains the failure of liberal democracy to take root. In the early 1960s hopes were high; an intellectual politician like T. O. Elias confidently looked forward to a new dawn for democracy on the continent (Elias, 1961); by 1982, when he had become the presiding judge of the International Court in The Hague, he was less sanguine and believed that Africa still needed many years before its institutions would be legitimated. Yet it should be remembered that the liberal democracy of the West did not appear full grown or develop from a political variant of the immaculate conception. It had a long and specific history, developing in response to changing needs and changing values. European states, for example, were usually liberal before they were democratic; they passed through the worst rigours of industrialisation before the working classes were granted the vote; they had the resources to 'buy off' disquiet (Potter, 1954; Macpherson, 1966; Lofchie, 1971). None of this was true in Africa. Leaders were faced with demands they could not meet; their people had before them models from the rest of the world which were manifestly beyond the means of their countries in the short term; the route to progress was defined in such a way that change had to be forced upon people who resented it. Liberal democracy, it is probably true to say, is a delicate plant and a luxury.

There can, however, be too great an emphasis on the continent's instability and lack of democracy. Continuity at the helm has been long in several countries; as the following chapter suggests, the degree of participation in politics is higher than unthinking models of authoritarian dominance imply. The new states of tropical Africa, it should be repeated, are still new; legitimation comes to institutions partly through the passage of time, when the inertia of loyalty becomes important, and partly through the success of the state in meeting the requirements of its people. Some hopeful signs may be discerned from Kenya which managed to transfer authority from her founder leader, Kenyatta, to a successor, or from Senegal where Senghor became the first president voluntarily to step down from the highest post (apart, that is, from a few military leaders whose intention had always been to give up power to civilians). There is little doubt that Africa needs more George Washingtons who can use their status and influence to consolidate a rule of peaceful transfer of authority (Lipset, 1964).

These examples bring into focus again the centrality of the personal dimension in African politics. The extent to which personal rule has become the norm limits the likelihood of establishing rules for the transfer of power which are seen as legitimate by aspiring politicians and the people alike. But there is nothing pre-ordained in this; it is people who hold offices and make choices. India had many more years' experience of imperial rule than Africa, is riven by quite as deep linguistic, religious and class divisions, and faces economic problems of similar magnitude; yet it regularly holds elections and, despite the robust use of men and media, the government can be, and has been, overthrown. The same could be said of Jamaica. What distinguishes these countries from Africa is not their degree of exploitation or inequality, but the experience of holding competitive elections in imperial days when governments fell, their members were not incarcerated or dispossessed and subsequent elections changed again the ruling party. Lust for power and fear for its loss cannot be ignored in any analysis of tropical Africa's politics. The replacement of the intelligentsia by power-seeking politicians in the 1960s has deeply affected the style and practice of politics (Ajayi, 1982); the fault lies as much in the new generation of politicians, who have no experience of the days of imperial rule, as in impersonal forces of the past still working themselves out in the body politic.

6 The View from Below

Common typologies tell us something about African politics. But the last chapter should have suggested that they do not tell us very much, unless they are considerably refined. The usefulness of typologies, of course, depends upon the questions to which answers are sought. These tend to cluster around two distinct concerns; the first seeks general characteristics of whole systems and has the state as its focus, or preferably several states, while the second is more concerned with parts of the state and has the specifics of individual states as its focus. The distinction between macroeconomic and microeconomic theories is not dissimilar. If, therefore, politics is interpreted essentially as the process by which competing demands in the public arena are mediated, then at the core of its study should be an interest in those demands and the policy outcomes which reflect the mediation process. In answering questions of this kind, a different focus from that which has so far been presented is required.

Every organisation has some formal rules by which the decisions it needs to make are reached. Some of these decisions are extremely visible and are unquestionably of nationwide, even international, significance; most, however, are concerned with fine tuning, with siting government capital-spending programmes, with hiring and firing individual personnel, and with deciding on the most appropriate means to implement agreed policies. For the vast majority of Africa's people, it is these decisions which so immediately affect their day-to-day lives, colour their political interests and fuel their political ambitions. How they are made and implemented is thus a question of substance for all those interested in African politics.

The formal arrangements within which decisions are taken cannot be sensibly ignored, but they are only the starting point.

Personal rule, patron – client networks and that whole set of values which may be subsumed under the phrase 'political culture' ensure that the formal rules are only guidelines. That would be true, to some extent, of any political system. In Africa, as in the more developed world, politicians must deal with a variety of interests; in Africa, too, there is an administration to manage, or be managed by; and in Africa, above all, the positive aims for social and economic change held by most governments require a change in behaviour from the majority of their subjects. What would be dangerously misleading would be to deduce from the lack of institutionalised conflict at the national level that Africa was short on political action. Nothing could be further from the truth; African politics are vibrant with the struggle for power and preferment, the determination to advance political interest, the readiness to use bureaucratic structures or to frustrate them, and the granting or withholding of support for government policies.

Decision-Making

Except in the most unusual circumstances, such as existed for a while in Amin's Uganda, national policy is not merely a matter of the personal ruler's whim. The skilled ruler, as Machiavelli well understood, is fully aware of significant groups' preferences and takes these into account when formulating his strategy and tactics. In any case, the focus on the capital and the making of national policy, although unquestionably important, does tend to ignore the range of decisions that are taken in the more humble arenas of region and village. One rationale for the single party is its alleged advantage as an institutional device to manage political tensions; one explanation for the military's failure had been its inability to control competing political forces. There is no escaping the simple fact that the states of tropical Africa need political processes of some kind, and at every level, to decide authoritatively on the questions of policy, personnel, or style which divide its people. So there is little sense in conceptualising African politics, as too many journalists do, as no more than the provenance of the leader, simply as Houphouet-Boigny's Ivory Coast, or Mugabe's Zimbabwe, or Banda's Malawi. It is, perhaps, proper that those individuals should be at the centre of the stage; but there are many other characters who play much more than walk-on parts.

As with all enduring systems, there is normally a set of rules which are known and which clearly indicate those people who are responsible for taking decisions on policy. Some of these rules are formal; others are informal. The quality which systems of personal rule emphatically stress is the tendency, on occasions, to permit the informal rules to take precedence over the formal rules. In most African countries it is simple to discern a basic set of institutions which structure the process of decision-making. There are ministries with public responsibilities; there are civil servants within those ministries to prepare position papers; there are Cabinets, by one name or another, to authorise the major decisions of the national government; there are legislatures to legitimise those policies. But where precisely within this recognisable, and widespread, formal position power *really* lies is a much less easy question to answer. The difficulty is compounded by an absence of that propensity to leak information, on which our understanding of American politics so much depends, or to record for posterity in printed form the trials and tribulations of the politician (rarely civil servants), a practice which has burgeoned in Britain recently. The British administration is famed for its ability to play its cards close to its chest, but it has been possible to persuade even some of its senior officials to talk publicly about the decision-making process (Young and Sloman, 1982). In Africa there is nothing like that (but see Kirk-Greene, 1972). And political correspondents lack the access, either from fear of retribution, lack of technical skill, or co-operation from insiders, to illuminate the recesses of the political process. There is virtually no equivalent to the lobby.

The formal situation provides only a guideline to the reality for it is, of course, distorted by the vagaries of personal rule. Presidents frequently make policy directly through public speeches which are interpreted not as kite-flying or indications of future policy directions but as directives. Presidents can equally countermand agreed policy by expressing their displeasure; indeed, this negative aspect of their intervention, so irksome to the bureaucracy, is probably more significant. When, for example, the Nairobi City Council had decided to bulldoze the shanty town which had grown up in Mathare Valley, it changed its mind once President Kenyatta had been persuaded to intervene on its inhabitants' behalf; some time later, when he saw the site and service developments which had been installed to improve their lot, his displeasure at what he reckoned to be the lowly standard of housing development there resulted in the scheme being stopped. Most senior administrators in African countries have several examples of this sort of quixotic behaviour. In the last years of the first Nigerian Republic, a senior civil servant who dared to offend a minister 'might run the risk of remaining permanently unemployed' (Adedeji, ed., 1968, p. 144). Under Amin, too, Ugandan civil servants ceased to make any decisions until a clear directive came from above. Administration thus atrophied and power shifted partly up to the President himself and partly down to whoever wielded the greatest physical power in the rural areas. Yet, day in and day out, the conclusions reached through the formal decision-making process provide the basic framework for action and indicate the individuals whose responsibility it is to formulate policy.

This perspective still neglects two other factors. First, it tends to downplay the importance of the party's National Executive Committee. In some states – Tanzania is the obvious example – the Constitution actually enshrines the superordinate position of the party over the government. In most civilian-run states there is a strong element of this. The shrewd leader can play party and government off against each other, on one occasion reminding the party that the government is the ultimate repository of political authority, on another using the party's preferences to push through popular policies challenged by the governmental system. At issue here are policies of high visibility (which is not always the same thing as highly important) in which powerful political figures have definite interests. Most decision-making, however, is not of that kind at all. The incrementalism associated with British decision-making has its counterpart in Africa, as does the discretionary authority permitted to the government's agents in the bureaucracy. It is precisely in this area – the granting or withholding of transport licences or permission to develop land, for instance – that a great deal of politicking goes on. What distinguishes much of

Africa from the experience of the developed industrialised countries is that many of these decisions, small in themselves but of central importance to those they affect, are taken by the party apparatus.

In the second place, concentration on central government itself and what might be termed macro-political policy issues eliminates from examination perhaps the most characteristic feature of tropical African states, the parastatal sector. Parastatals come in several guises. Some are instantly recognisable as nationalised industries; others are clearly public corporations; yet others are more difficult to categorise, stretching from monopolistic commodity associations to quangos overseeing the distribution of imported films. The enthusiasm for parastatals derives from a combination of factors: the inheritance from imperial days already included a number of institutions (Lint Marketing Boards or Electricity Supply Commissions) which were essentially part of the government structure; the ideology of African nationalists stressed statism and embraced that part of the socialist tradition which equates the people's control with government control; the logic of positive development aims and the paucity of local indigenous capital necessitated some sort of move towards state capitalism and association with outside investors. The ubiquitous presence of these institutions brings under the government's potential control an extraordinarily high proportion of the economic activity of the country and thus provides the government with a virtual monopoly of salaried employment and resources. If success is measured solely by growth, the parastatals have been Africa's success story. In Tanzania, for example, the number had reached 142 by the middle of the 1970s and a parastatal organisation, the Standing Committee on Parastatal Organisations, was established, primarily to keep the pay of employees down (Jackson, 1979).

Growth in numbers, however, has not brought economic growth. In the haste to harness these new instruments to the developmental process, African governments were forced to turn to outsiders to manage their public corporations and jointly owned public companies for they lacked technical, marketing and managerial skills and knowledge. In the late 1960s there developed what can only be called a form of 'crude private neo-imperialism' (Schatz, 1969) in which dishonest practices, overhard bargaining and selective suggestions for purchases and prices found no countervailing expertise. The drug companies have been some of the worst offenders (Muller, 1981). There were, of course, forces indigenous to Africa which encouraged these practices; intranational rivalries (especially in Nigeria) encouraged state governments to set up enterprises without appraising their cost or worth as a matter of pride, while some venal politicians and bureaucrats were happy to give their signatures to contracts they knew to be exploitative. Times have changed; more trained local accountants, a more moral attitude on the part of expatriate companies and advisers, and a greater awareness of the possibility of being hoodwinked have helped. In 1982, for example, Dr Herbert Ushewokunze, then the Zimbabwean Minister of Health, banned the use of the injectable contraceptive Depo-Provera (which was extremely popular among rural women because it was effective for three months and was undiscoverable by husbands). His reasoning was simple; although the International Medical Advisory Panel of the International Planned Parenthood Federation (IPPF) had cleared it, the refusal of the United States Food and Drug Administration to approve it suggested to him that the women of the Third World were being used as guinea pigs for the drug company manufacturing it.

But the parastatals have not been successful at developing a more self-reliant and productive national economy. It is not always clear whether social or financial criteria should predominate; they have a tendency to self-aggrandisement and self-defence which is often not in the national interest; they still strike bargains with overseas companies which are not to the African state's benefit; they are frequently grossly overstaffed and undertrained; they seem unable to achieve economies of scale, yet succumb to the hardened arteries of size; their employees often lack the confidence to take hard decisions; they are sometimes (which will come as no surprise to chairmen of nationalised industries in Britain) used to ease a government's political problems (Killick, 1978, on Ghana; Coulson, ed., 1979, on Tanzania; Turok, 1981, on Zambia). Besides those obvious problems associated with the parastatals, there is another one. For many administrators and politicians there is little positive and readily available guidance to action. Most ideologies are negative, often eclectic to the point of incoherence, strong on the rhetoric of romantic anticapitalism, and generally of little assistance to men and women facing the necessity to take decisions on real issues which are immediately before them demanding specific responses couched not in theoretical terms but in manageable instructions comprehensible to subordinates expected to implement them. In these circumstances, it is difficult to determine where power lies because it is often not exercised.

In the liberal democracies of the West, parties or presidential candidates offer their electorates a package of policies which provide, in theory, a programme for action to cover the years until the next election. The debate over policy is ongoing, but it reaches a pitch of intensity at election time. Although even the central features of the debate remain a mystery to a depressingly large proportion of voters, there is left a sizeable body of articulate citizens and an active, if by no means disinterested, press to ensure that most policy issues remain on the political agenda. This is markedly different from tropical Africa. It is very much the exception for elections to be fought over competing visions of appropriate government policies, while in few countries is there a lively press constantly drawing attention to what it sees as government shortcomings (Hachten, 1971; Wilcox, 1975; Barton, 1979). The press in Africa, for instance, does bring to the surface a number of issues which divide the politically aware, but the majority of stories are highly personalised and interpreted in terms of the strength and weaknesses of individuals. The Nigerian press, which is comparatively unrestrained even by some European standards, is essentially concerned either to denounce particular individuals and the policies associated with them or to reaffirm faith in the virtues of the state government; its focus is rarely on positive alternatives and its local focus tends to limit the attention given to matters of international significance. In the multi-party states almost as much as in the participatory single-party states, disputes revolve around personalities or matters of local allocation. What, then, takes the place of the programme, the manifesto, or the State of the Union Message?

The answer would seem to be the five-year plan. The argument for this view might go something like this. The sectoral aspirations written into these documents provide, in so far as anything does, the guidelines to which civil servants and their ministers work. The allocations between expenditure on health, transport, housing, or education, for example, represent the government's public expression of its priorities. Yet these documents are rarely the result of Cabinet discussions or party committee deliberations. Especially in the initial years of independence, expatriate advisers played a central role in drawing up these plans, sometimes as outside consultants, sometimes as contracted employees of the President's Office or the Ministry of Development and Economic Planning. If the nodal point of the policy-making process in Britain is effectively the Treasury, in most of Africa it is the organisation responsible for planning, usually dominated by expatriate advisers or local economists trained in the assumptions of Western economic theory.

But this is not what usually happens. Economic planners and plans are carefully consulted and take on a great significance to outside donors, but they rarely dominate what happens within a country. In Malawi, for instance, there has been little attempt to check whether policy conformed to the priorities and projections of the country's *Statement of Development Policies*, while one economist has observed that in 1975 he was left in no doubt that the Zambian government 'neither knew nor cared what the twenty-five economists in the Ministry of Development Planning got up to, so long as they produced a volume for public consumption to be called the *Third National Development Plan*' (Giles, 1978 – 9, p. 217). Within weeks of a plan's publication, the ministries return to their central function of arguing for resources and negotiating with outside bodies for the funding of programmes. The data behind plans are, in any case, unreliable and the assumptions of external constraints too often unrealistic; within a short time, the struggle for those scarce resources which do actually exist is resumed. Central participants in this process are the experts within individual ministries, in the early days of independence often expatriates, and the negotiators representing the organisations or states providing the development funds.

The question therefore arises: to what extent do these outsiders impose their values and preferences on the new states? It would be absurd to pretend that they have no impact, but it is too simple to presuppose either that they dominate the planning process or that their suggestions blunt the radical inclinations of their political masters. For one thing, their political masters are by no means universally radical; for another, many who offer their services to the Third World are committed to a more liberal vision of its future than the word expatriate, with its settler overtones, might suggest. Few, it is true, escape from the intellectual constrictions of their own upbringing; most bring to their tasks the orthodox assumptions of the mixed economies and social welfarism of Western Europe. In French-speaking Africa a large number of imperial servants stayed on to serve the newly independent states; unsurprisingly, their propensity to overthrow the policies they had themselves developed and championed was low (W. B. Cohen, 1971; R. C. O'Brien, 1972). In English-speaking Africa the continuity of service was less marked. In the more conservative states, such as Malawi or Kenya, many expatriate advisers were distinctly more liberal than their presidents. The word 'liberal' is the operative one. African policy-makers in the higher echelons of government service in the 1970s were not putty in some outsider's hands; indeed, some had the brash confidence of the ignorant which is not easily gainsaid. Their economic and political values, learned in the universities of the metropolitan power, were largely mirrored by those who advised them. The influence of the expert was, therefore, indirect, confirming and reinforcing a set of assumptions which, arguably, were appropriate for different conditions (Nellis, 1973). These values were essentially liberal. And this was true, to some extent, of outside bodies, such as the International Labour Office or World Bank. Although the ILO Report on Kenya ran into radical flak (ILO, 1972; Leys, 1973), those proposals which would have shifted the balance of economic gain from a small, already affluent class to the broader mass of the people were not accepted. The World Bank, for its part, had almost insuperable problems in persuading the Kenyan negotiators to shift their emphasis on housing development from middle-income groups already in receipt of government allowances to low-income groups. It was the Kenyans, not the World Bank, who objected to site and service schemes. In the Cameroon petro-revenue went straight to the president's own account. It was French businessmen who persuaded the government to raise workers' pay and to consider the tensions created by the conspicuous affluence of the few.

The new states of Africa lack expertise in a range of issue areas where expertise is essential. Town planning, steel making, forestry, and so on, can only be successful if organised by skilled men and women. The impact of this technical input can be high – as the often unsatisfactory ecology of African capital cities designed by outsiders indicates – and there is no doubt that the presentation of a limited range of options or the monopolisation of the ministry's agenda seriously reduces the options open to the local policy-makers. The line between technical and general experts cannot easily be drawn; it must be remembered that most decisions are political in the sense that they express preferences based upon essentially ideological, or value, arguments and contribute directly to the precise distri-bution of resources in a country. Because there is little institu-tionalisation of interest group input in most African states, there is room for considerable ideological autonomy and thus one of the constraints of pluralist political systems, which are designed to mediate between conflicting groups, is removed.

This relative autonomy gives politicians a certain freedom to pursue their own ideological preferences, but it also makes them susceptible to the arguments of experts at home and outside pressures at times of crisis, which are frequent and frustrating. Acute balance-of-payments problems, massive hikes in the price of oil and a world recession have all made an immediate and depressing impact on development plans. Inevitably, many governments have turned to international organisations like the International Monetary Fund (IMF) or the World Bank for help and, not unnaturally, have found themselves subject to externally imposed conditions. Without vociferous parliaments to placate, political leaders have only their own will to employ in argument against the international experts for they cannot plausibly plead that unpopular policies will necessarily be politically impossible. Tanzania did exercise this will against the IMF and, in part, prevailed; but that was a rare occurrence and reflects the very special standing Tanzania enjoys in the international community as well as a certain softening of IMF attitudes.

In examining the decision-making process at the national level, a number of themes have emerged. Essentially, there is a perfectly recognisable formal set of procedures through which policy is made. This indicates that very considerable power rests with a few significant individuals, the president above all, some of whom are politicians and some bureaucrats. In a system which lacks parliamentary scrutiny, competitive party politics and a questioning media, decision-makers enjoy, in theory, a considerable latitude in the exercise of their power. This relative autonomy is limited in part by the very real physical constraints already described in Chapter 4, in part by a lack of expertise which necessitates the employment of expatriate advisers and in part by the political need to ensure support from significant sections of the polity, to which the next section is addressed. This relative autonomy has two further consequences: first, it permits a greater freedom to indulge in abstractions and ideologically directed policy-making than in a more circumscribed pluralist system for it is not constantly forced to arbitrate between powerful, legitimate and enduring interests; secondly, it can weaken a government in the face of external demands for it cannot easily mask its own opposition behind the voice of the people's representatives in parliament or in an open and responsive party.

Representation of Interests

As has just been indicated, African states do not share the British and American tradition of incorporating formal pressure groups into the decision-making process. There is no felt necessity to consult the spokesmen of representative bodies during the period in which policies are worked out and their administration considered. Nevertheless, an acknowledgement of the importance of sectional groups is illustrated by the way in which some African leaders have inherited and adapted the imperial practice of nominating individuals as representatives of particular groups to the legislature, for some states do permit heads of government to appoint a few members to the National

Assembly and this has been used to ensure that women or trade unionists do have some form of representation in the national political structure. For the most part, however, governments have frozen out the formal organisations which try to advance the interests of their members and have preferred to see policy-making as an intellectual act in which the government's will should prevail over the compromises and bargains necessary in a pluralist system. The failure of so many policies is not unconnected with this preference.

A casual visitor to most African states and, indeed, the scholar who riffles through the academic literature on African politics may be forgiven for thinking that the continent is a singularly barren place in which interest groups can grow. That would be an error. During the years of imperial rule, voluntary associations grew up all over the continent to cater for the needs of the people. They tended to be multifunctional, although some were consciously social, concerned more with the rituals of births, marriages and deaths than anything else, and others were mainly economic, catering to the new cash-crop farmers or the wage-earning urban labourers. But all had a political tinge to them; if only to the extent that they provided experience of running organisations for would-be politicians. The nationalist parties often grew out of these voluntary associations and they depended upon them for the recruitment of workers, for the dissemination of information and for politicising the population (Wallerstein, 1964; Hodgkin, 1957). By independence, therefore, cocoa growers, taxi drivers, women's groups, tribal groups, and so on, all had experience in setting up, running and using voluntary organisations. They did not disappear at independence.

The function of some of them undoubtedly changed. What happened to the trade unions provides a good example of the way in which many organisations created to articulate their members' interests were 'nationalised' by the new governments. In the period of nationalist agitation before independence, the unions provided considerable support in terms of leaders, a mass following, money and muscle. They saw their sectional interests as being intimately linked to the aims of the nationalists. After independence, however, the situation changed radically. While union leaders and, even more vociferously, their followers continued to make consumptionist demands, the new governments soon came to treat them with acute suspicion. In part, this was yet another manifestation of so many politicians' inability to come to terms with a potential alternative centre of autonomous power; in part, it represented a genuinely egalitarian philosophy which conceived of trade unions as the means by which a labour aristocracy retained its comparative advantage over other workers; in part, it reflected the obsession with a centrally directed development ideology. The unions thus came to be seen as sectional interests whose consumptionist demands should be subordinated to the national interest in production, of which the unions were to be, to some extent, government agents.

In many states, therefore, legislation was introduced which established an umbrella national organisation closely identified with, and often controlled by, the central government. This happened more fully in the radical states whose leaders certainly did not see the urban proletariat as a progressive force. In Tanzania, the Act setting up the umbrella union permitted the President to appoint the minister of labour as general-secretary of the organisation; in Ghana, too, the freedom of the unions was emasculated so that its TUC became something very close to a government office (Friedland, 1969; Jeffries, 1978). In almost all countries the right to strike and to engage in 'free' collective bargaining was severely limited. This might be seen as the essential neutering of the unions in their role as defenders of working people's interests. But they were never entirely castrated; strikes did happen on occasions and any liberalisation, such as the establishment of workers' committees, was seized upon to express demands. Nor was it entirely a matter of control. In Tanzania, for instance, workers were given many new and substantial rights, including the introduction of incremental payments, financial and tenurial security, industrial democracy and workers' education (Jackson, 1979). In Kenya tripartite agreements between organised labour, private employers and government attempted to reverse the tendency towards unemployment and diminishing wages. On balance, urban workers managed to preserve their standards of living, benefiting not only from comparatively high wages but also from the better schooling, recreational, health and shopping facilities to be found in urban areas.

Two partial exceptions to this picture can be found in Nigeria where something approximating to a labour movement complete with unions, a party and financially supported radicalism has existed, and in Zambia where the Mineworkers' Union has retained its autonomy and has been a consistent thorn in the government's side. In both cases, the dominant party failed to corral the union leaders and incorporate them into the government structure and in both countries the central government lacked either the will or the power to force unions into a government-dominated nationwide Trades Union Congress (Hughes and Cohen, 1978; Bates, 1971). The general rule, however, is co-option.

And this applies not only to trade unions but also to co-operative associations, youth movements and women's movements, which have been stripped of their formal independence and integrated either into some central ministry or into the dominant party. This was due largely to the *dirigiste* assumptions of most leaders and to their fear of countervailing political forces; but it was also assisted by ambitious leaders of the formerly independent organisations. Given the overwhelming monopoly of resources enjoyed by government, ambitious young men sought to become part of that governmental structure rather than oppose it, to be embraced by its glamour and resources rather than struggle along in organisations whose financial base was often weak and whose offices and perquisites were meagre. Ambition thus cut across the duty of reflecting members' urgent needs and demands. Certainly, voluntary organisations could be, and were, used to raise individuals from a lowly status to something altogether more exalted. These 'spiralists' employed their positions in, for example, a local co-operative association to enhance their visibility, prestige and importance, ready for the transition to party or government service (Vincent, 1970). Many voluntary organisations thus became avenues for social and economic advancement rather than institutions whose leaders were pledged to work for the interests of their members. Of course, this was not universal (some of the union leaders in Nigeria never succumbed to the blandishments of the government sirens), but it was extremely common.

The monopoly of power enjoyed by the state was not only a cause of the declining significance of interest groups; it was the very expression of a society lacking strong and enduring interest groups. By definition, a pluralist society consists of a great many interests, often competing among themselves, sometimes coalescing to form powerful pressure; in a monopolistic society such organisations are fewer and weaker. Influence flows from direct access to senior politicians and civil servants, not from the number and status of the group's members. In this way, many outside bodies and individuals enjoy greater influence than most of the nationals. Chairmen of multinational companies, officials of the World Bank, economic councillors in embassies, expect to have direct access to the appropriate minister and expect to be treated seriously when they discuss matters of mutual interest. There is no escaping the truth that transnational corporations and foreign governments often have a more direct input into the policy-making process than citizens of the African state. The representatives of a rural local government, or of the primary school teachers, or of the local, independent road hauliers, do not enjoy such an implicit right.

This does not mean that they have no access. The personalised system of government and the nexus of patrons and clients are essential in this process. Interests do have their spokesmen; some are fortunate to be represented by a 'big man', others are less fortunate as their patron carries little weight in the centre. Such representation has a certain random quality to it, in that governments rarely seek the advice and support of an organisation and the representatives themselves do not always reflect the wishes and interests of the members.

In European studies there is a tendency to categorise interest groups according to whether they are established to defend and prosecute the interests of a particular class of individuals or whether they are established to advance a particular cause. In Africa these latter kind are rare. Of those consciously established to advance the interests of a group, two kinds can be discerned: on the one hand, there are the familiar groups representing particular professions, categories of workers, taxi drivers and other occupational categories; these are horizontal – and largely urban – in that their membership tends to be drawn from a single class but from many tribes. On the other hand, there are locally based tribal organisations or their equivalents in the cities, such as the *associations des originaires* in French West Africa; these are vertical, in that their membership tends to cross class divisions and to be drawn from a single tribe. The dominant parochialism of so much of Africa is well represented in Western Nigeria where the agent for interest aggregation and expression was a geographical unit, the town. Individuals looked to the town's notables to act as their spokesmen rather than to the presidents of their occupational organisations which barely functioned on a regional level (Murray, 1970). However the classification may be done, organised interest groups exist in profusion.

Most are multi-functional. In an essentially patron – client system of politics, these associations have three basic functions – to act as channels of information and communication, as repositories of votes, and as barometers of popular feeling. Newspapers in Africa are normally capital focused, pro-government and read by a small proportion of the population as a whole. There are wide variations between the empty record of President Banda's utterances, which dominated the Malawi press in the 1970s, and the rumbustious, partisan newspapers of Nigeria in the early 1980s, yet they are all focused upon a small part of a country's population, the literate white-collar workers of the urban centres. Reports from the rural areas are more usually concerned to reflect ministers and government officials in a good light than to chronicle the struggles and deprivations of the rural farmers; information of direct relevance to Mali peasants is more likely to be acquired from BBC 2 than from the newspaper stalls in Bamako. The informal associations, however, do much to make up for this partial representation of events. They act as the carriers and disseminators of news, often gossip and rumour, from the city and bring back to the capital the hopes and grouses of the rural areas. Whereas in Europe the peasantry was driven permanently from the land into the cities, in Africa the migrant worker is an inhabitant of both town and country. In most cities – and this is increasingly the case – there is a small, permanent number of urbanites; but the majority of city residents, at any one time, are temporary sojourners who can, because of the vastly improved transport technology of the 1980s over the 1920s, return regularly to their families in the countryside for a week-end here, for a month there, perhaps for a year or two on another occasion. The tribal and welfare associations, the secret societies, the masonic lodges and even sports teams provide information and comment, affect attitudes and communicate feelings from the rural areas and the small towns to the capital city where the seat of government is.

In the second place, voluntary associations can act as the giver, and taker away, of votes. In the Kenyan primary elections, for example, the significance of clan associations is crucial in the final disposition of the vote. In constituencies where many different tribes live, the solidarity of tribal unity is frequently the basic building bloc for political advancement. Richer traders and store-keepers might favour one candidate, the homeless and low paid another. The process by which the ultimate decision to vote for one candidate or another is taken includes a good deal of discussion within the primary social groups of each individual elector. Obviously, in those countries where there are no competitive elections and where the party is very centralised, the question of delivering and taking away votes hardly arises. Yet, the status – and consequently the power – of individual politicians can depend largely on the extent of the clientage and the degree to which that loyalty is known and feared. The intermediaries who provide the link between the 'big man' and the small, often locally based, associations enjoy a certain leverage and hence power.

They are, in the third place, barometers of popular opinion. Their role as communicators and bases of political support already suggests this. The very visible declaration by professionals in Ghana that the disastrous state of affairs in that country owed much to Acheampong's government made a profound impact both internally and externally. In Nigeria, perhaps more than in any other country, there exists a plethora of associations whose representatives contact politicians, put out statements, distribute pamphlets, lobby councillors and generally ensure that their views are publicised (Peil, 1976). On the other side of the continent, the enduring conflicts with the Kenyan trade union movement are keenly reported in the press and discussed in the National Assembly; in the early 1970s the secretary-general, deputy secretary-general and treasurer-general of the Kenyan Federation of Labour were all MPs and hence ensured that labour matters were aired. The personal contacts between associations, whether of the horizontal or vertical kinds, and politicians bring to the capital some idea of what is being said in the districts. But it is in the urban areas, on the whole, that voluntary associations really flourish; the British penchant for committees is another part of the imperial heritage to which educated Africans have taken with alacrity. They allow people to participate in communal activities which give meaning to their lives and, as the formal departicipation of the 1970s took place, offered an avenue for participation and the expression of grievances (Chazan, 1981 – 2).

It is in the smaller towns that the voluntary associations play a more obviously significant role. Local politicians lack the quantity of disposal resources and the ideological guidelines which insulate national figures to some extent from the pressure of interest groups. They are, therefore, more amenable to the demands of vocal, or numerous, groups in their patch. This can be seen in the struggles for influence and the distribution of resources on the Nairobi City Council (Greenstone, 1965 – 6; Werlin, 1974); it can be observed, too, in the small Ghanaian town of Ahafo where the manipulation of local associations and their leaders was central to the acquisition and retention of power (Dunn and Robertson, 1973); it can be found also in French West Africa. Kita, in Mali, witnessed a high level of local involvement in politics in which cliques and factions dominated local events and officials were relatively responsive to popular demands (N. S. Hopkins, 1972). This is particularly significant given the monolithic nature of the single party in Mali at the time. Mali gave the outward appearance of a political system in which a single authoritarian organisation drove along a determined socialist path against all opposition; but this was to misread what was happening and to emphasise the hopes and assertions of the politicians in the capital over the reality of competition in the rest of the country.

This point illustrates an important truth of politics in societies lacking institutionalised opposition forces. Monolithic structures and vanguardist parties do not inevitably mean the demise of voluntary associations or of group pressure. Enduring governments operate on the principle of anticipated reactions. That is to say, the retention of power is assumed to involve the placation of significant groups, both tribal and class based. The potential threat from a disgruntled urban proletariat is rarely far from leaders' minds and their policies – keeping the price of basic food down at the expense of rural incomes is the most obvious one – are designed to defuse possible opposition from that quarter. Governments can only be successful if they carry most of the people with them most of the time. Students may be roughly treated because they enjoy a transitory status and have little broad support and peasants, as a class, can be ignored in the short run because they cannot easily be organised; the urban workers, the bureaucrats, the military and tribal groups whose loyalties might be harnessed in opposition to the regime are taken care of. The interests of some groups, therefore, are an integral part of the political process in African states and in Africa, as in the rest of the world, some groups manage to gain advantages incommensurate with their numerical strength.

Bureaucracy and Local Government

At independence the governments of tropical Africa inherited not only the personnel of pre-independence years but also an established bureaucracy and local government systems which had been designed on the model of the imperial powers and with the purpose of carrying out imperial needs. Unsurprisingly, changes were urgently demanded and many changes were made; however, what is perhaps most striking is the continuity between the last years of imperial rule and the first decades of independence. This is most noticeable in capitals where the presence of ministries with their permanent, generalist civil servants advising and assisting political superiors would be familiar to any imperial official; in the districts, too, the form and often the style of administration associated with the British or French was continued; the one major innovation concerned the role of the party which became less an articulator of demands and a pressure upon the governmental structure and more an agent of the government in the field. Each of these three aspects of administration warrants some consideration.

One of the first imperatives perceived by the new governments was to localise the civil service and to reduce the visibility, and power, of the expatriates. In West Africa much progress had already been made in this respect and there were only a few positions, in sensitive areas like security or economic management, in which whites remained. In East and Central Africa, where the indirect consequences of settler society slowed down change, the process of localisation was much less advanced. The rapid localisation, in effect the Africanisation, of the administration thrust into important positions many people who had very little experience of running a department or overseeing a large budget. Paper qualifications, although perhaps necessary, were certainly not sufficient for the efficient performance of duties. A doctorate in international relations and some teaching experience in a small liberal arts college in the United States, the sort of qualifications with which many senior Zimbabwean civil servants embarked upon their administrative careers, is barely an adequate grounding for managing, for instance, a national health programme. Inevitably, there was a general diminution in the quality of administration, another legacy of the imperial powers' failure to train future bureaucrats and give them genuine experience of responsibility. In West Africa, both among the English-speaking and the French-speaking states, the longer period of tutelage meant that there were, by comparison to East and Central Africa, more experienced bureaucrats.

These notions of experience and quality employ criteria which are very much European criteria. The models which African bureaucrats followed were mainly those of their imperial masters; the skills they were taught and the values they imbibed were the skills and values highly respected by the imperial powers; the procedures followed and the relationships with politicians and the public were the procedures and relationships approved of by the imperial powers. This tendency was strengthened by a further factor, itself ironically designed to reduce dependence on imperial influences. Conscious of the lack of skilled manpower, the new governments often set up Institutes of Public Administration to train civil servants and diplomats; these were financed and staffed by expatriates who unashamedly taught the ways and attitudes of their own countries. The picture which Adu draws of the bureaucracies in the Commonwealth at the end of the 1960s is instantly recognisable to any observer of Whitehall (Adu, 1969). Senior civil servants generally enjoy a high status, act as the handmaidens of their political masters, see their function as warning too imaginative politicians against too radical innovations, and so on. Because African civil servants tend to be much better educated than most of the politicians, they come to dominate the decision-making process outside those areas colonised by the president himself and a few unquestionably powerful political figures.

Bureaucracies not only tended to reflect the models of European bureaucracies. They also grew enormously. By 1972 over 65 per cent of all formal employment was public employment in Ghana, Tanzania and Zambia. Even in those countries like Malawi and Kenya, where the private sector found greater favour, virtually two-fifths of wage and salary earners were government employees (World Bank, 1981, p. 41). There are two aspects to this. The new governments were much more wedded to the notion of development than their predecessors; they may often have failed to think through precisely what development might mean and what the consequences, both financial and human, of development might prove to be but they were convinced, and rightly so, that the state had to take the lead in the transformation of their countries. They thus needed a good deal of manpower in the expanded ministries of economic development, education, health, and so on. This ensured that in the short run the demands of most of the articulate and educated were met. For, in most African minds, the purpose of independence remained the opportunity to obtain employment in jobs commensurate with their formal qualifications. It was not only Nkrumah who made this point, after those same public employees had apparently welcomed his downfall. Nyerere had been conscious of the reality in the earliest days of Tanzanian independence and had tried to shape the education system to undo this perception. But white-collar ambitions remained strong among schoolchildren and students (Prewitt, ed., 1971). Thus, the commitment of the majority of new bureaucrats was not to a particular type of development —

say a socialist kind – but to the opening up of jobs to Africans in their own countries. As a result, African states, whatever the rhetoric of their political leaders, found themselves with large bureaucracies (the more radical the leader, usually the larger the bureaucracy) manned by people whose ideals increasingly came to reflect the models of their superiors, themselves modelled on the departed imperial administrators.

The essential conservatism which this represented was strengthened by the simple fact that employment in the public sector was a considerable privilege. The rates of pay were high, for the most part reflecting those of the expatriate officers being replaced; the assumed need for relatively high payments as inducements to Europeans to work in the tropics was thus retained for indigenous personnel. In addition, civil servants had enjoyed a number of perquisites which were continued into the independence age. In Zambia, to take one instance, the Committee of Enquiry into Public Service Salaries of November 1980 proposed allowances of 300 kwacha (£170) per month for a person living in a house valued at over 35,000 kwacha, or four and a half times the salary of an ordinary worker. A number of senior officials were to receive free transport, fuel and a driver, as well as an entertainment allowance, which would bring them into line with the perquisites proposed for the Zambia Industrial and Mining Corporation (Turok, 1981). The bureaucracy, therefore, became a privileged stratum whose self-interest could usually be preserved by their pivotal position in the country's political system.

The growth of the public sector, however, came in time to produce tensions which were not so easy to manage. The early localisation had meant that senior positions in the administration were taken by comparatively young men, frequently less educated than the next generation of university graduates who began to appear in large numbers in the late 1960s as the expanded university systems of the continent started to produce their graduates. To some extent, the public sector could absorb, due to its size, the less able senior figures into symbolic posts within the parastatal sector or the diplomatic service. But there was a limit to what could be done by these methods. Consequently, the new generation of educated young people, often the receivers of an education more radical in orientation than their elders, ceased to look upon the public sector as the natural route to self-improvement, but challenged the manifestly privileged position enjoyed by its incumbents and readily espoused causes that might upset the stable and mutually satisfactory alliance between the bureaucracy and the politicians of the day. Africa does more than mirror the nearly universal fact that students tend to be more radical than their elders, as they have yet to learn the realities of power and politics; attacks on governmental corruption and governmental complacency are the rational response to arriving on the job market a generation too late.

The privileged position of the bureaucrats further illustrates one central feature of the African scene. With their access to high salaries, private information, loans, and so on, entrepreneurially minded individuals can use their position to advance themselves financially. For instance, provided with government housing and the prestige that is associated with high positions, a permanent secretary could borrow money to buy not only a small home for himself but also another property and thus let out, at high rents to international companies like the airlines, two houses. The profits from these enterprises can then be invested in further housing, probably at the lower end of the market where the demand for homes is so very high, and so make the bureaucrat or politician a major rentier in the capital city. Housing, and transport too, are the bedrocks of capitalism in the continent and the foundations on which the wealth of many a politician and public servant are based. Political connections and the plethora of parastatal organisations can accumulate power and wealth in the hands of a few. In the Cameroon, for instance, El Hadj Fadil, chairman of Société Nouvelle des Cocotiers, sat on sixty-three other boards, owned the Meridian Hotel, yet could not read or write. In European societies it is often assumed that political influence flows from economic wealth; in Africa economic wealth tends to flow from political influence. The cumulative inequality that was one of the central legacies of the imperial intermission is thus carried forward and extended into the post-independence years.

To say that many civil servants use their position in an extractive way to assist themselves, their relations and localities is not to say that they all lack bureaucratic skills. Indeed, the instability associated with unconstitutional transfers of power from civilian politicians to military leaders (and back again, in some instances) is less disturbing than it might seem because the senior civil servants are, in many cases, extremely competent and able individuals, well able to ensure that the machinery of government continues and that the services for which the state is responsible are largely delivered. At the same time, stressing the conservative aspects of the civil service is not to say that its members are unaware of the developmental needs of their countries. The local official of the Ministry of Agriculture, resplendent in suit and tie, may appear to be interested in no more than monitoring the coercive sections of the law affecting agricultural production; the permanent secretary arguing with a minister that collectivisation may not increase total yields and production may appear to be using his advisory capacity to prevent radical change. They are fulfilling their roles as bureaucrats. But many of them are well aware that this particular conception of the role may not be the most appropriate one. The regular meetings between the senior civil servants of the English-speaking countries of Africa indicate a continuing concern with the proper role of the civil servant (Kirk-Greene, 1972). Here are expressed concerns about the ideological inheritance of the imperial years, about the civil servant's duty to warn his political master of the possible difficulties inherent in his policy, about the lack of a commitment and a constructive role in the development process, and about the emphasis on the apolitical nature of the ideal civil servant.

Generalising about bureaucracies in Africa is quite as dangerous as generalising about any other aspect of the continent. With a few exceptions, such as in Benin (where the telephone in the ministries is answered with the question: 'Are you ready for the revolution?'), the bureaucracy is a recognisable imitation of its metropolitan models. At the highest level, it is staffed with experienced and skilful operators, some of whom are unquestionably venal but most of whom are serious and committed public servants. The lower down the hierarchy that one passes, the less confident and skilled the bureaucrats become and the more they rely on the letter of the regulations rather than their discretion or on the principle of putting off decisions until they are forced upon them. As the public service has grown and governments have enlarged their area of operation, both in terms of subject-matter and geographical reach, the tentacles of the central bureaucracy have spread further and further into the rural areas. Here the pressures of the local community and local obligations begin to bend the rules of rational, apolitical decision-making (Riggs, 1964). Caught between two value systems, the Weberian bureaucracy of the European model and the personalised African principles of mutual aid, many civil servants operate two distinct systems of values and behaviour. Because they are potentially so significant, on account of the discretionary powers they exercise in a number of areas, they are put under intense pressure by local people; and few can stand their ground. The distributor of small benefits is thus caught at the very interstices of tribalism, corruption and the extractive view of politics which dominate the political process in most of tropical Africa.

The extension of the central government's bureaucracy into the districts has inevitably reduced their autonomy. It was in the decade after the Second World War that a degree of democratisation came to local government structures. These councils were designed to increase participation and to provide an input into the political system from local notables. Both these functions were enthusiastically embraced by the nationalist movements which used them to advance their own claims to increased recognition and independence. The principles behind the developments which took place in the years immediately preceding independence were those of the metropolitan local government systems. In the British colonies there were at least four distinguishable themes: the granting to local authorities of powers in areas distinct from central government; the creation of a local source of funds; the establishment of a localised rather than a national bureaucracy; and an elected and therefore accountable council (Mawhood and Davey, 1980). The ideal, therefore, envisaged a large number of local government authorities responsible for important services, responsive to local demands and, to a large degree, independent in financial and policy terms from the central government. In some extreme cases, this independence was institutionalised through the creation of federal structures which were intended to insulate some regions from central government intrusion.

The federal structure in Nigeria is the most obvious case, the quasi-federal arrangements in Uganda the most bizarre and the devolution, or *majimbo* constitution, of Kenya the least operationalised. Implicitly behind all these schemes in English-speaking Africa was a derogation from the central government's authority.

From the start, national governments found the existence of local governments, with their potentially countervailing centres of power and opportunity for patronage, uncongenial. Although it is something of an exaggeration to assert that politicians were concerned with nothing more than the acquisition and retention of power, there was a strong element of this in their outlook. Centres of countervailing power, whether parties or local governments, were always suspect. Certainly, the victorious Kenyan African National Union had little intention of devolving power to the regional authorities dominated by the opposition party as the Constitution theoretically required. There were, in addition, two further factors which tilted the balance of power irrevocably towards the centre. In the first place, virtually all governments, whatever their ideological hue, accepted the primary role of the government as the engine of development. This statist ideology, which was socialist only to the extent that it emphasised the centrality of the state, resulted in a continued emphasis on national planning, a national bureaucracy to administer the plan and a national uniformity to ensure best use of resources. In the second place, some local governments proved themselves inefficient, and extravagant, institutions.

The fate of the four pillars of British policy can be quickly traced. The first pillar crumbled before the inability, or unwillingness, of central government to permit local governments a constructive role. The areas of responsibility permitted to local authorities were steadily reduced. At independence most local councils controlled their primary schools, were responsible for health clinics, for the siting, building and maintenance of minor roads, and for the licensing of business activities. As decisions in these areas directly affected the distribution of resources in their localities, the councils were the focus of considerable political activity (Leys, 1967). Over the years, however, the central government increasingly colonised these areas of responsibility so that the Department of Education took charge of educational policies, the Department of Health allocation of health resources, and so on. The function of local councils shifted to an advisory one; as governments became dominated by their attempts to develop their countries, they came not only to take the major allocative decisions and to appropriate the bulk of available tax revenue, but also to oversee the local distribution of central government benevolence, leaving local committees, variously called, to argue over the siting of projects, the provision of voluntary labour and the priorities for future development plans. The active interventionist position of the state in a proliferation of functions directly acting on all aspects of village production, as Bryceson has shown, actually leaves little autonomy or self-determination to the village councils (Bryceson, 1982). This major shift in the function of local government was accompanied, not surprisingly, by a reduction in its perceived significance.

Some governments, indeed, felt that the logic of centrally planned and administered services should lead to the elimination of local councils altogether. Military governments were the most obvious examples of this. But, in Tanzania, the government put an end to urban local government between 1972 and 1978, administering these areas centrally. In the case of the capital, Dar es Salaam, the city was divided into three competing development districts, to be planned and administered as a corporation. When this was unsuccessful, the city council was reintroduced and a new 'urban' bureaucracy had to be trained.

The shift of emphasis away from local government was only partly due to the politicians' desire to control to the limit the provisions and distribution of government services. It was also due to the failure of the second principle of local government, the establishment of an independent financial base. In any case, the tax base of the local authorities, especially in the rural areas, was weak. Personal tax (a very unprogressive form of taxation), together with fees, licences and government grants formed the basis of their financial resources. And these were very inelastic. Ambitious councils thus found themselves quickly constrained by the paucity of funds; although self-help projects were, in many cases, successful, their financial consequences were not always thought out. Thus, *harambee* (or community) schools were built in Kenya but there was often insufficient money to pay teachers after the building of the schools. The cities, with a more developed business community and even an industrial area to tax, together with rents from municipal housing and levies from the sale of liquor, were in a stronger position to increase their incomes and were, because of the comparatively stronger tax base they enjoyed, better placed to raise loans for housing projects and the like. But in the towns, too, most major developments required central government financing, either through the public expenditure channel or through loans and grants negotiated by the central government from outside donors. The central government, as the major provider of resources, also wished to have the major say in what was done.

The tax base was one constraint. But it was compounded by two other developments. On the one hand, local councillors, conscious of their electorates and desirous of repaying the favour of the vote with other favours, were often remiss about collecting tax. This was, in part, the result of administrative failings pure and simple but it was also, in many cases, a conscious decision. The management of funds was almost uniformly lax; rents and licences were waived, while expenditures were incurred without authorisation or without reference to budgets and estimates. Many a council was soon bankrupt, overcome by its own generosity. The central government was thus forced to intervene. On the other hand, the central government, although relatively advantaged in the matter of raising tax, was jealous of even those meagre resources available to local councils. Thus, some of the urban authorities found that one or other of their basic sources of finance would be appropriated by the central government. This, too, reduced the freedom of the urban areas to act as independent bodies. Yet, so long as they were not wholly eliminated and they retained discretionary control over some resources (such as the granting of licences to transport operators, publicans, or market stalls), the local councils retained an autonomy of their own which was impervious to outside attempts to infiltrate. Even in a very centralised single-party state, such as Kéita's Mali, the small towns were never entirely absorbed into a unified system of government; they remained centres of power, meagre though it might seem in absolute terms, and were used by people as a buffer against the further intrusion of the dominant party and the all-pervasive state apparatus (N. S. Hopkins, 1972).

A weak tax base prevented local councils from becoming very independent from the central government. The extreme paucity of skilled manpower added to their dependence on the centre. The idea of a localised bureaucracy (which was, in any case, much more British than French in conception) was never implemented. What happened was that the ministries of the central government established local officials with responsibilities for agriculture, education, health, co-operatives, or whatever. Some countries became very much administrative states where the important local officials owed allegiance to their superiors in the capital, and whose local boss was not the chairman of the local council so much as the successor to the imperial district commissioner or *commandant de cercle*. As an acknowledgement to the new independent status, these names were sometimes changed – the district commissioner, for instance, becoming the district administrator in Zimbabwe and the area commissioner in Tanzania. But their functions were broadly similar. In Kenya the central administration was the basic co-ordinator and instrument of the state's development policies (Gertzel, 1966). In French West Africa the same was broadly true. Local government ceased to make the most significant decisions for the local people; this task was taken over by agents of the central government, responsible to no local electorate.

The electoral base of the ideal British local government system was also eroded. Councils, reminiscent of their imperial past, often enjoyed hybrid membership. Some members would represent wards; some members would sit on the council by virtue of their administrative positions as local educational officer, and so on, while others would be party officials, themselves sometimes appointed and sometimes elected. Even in Botswana, where local councils survived more actively than in most of tropical Africa (Picard, 1979), the central government had the authority to appoint members to the council to ensure a majority for the government party, an authority which the majority Botswana People's party did not gainsay. Changes in the membership of local councils reflected changes in their functions. Where once they had been avenues for local politicians to advance and centres for the airing of local complaints, they became, in essence, agents of the central government's development efforts. Yet, the democratic assumptions of representation were not entirely lost. In Tanzania the incipient conflict between the roles of people's forum and government's spokesman has been clear. Just as the chiefs in the imperial years were caught between their role as people's tribune and administration's agent so, too, the cell leaders in Tanzania are torn between their dual functions (for example, Ingle, 1972). It is now, as it was before, an insoluble dilemma. Just as the call for unions to be productionist rather than consumptionist was to emasculate the central function of a union as the organisation promoting the sectional interests of workers, so the desire for local councils to adapt their local detailed knowledge in the interests of central government policy negates their function as local institutions representing local wishes.

What have emerged, therefore, are institutions which, on the surface, seem to be local government structures. Councils, chairmen, committees, local taxes, even mayors in some cases, offices with local titles, all can be seen and touched; they undoubtedly exist. But they are, as Tordoff has put it, examples of 'local administration' rather than 'local government' (Tordoff, 1980, p. 389). The British experience has thus come to mirror the French. The tradition in French-speaking Africa was metropolitan France's with its centralising principles and its suspicion of too much local autonomy. Ridley and Blondel's description of French administration in the pre-Mitterrand years would apply equally well to French-speaking Africa and, increasingly, English-speaking Africa too; they noted that central control of local government

follows from the unity of the state. Clearly, the central government is the higher organ: in modified form, the principle of hierarchic subordination still applies . . . local authorities . . . are branches of the state, just as the central government, and indeed public corporations, are branches of the state. They are responsible in their sphere for the organisation of those state functions which are local in character. (Ridley and Blondel, 1964, p. 87)

The structures developed for administering countries, and the values that lay behind them, emphasised the primacy of the governors and their ideas; an enduring difficulty arose because the governed did not always see things in the same way. And they often enjoyed an autonomy and political influence which could not be ignored.

Government and the People

Parliament buildings in Africa may be generally underutilised; government offices are not. In virtually any capital city of Africa, large numbers of civil servants, usually well turned out in dark suits and sober ties, can be seen going around their business with the assurance associated with important people. There are regular international conferences and official visits in which a goodly number of supporting actors appear. International hotels, with their lifts, air-conditioning and mid-Atlantic cuisine, exist in abundance to replenish the energies of the businessmen, diplomats and international experts, as well as the tourists, who arrive in their hundreds at the modern airports which national pride has made resplendent. It is easy for visitors and locals alike to succumb to the atmosphere of the city and to believe that it is there that the political heart of the country lies. In some ways they are right; but the cities are Europe in Africa, an aphrodisiac to which many educated Africans have become addicted.

Outside the city and the line of vision of the casual visitor (and of the self-important politician, too) live 80 per cent of the country's population. The annual growth rate of the urban areas is now about 6 per cent, stretching from the 15 per cent in Botswana to the 2·5 per cent in Burundi, for the most part, therefore, appreciably above the rate of population growth; the balance between rural and urban sectors is thus slowly shifting as some rural residents gravitate to the urban areas. Yet there is a tendency to see the two as quite distinct. In the cities are the 'élites', the professional, salaried and educated classes, while in the rural areas are the peasants, smallholders and subsistence farmers. Such a dichotomous conception of African societies is now grossly oversimplified, as it always was, for it ignores the variety of African social and political arrangements. Within the cities are also, indeed predominantly, large numbers of workers, the labour aristocracy of the permanently employed as well as the temporary sojourners, the independent entrepreneurs in the informal sector, and the transient migrants in desperate search for work. Despite a tendency to decry the economic performances of tropical Africa, the new states, in fact, grew fast in the 1960s on average, although more slowly in the 1970s, and villages became small towns and small towns became urban centres. In the countryside, too, changes have taken place. Some have been enforced; some have happened naturally. In Tanzania, for instance, the dispersed settlements which are the hallmark of the African 'village' (the green with its spreading chestnut tree and surrounding workers' homes, church, pub, blacksmith and small store was never the norm in Africa) have been transformed into nucleated settlements where the increased range of services can be made more easily available. In most of the rest of Africa, however, the pattern of landholdings and dwellings has been less radically altered, although the extension of water supplies, health facilities, government agencies, provision of schooling and leisure activities in the form of bar and football field have certainly given rise to an increased number of small centres whose inhabitants are more than merely small-scale farmers.

The consequence of these changes and the essential continuity of the family farm is to produce a very differentiated society, a veritable kaleidoscope of different occupations. No study of the political environment in tropical Africa would be complete without some awareness of the Djilas-like new class, to which access was originally quite open but which has begun now to consolidate itself even to the extent of espousing private schooling for its children; or of the many-faceted intermediate group of clerks and local party officials whose comparative affluence and discretionary powers make them 'big men' in villages; or of the increasing number of small traders and store-keepers, bar owners and transporters without whom the nexus between the primary-producing villages and the outside world would be broken; or of the variations within the peasantry itself, some of whom can barely survive on their smallholdings, whilst others actually employ the less fortunate on their lands; or of the flotsam and jetsam of the urban areas, men and women whom village life has pushed out, either by its seeming lack of excitement or by its real lack of economic opportunity, to seek money in the inhospitable ghettos of the growing towns.

Given the range of occupations from the 'traditional' wife pounding maize on her husband's land in the rural areas to the 'modern' bureaucrat in his Mercedes-Benz (together with every conceivable position between the two), the question naturally arises: How, then, should the new states of tropical Africa be analysed? This has produced one of the most heated academic debates of recent years, where faith as much as evidence has been in the driving seat. There are obvious problems for those nurtured on the European experience, where the peasantry, if not extinct, is clearly dying and where urban society has developed recognisable and enduring patterns of social division and reproduction. It is impossible to comprehend contemporary Africa without being acutely aware of the variety of analytically separable categories, to which attention was drawn in the previous paragraph; but whether they are classes in the Marxist sense is something else. Much depends, of course, on how tight or loose are the criteria used. On the one hand, there are millions of peasants with their own access to the means of production, their land and their labour, able to survive and reproduce without giving up control of either; on the other hand, there are thousands of politicians and bureaucrats who achieved power by using their skills of persuasion and oratory or their educational achievements, and used that power to establish their economic strength. Are these classes or merely strata (Kitching, 1982)?

Despite the fascinating, subtle and illuminating work done by several scholars in the Marxist tradition, my own view remains that class analysis is inadequate to manage the political relationships between these analytically separable categories. This is only partly because an individual's class position is often by no means clear. As important is the fact that the first generation of political leaders, catapulted into power by the granting of independence, did originally order their policy priorities as an intellectualised vision of the ideal society rather than an expression of their interests as a corporate and self-aware class. A connection between economic needs and ambitions, on the one side, and political action on the other, as any liberal will assert, needs no defence. In Africa, however, additional layers of social relationships exist to weaken too close a linkage between economy and politics. In some parts of the continent, race obtrudes (Nolutshungu, 1982); in most parts, tribal loyalties overlay the simplicities of economic self-interest; in others, religion plays a significant part. Abdul Nasser's analogy of the individual's being *inescapably* caught up in several 'circles of identity' remains apposite because African political systems are still essentially syncretic. It takes time to adapt existing practices and beliefs to the explosion of fundamental changes caused by the continent's forced incorporation into the European empires and then hasty extrusion into a world of sovereign states dominated by the industrialised and essentially capitalist economies of the developed world. Individual behaviour can only be explained through an awareness of that individual's conception of the issues involved.

Africa's refusal to be engulfed entirely by the tide of externally induced change is well represented by the survival of chiefs in much of the continent as significant political actors. Of course, the scale of political society has altered their reach and the intrusion of central ministries, national parties and a certain degree of separation of powers have done much to undermine their pre-eminent position. Yet neither these changes nor the nationalist movements' generally antagonistic position to the chiefly hierarchies have altogether eliminated their political authority. The chiefs, too, had adapted in many cases to the new ideas; a few threw in their lot with the nationalists, some remained the faithful servants of the imperial power and forfeited much of their respect in their own community, others tried hard to play both the incompatible roles of people's spokesman and government agent with delicate skill, and a number cracked up under the competing pressures and took to drink (Weinrich, 1971). Most of the nationalist parties had inveighed against the chiefs and promised to abolish their special status, for they claimed with much justification that the battery of administrative orders which had so antagonised the peasantry in the terminal period of imperial rule – regulations enforcing terracing, destocking, limitation of crop production, as well as payment of taxes – had been effected with the co-operation of the chiefs. They were therefore suspected of being less than fully committed to the nationalist cause and their removal from positions of authority became a major demand of the new nationalist leaders.

But their powers have not been abolished. There is a continuum extending from those, like the emirs of Northern Nigeria, who have continued to carry great political weight to those, like the small chiefs of Tanzania, who wield little independent power. The emirs had exercised genuine power, even over those developmental areas of policy which were such important catalysts of political protest elsewhere in Africa; they *were* the administration; their legitimacy pre-dated the imperial era; they recruited into their ranks men of their own kind; in short, they controlled their fiefs. Their opponents were weak in Northern Nigeria, an electoral weakness which the emirs' control of the administration, and thus the electoral machinery, did much to enhance. Finally, their own standing in the Islamic North was very strong, based on a history of temporal dominance as well as spiritual pre-eminence as the religious heads of their people and the appellate court in all matters of custom and native law. Neither independence, nor coups, nor military rule, nor recivilianisation have much weakened their position (Panter-Brick, ed., 1970).

In Uganda there can be found an example which lies in the centre of the continuum. The kabaka of Buganda's government preserved considerable independent powers during the imperial years, but these powers were not extended to include the new range of administrative action rising from the policy of positive development inaugurated by the British after the Second World War. Consequently, it was less central to the life of the Baganda than the emirs' governments in Northern Nigeria. The opponents of traditionalism within Buganda were weak, but the opposition outside the region was strong; although the Ganda people tried, by the establishment of a party committed to the preservation of the kabakaship and a quasi-independent Buganda in the form of the Kabaka Yekka (the King Alone Party), Obote's ability to build a majority outside Buganda and his control over military force did, in

1966, drive the kabaka into exile; yet, attachment to the notion of kingship did not die. The kabaka's downfall was, in part, due to his forsaking the second law of Ganda political culture, namely that flexibility before outsiders provides the key to survival (Low, 1971).

In Tanzania there is a third position. The power of the chiefs, both in terms of constitutional authority and legitimacy, was not strong as the major decisions, except for a brief period in the 1930s, were taken and administered by other government officials and there was little loyalty, cemented by the passage of time, for the successors of the early appointed chiefs. Opposition was stronger than in many countries and there was little generalised support for their retention among the political élite. Soon after independence they were 'abolished'. Yet they did not thereby cease to be important. Although their formal authority might have been destroyed, local headmen in particular retained a following and were, in many cases, elected to party and political office (Miller, 1969). Even after independence, the chiefs retained two important qualities: their experience and skill as intermediaries with outside forces and, in most societies, the respect reserved for senior members of high-status clans whose duties included judgements on many matters of intimate social concern to the rest of the village. In disputes involving marriage, land rights, or custody of children, for example, the traditional importance of the chief as judicial officer, whatever the new 'modern' court system might be, is often central to any resolution. He no longer had a *right* to a political position; he had to earn the support of the ordinary people. But he started with some strong cards. In Mali, to take another example from a very different part of the continent, despite considerable efforts by the radical single party to create a rural socialism which destroyed the ascriptive authority of elderly chiefs, in village elections the traditional gerontocracy maintained itself; indeed, the average age of elected chiefs was 75 (Jones, 1972)!

The geographical focus of the observer colours the attention given to the traditional authorities. In Malawi, for instance, the government has consciously restored to the traditional chiefs and headmen some of their former authority and the traditional courts, employing very different rules of evidence from the 'modern' courts, have taken on a new lease of life. Zimbabwe watchers would observe the more obviously democratic, but not necessarily more just, shadow of people's courts; they would also note the competition for chiefly office together with the lack of obvious power that successful candidates could then wield. Slightly further south, however, the picture is very different again. Although the principle of hereditary power may be in retreat before the egalitarian philosophies spreading through Africa, it is far from dead. In Lesotho, Swaziland and Botswana it remains of central importance and the configuration of power is largely determined by the status of the individual within the traditional political hierarchy (Proctor, 1969; Gillett, 1973; Proctor, 1973). The death of King Sobhuza in 1982 galvanised the Swazi peoples into a reaffirmation of pre-imperial practices and procedures for choosing a successor. And even in those countries where the modern sector of society, the sophisticated intellectual and politicians of the capital cities, are so much in evidence, in the rural areas it matters very much who is one's father or mother. There is no escaping the fact that in so many walks of life the African peoples have adopted and adapted over the years. Abrahams has described the Nyamwezi response to Christian and Muslim religions as 'flexibly accretive' (Abrahams, 1981); much the same could be said of the responses to political penetration from outside.

Where once that penetration came from the varied faces of imperial overrule, it now comes from the conscious desires of the independent governments who are all committed – to a greater or lesser degree – to something called 'development'.

There is no agreement on precisely what this means; indeed, for most politicians, there is little inclination to agonise over its meaning. The overwhelming assumption is that development is, at the very least, the quantitative leap forward associated with an increasing GNP; it also includes the establishment of institutions and values associated with the concept of modernisation, itself a vague idea redolent of the small towns of middle America. More schools, better health facilities, more advanced agricultural techniques and higher levels of production, a wider range and distribution of consumer goods, a more depersonalised bureaucracy, the outward and visible signs of advanced societies, these are the assumed constituent parts of the modern society. Among many commentators, more than among the African politicians themselves, questions have been raised as to whether such things truly constitute development. A qualitative, indeed normative, element is introduced which implicitly challenges the virtue of the industrialised model of society, questions the emphasis on the external manifestations and calls for inner values of egalitarianism and justice, of self-reliance and self-pride. Both schools, caricatured as they have admittedly been, hope for changes among the majority of the African people; the modernisation supporters want a radical change in attitudes and practices but so, too, do their critics who fear the corroding influences of the market-oriented and consumer-dominated preconceptions of their opponents.

Whatever is meant by development, most governments are keen to alter the way in which a majority of their subjects live. A fundamental question therefore arises: How can this be done? There are almost as many answers on offer as there are political leaders to give them. Politicians are grappling here with one of the disputed areas of the social sciences for there is still no accepted explanation for people's motivations. Fear and force have their effects, but they are essentially negative; put crudely, an executed farmer cannot increase his output of coffee. Although in the short run, and in special circumstances, the state's coercive powers employed by a government may extract reluctant co-operation from citizens, throughout the continent such a policy has proved of only limited value. The alternatives fall broadly into two categories: those which assume that a people can be inspired to change and those which assume that change can only be induced by a people's perception of self-interest.

The inspirationalists have attempted to create a new fervour and commitment to work and production, as well as a deeper understanding of socialism and other progressive ideologies. But they have tended to be short on detail and practical policies; they have often been obscure; they have addressed the intellectuals rather than the workers and peasants in a language more suitable for the seminar room than the factory or field; they have resorted ultimately to the repetition of the slogan in place of conversion. There is no doubting the problem such politicians faced. At independence, the dominant ideology was

African nationalism, but the very eclecticism which made it so suitable for its time rendered it less useful in the post-imperial era. Attempts to graft on to it the bogey of neo-colonialism and the ideal of Pan-Africanism were unsuccessful. Such ideas might speak to the intellectuals; they lacked the direct relevance and simplicity of message which had made African nationalism so effective a mobilising cry among the people. Middle-level leaders in Africa are not ideologically sophisticated; hence ideological institutes such as the Wineba Institute in Ghana and Kivukoni College in Tanzania were established to inculcate a deeper awareness of the governments' philosophical positions. The mass of the people, like ordinary people everywhere, have rarely intellectualised their conception of the political order and their vision of the ideal; they have an ideology in the loose sense of a general, normally implicit, orientation towards power, stratification and political structures (along the lines set out in Chapter 4), but they lack an ideology in the strict sense of a conscious, explicit, more or less internally consistent set of values and beliefs which at once both explains the present and directs the path to the future. But it was precisely this second type which many African leaders felt was needed.

There were great difficulties in doing this. The political élite was usually itself divided. But there was also an insurmountable problem arising from the quite different family of ideas which predominated in the mass of the population and in the political élite. The rank and file of the nationalist movement had been essentially populist (Saul, 1969), opposed to large-scale, centralised economic structures and in favour of devolved power, while political leaders were almost invariably statist, favouring centralised economic and political control. A response to this was to appeal not to the head but to the heart. A search was on for uniquely African factors to regenerate and provide the mainspring of a new nationalism. This can be seen in Nyerere's early writings on African socialism, Mobutu's concern for authenticity (shared for a while by Banda, too), Nkrumah's reference to the African personality, Kaunda's humanism, and Senghor's stress on *négritude*. All appealed to a mythical past which the imperial years had partly erased and for which modern society had created inhospitable conditions. Much of

African political theory is, in any case, rationalisation of short-term political needs (Clapham, 1970). To be successful, an ideology must tap a wellspring of existing ideas and few have done that. Too often, they have developed into a sterile plethora of slogans and aphorisms. Leaders are caught in a bind; they tend to assume a community of interest and their own assertions about the progressive nature of the people, yet they need simultaneously to build that community of interest and convert people to progressive ways. The ideas, the language, the behaviour of the committed enthusiasts and the suspicion of ordinary people towards the distant government have all contributed to general failure of the inspirational model.

The more pragmatic approach has its roots in a less optimistic view of human nature. On the one hand, there is little doubt that a popular readiness to produce more, or to switch between crops, owes a great deal to the prices offered. In those French-speaking African territories where the integral link through currency valuations with the French franc has enforced certain constraints on government pricing policy, farmers have produced food crops more successfully than in those English-speaking states which have artificially depressed the price of food at the farm gate to satisfy the demands of urban workers. The total exports of Tanzania's major commodities in 1980 were 34 per cent lower than in 1973; as a percentage of GDP export earnings fell from 25 per cent in 1966 to 11 per cent in 1979. In 1965 farmers produced 566,000 metric tons of cocoa for sale in Ghana, while in 1979 this had dropped to 249,000 tons (much being smuggled abroad where prices were higher). Between 1963 and 1979 the price index for consumer goods and food prices rose twenty-two times, but the price of cocoa rose only six fold, compared to thirty-six fold in neighbouring countries (World Bank, 1981, p. 26). Although adverse weather conditions and some deterioration in the terms of trade have played their part, one primary cause of both Tanzania's and Ghana's economic difficulties has been pricing policy. Peasant producers are neither non-numerate nor ignorant. The effort price, to use Arrighi's phrase in a different context, is palpably too high when the reward for cultivation is so low (Arrighi, 1969 – 70). The propensity to smuggle is greatly enhanced by the vast disparities of price on either side of a border which could not be easily policed even if the officials were prepared to forgo the pecuniary advantages of permitting trading across the boundaries. By 1981–2 most of Ghana's cocoa was being sold in Togo or the Ivory Coast; it would have been an odd farmer who did not act in this way. This encapsulates one central fact of rural life – the essential rationality of the inhabitants. They respond to rewards when they see a use for added income (Acholi farmers were quite prepared to let cotton rot on the plants once the money they wanted for the labour they were prepared to give had been achieved); they select representatives with a view to their usefulness, staying loyal to Cabinet ministers but punishing others unable to extract resources; and they keep government at arm's length with great skill and politeness, safe in the knowledge that their effective 'ownership' of their land is itself an assurance against adversity.

Short of adequate disposable rewards or a unifying ideology, and unable to tap a deep natural loyalty to state and party, political leaders are inevitably short of resources to build up, and keep support for, the government. There is, therefore, a quite understandable tendency to scapegoat and to trade in symbolic rewards. Bogymen – sometimes external neo-colonialists or imperialist lackeys, sometimes indigenous troublemakers and sowers of 'confusions' – are created. What ensues is more often a witchhunt of the unconventional than growth of patriotic idealism and self-sacrifice. An alternative ploy is to satisfy a popular prejudice by using state power to satisfy it. The anti-Asian prejudice of much East African political rhetoric and action is rational ultimately only in this perspective. Wholesale expulsions from Uganda by Amin, while they satisfied a widespread antagonism towards the closely knit and relatively affluent Asian community and provided opportunities for black Ugandans, were ultimately economically self-defeating. In neighbouring Kenya in January 1972, an MP could say to loud applause: 'Look at the Olympic team today. A Singh here and a Patel there – even in the East African Car Safari it's all Singhs. I look forward to the day when there will be no more Singhs in the Olympic team, only Africans.' It is little wonder that Furedi commented: 'Anti-Asian ideology is the bread and butter of many a local politician. This rhetoric not only diverts attention from the real problems facing Kenya but also provides a part of the Kenyan bourgeoisie with profitable opportunities.' (Furedi, 1974, pp. 357 – 8)

Diversionary and symbolic policies are to be expected. But they do not solve the central problem of mobilising the peasantry. It is the relative autonomy of the rural areas which necessitates a less coercive and more co-operative approach than is customary from the politicians. The readiness, and the ability, to withdraw from the wider economic and political system into subsistence agriculture and a social life of an essentially local character has been one of the most significant features of the 1970s. Imperial rule, the market economy and the new nation state have yet to break the ties which bind a majority of the rural populace to 'home', through an enduring network of family links, emotional bonds and economic self-sufficiency. The peasantry, to a significant extent, remains uncaptured (Hyden, 1980). The anarchy of Uganda in the late 1970s and 1980s produced much human misery and suffering, yet most Ugandans, turning away from growing coffee and cotton to the production of food, survived. Farmers in Ghana or Guinea in West Africa, or Tanzania in East Africa, have responded to their fundamental exploitation by withdrawing their efforts from the national economy, reducing the production of export crops (whether intended for overseas markets or home towns), and concentrating on their own survival. Farmers are not easily deluded and they are largely their own masters, well able to calculate the costs and benefits of their own labour. Too few governments in tropical Africa realise this.

Conclusion

Governing any tropical African state is difficult. Three types of problem are almost universal. First, there is the problem of continuity. Existing administrative structures, existing local government arrangements, existing philosophies concerning the separation of party and bureaucracy or the role of civil servants are all inherited. Although the logic of the independence struggle requires a change, or at the very least the illusion of change, in order to translate the constitutional independence into a visible independence, meeting such a requirement is not easy. Government has to go on; structures generate a momentum, or an inertia, of their own; within a few years, the system has settled down operating along lines virtually pre-determined by the practices of the 1950s. The leaders of independent Africa did not enjoy a *tabula rasa* upon which to imprint their own ideals. Furthermore, the range of ideas available to them at the time was limited; many of their advisers were themselves expatriates and most of their educated locals had been trained in the universities of Europe and North America and had, to some extent, imbibed the implicit assumptions that underlie the political systems of the indus-trialised world. The available models were overwhelmingly European in origin. This explains, in part, the fascination with China as a possible alternative model. By the time leaders, academic commentators from outside and intellectuals within the countries had come to feel that the conditions of Africa might dictate different kinds of political institutions, it was almost too late. There were already vested interests well entren-ched to defend their positions, and the assumptions on which Western organisations are based were quite widely dis-seminated through the educational system and the media. The problem of continuity thus stands as one obstacle to the radical changes which might be thought appropriate for the new states.

Second is the problem of experience. At the most obvious level, this is represented by the dearth of technical expertise and knowledge and the consequent dependence upon out-siders. Imperial rule largely failed to produce the accountants, technicians, managers, and so forth, which are essential for the smooth operation of any large organisation. The emphasis on local government and the 'benign neglect' of British rule thus came home to roost; the French heritage was, perhaps, less obvious in this respect, but there was still a dearth of necessary indigenous skills. More significantly, there was a lack of experi-ence of ruling and being ruled under a democratically based political system. There is much to learn both about running a country and also about being a citizen in a participatory democ-racy; the imperial powers had trained very few in these skills. Whereas in India and, to a lesser extent, in the West Indies there had been many years of responsibility, both as rulers and ruled, in Africa there was little time devoted to that training; it is no accident that India and the West Indies (despite their poverty, ethnic and linguistic divisions, and dependence on outside powers) have, by and large, managed to ensure the survival of a political system in which governments are actually held accountable to their electorates. African leaders knew only an essentially authoritarian system, an amazingly rapid achievement of political aims and a seemingly united popular feeling. What they were asked to oversee was a system of democratic controls set in an environment where demands would inevitably be very difficult to meet and in a social milieu where the unity represented by the search for independence gave way to the divisions of class, tribe, ideology and personality. The problem of experience thus stands in the way of operating the inherited institutions in the essentially liberal way for which they were designed.

Third is the problem of support. The new states lacked an internalised popular attachment to the nation, lacked parties based upon the loyalty of long association, lacked a political culture which saw politics as just one of many ways to advance self-interest, and lacked a common political language to bind the mass of the people and the political élites into a single community. It is dangerous, however, to focus entirely on the central organs of the state, on the party, the governmental apparatus and the military. Obviously, it is there that the political disputes have centred and struggles for power have been located. But in the small towns and in the rural areas there is, in many countries, another layer of political systems in which citizens find fulfilment, achieve their ambitions and feel involved. The stability of some states can, therefore, be explained by the extent of the vibrancy of these systems. In essentially conservative regimes, the problems of support are less crucial than in those countries whose governments are committed to fundamental changes in the course of their development. Social and economic changes require commitment from the government agents appointed to implement them and supportive behaviour from the mass of the people; in much of Africa, the agents are underpoliticised for their vanguardist tasks and the people are rationally calculating, and cautious, in their take-up of new ideas.

On balance, therefore, the more conservative regimes have survived better than the radical ones. The price of continuity is less high since they place some value on continuity; the price of experience is less high since they are ready to employ outsiders; the price of change is less high since the changes they seek are broadly in accordance with the values of the major trading powers in the world and support is easier to retain because the demands made upon the mass of the people are less. It seems to be a general rule that under conservative regimes (which should always be distinguished from reactionary or tyrannical regimes) more distributable wealth has been created than under radical regimes. The balance of the equation is not all one way. The cost of conservative policies has often been the exaggeration of the process of cumulative inequality, the alienation of the intellectuals and progressive forces within the country, and a greater dependence upon the former imperial powers. It is to this external dimension that we must now turn.

7 African States and the External World

The granting of independence to the new states of tropical Africa did not end the close links between them and their former colonial masters. Over a wide range of activities (finance, trade, education, technical expertise, military training), the links remained strong and it was to the metropolitan power that most African leaders looked in times of trouble. When mutinies broke out in East Africa in 1964, the British were called in initially; when disturbances rocked some of the French West African states, French assistance was soon at hand. In terms of tangible contributions – to training schemes, to the establishment of new universities, to the drawing up of development plans – these imperial associations remained the primary external links of the new states.

There was, however, something plainly unsatisfactory from the point of view of the nationalist leaders in being politically independent yet still dependent in so many other ways on the former imperial powers. Attempts were soon made to diversify their external links, not only as a visible sign of independence but also as a conscious policy designed to maximise assistance for development programmes. At the same time, the awareness of being African, as well as recent imperial possessions, created a widespread desire to enshrine continental unity in some organisational form and to use African means, if at all possible, to resolve African problems. The creation of the Organisation of African Unity (OAU) in 1963 was the most obvious symbol of this desire, but there have been many attempts to create smaller groupings of states in regional organisations for mutual co-operation.

The weakness of tropical African states acting singly was one reason for the search for continental unity. It also gave rise to the ambivalent relationships between individual states and the much more powerful states of Europe and North America. On the one hand, it forced states to look for external assistance to help the development of their internal economies; on the other hand, it permitted not only the rich states but large transnational corporations to strike often unequal bargains with African governments. The search for help was sometimes the handmaiden of exploitation. The superpowers for their part did not always recognise the claims for independence and non-interference and their rivalry spilled over into the continent, sometimes in spite of African efforts but sometimes, too, as a result of invitation.

This final chapter thus looks briefly at the states of tropical Africa in their varied and complex relationships with the wider world. Governments retain the sovereign prerogative of choice, but this choice is limited by the felt needs of the African countries and the self-interests of the rich nations. While it is essential to comprehend the constraints, it is as important to recognise that governments still have some choices and different governments thus pursue markedly different policies.

The Context of International Relations

The classic studies of international relations dwell on the relationships between sovereign states. The appropriate model was one composed of independent states employing their varied resources (wealth, manpower, technology, strategic position) to advance their national interests in a world of independent states. To a very large degree, domestic matters were insulated from direct external interference; that situation, after all, epitomised sovereignty. Order in the international system was essentially preserved by balancing competitive powers. In the aftermath of the Second World War, a bipolar system grew up in which every state was thought to rotate either round the Washington pole of Western liberal interests or the Moscow pole of socialist interests. To some extent, this represented the truth, especially while the empires survived. But the end of empire, which coincided largely with a peak in the Cold War relations between East and West, gave birth to many states whose allegiance was not immediately clear.

At independence, the states of tropical Africa had no time-honoured interests to be preserved. Foreign-policy aims were often more symbolic and psychological than pragmatic continuations of practices already legitimised by time. Much of Africa's behaviour in the international community can only be understood in this perspective. The language of anti-colonialism and sometimes that of anti-capitalism, the instinctual sympathy for the Soviet Union with her claim to be the leader of progressive forces, and the deeply ingrained antagonism to apartheid and any surviving manifestations of imperial rule reflect this need. Speeches at the United Nations or in the home legislature again often represent a public posture rather than a true presentation of government policy. But international relations, although fuelled by passion often enough, have a harder quality than the trading of ideals.

The first two decades of tropical Africa's independence have coincided with a collapse in the political order of the international system. Four themes need stressing. First, both the assumptions and the reality of bipolarity have been called into question. The communist world has itself become divided, most obviously illustrated by the Sino-Soviet split and the independent line pursued by Albania, and there are stresses within that bloc which permit a greater degree of autonomous behaviour than in the 1950s. The positive role played by Cubans in Africa is a function quite as much of Cuban will and need as of Soviet pressure, while the Hungarian decision to affiliate with the IMF is another instance of the general collapse of the monolithic Eastern bloc. At the same time, the unity of the Western bloc has been sorely strained. The relatively independent role of France, the tensions between Europe and the United States, the independent behaviour of Iran, or South Africa, or Japan, all testify to the dissolution of the Pax Americana. It is no longer true (perhaps it was never entirely true) that the superpowers can settle the conflicts between states. Certainly, the plethora of international disputes which neither the United States and her allies, on the one side, nor the Soviet Union and hers, on the other, have been able to resolve is a distinguishing feature of the 1970s. To some extent, the world is therefore a less stable and less predictable place.

This is closely associated with the second theme. The assumption that peace could be preserved by a bipolar world resting on the basis of balanced nuclear terror has been proved incorrect. The horrific level of destructive capacity available to the superpowers may so far have prevented a nuclear holocaust, but it has manifestly failed to prevent conventional wars. The very level of destruction associated with the nuclear weapon means that it no longer provides a credible threat; weaker nations know that the issues involved in the small wars which occupy them are of insufficient significance to warrant the start of a nuclear war. Furthermore, the unwillingness of the United States (in particular after the tribulations of the Vietnam War) to use its massive conventional power to impose local solutions has added further to the likelihood of local wars. In addition, the availability of arms, often of a very sophisticated kind, has been encouraged by the great powers both for political and economic reasons. The end result has been an increasing number of 'small wars'; in the Ogaden between Somalia and Ethiopia, in Uganda between the Tanzanians and Ugandan liberation forces against Amin's army, in Chad between various factions variously supported by French or Libyan expertise and material, to take but three examples. The ensuing destruction of the terrain over which the fighting takes place, the cost in lives and money, the creation of a large and growing refugee population, and the shift in emphasis from development to destruction or survival has clearly laid a heavy burden on many countries, not a few of which have little stake in the crisis which causes the disruption.

Thirdly, the 1960s saw the full maturity of the penetrated state. Of course, the tradition of state autonomy and the principle of non-interference in the internal affairs of a sovereign state had never been absolute, but they represented broad principles upon which behaviour in the international community could be predicted. But that is a thing of the past. Rival claimants for office now operate from outside state boundaries, assisted by other states and linked to similar groups challenging the existing *status quo*. Terrorists, liberation movements and general revolutionaries have increased in number, and their political aims are prosecuted now on a wider stage than ever before, spilling over into countries unconnected with their disputes. Transnational ideas and movements, such as the rise of Islam or Pan-Arabism, have ramifications far from the countries where their leaders may live. The enormous growth in the means of communication through the world media has resulted in the rapid dissemination of ideas, of news, of examples to be emulated. The days of the impermeable state are gone. Once the People's Republic of China opened a chink of light on to the wider world, the last bastion of controlled self-sufficiency was breached. Burma and Kampuchea may try to insulate themselves from the events and ideas of the outside world, but it is not wholly successful and the consequences are dire. Both physical and ideological interference is now more possible and less preventable.

But there is another development of perhaps even greater significance. This is the emergence and proliferation of trans-national companies, the great mining conglomerates and multi-purpose trading companies, with enormous capital resources and scarce skills. The expenditure of a company like Exxon, ITT, or even Unilever is many times greater than that of the average tropical African state. As capitalism has developed from the still largely labour-intensive operations of the nine-teenth century into the many functional, highly capitalised and ubiquitous companies of the late twentieth century, a great concentration of capital and technical expertise has taken place. Without the participation of these enterprises in their econ-omies, the poor states of the world would lack the essential resources needed for the sort of economic development they have in mind. Yet it is the large corporation that can usually call the tune. It enjoys the technical superiority; it offers the capital and expertise the new states seek; its needs are its share-holders', not the African states' interests; on balance, the poor states need its involvement more than it needs to produce or locate in the poor states. In many ways, therefore, the direction – and, more to the point, the detail – of an African country's economic strategy may be dictated by the external forces of the transnational companies, able, through their various sub-sidiaries in many parts of the globe, to limit their tax liabilities by transfer pricing (selling goods in high-tax countries cheaply to themselves in low-tax countries, thereby maximising their profits). At least, this is one of the images.

The fourth theme is the increased problem of internal con-trol. In imperial days there were scattered problems of this kind, but the local administration saw its primary task as the establishment and preservation of order, a task which the central government supported with military strength. The emphasis in the post-independence years on the developmental role of the administration and on its integration with the party or the local political élite has reduced the confidence, and the ability, of local administrators to ensure the continuance of order. Kenya is one of the few exceptions, where the role of the provincial and district administrations remains consciously that of supporting the state and bolstering up the government's authority. This reflects both the colonial tradition and the 'inherent insecurity of government in a society where rapid social change continually threatens to upset the delicate political equilibrium so recently established' (Hyden *et al.*, 1970, p. 334). Unsurprisingly, the disaffection in most African countries has been on the increase. Once the honeymoon period of the immediate post-independence years had ended, the reality of disappointment began to set in. There was not a true revolution of rising expectations (or frustrations, as it should be), because expectations among the majority of the rural people remained realistic (Oberschall, 1969–70). In time, however, even those who had done comparatively well out of independence began to fret. Some of the problems were externally generated: the rise in oil prices, recession in the developed world, the stagnation of primary-producer prices and the technical impoverishment of most African states inevitably affected the quantity of resources available for distribution. But there were also endogenous factors: inefficiency, corruption, selfishness, peculiar priorities, tribalism, all played their part. The tensions that were so aroused, when combined with the weakness of the state and the means available to dissident groups to disrupt the smooth working of the state through strikes, boycotts, demonstrations and armed physical uprisings, provided the preconditions for much destabilising activities. The other factors in the international scene, of which mention has already been made, added to the difficulties. Without the great powers to force order on to parts of the continent, without the threat of external involvement to act as a brake, and with the proliferation and easy access to arms, there was little to stand in the way of groups who challenged the hegemony of a ruling group by force.

The eclipse of bipolarity and the emergence of the penetrated state naturally called into question the traditional way of viewing international relations. In its place a new conceptual framework became popular which envisaged the world not so much as a set of individual and sovereign states but as a single economic and political system in which the states were linked to each other in often unequal relationships. The peripheral states were seen as so dependent upon the giants of the industrialised West that their freedom of action, in short their very sovereignty, was compromised. Indeed, some have argued that the structural imperatives of the relationship actually prevented the possibility of true independence for the peripheral states, partly because the metropolitan countries' self-interest dictated a policy of denying the poorer states the technological and financial resources to break the dependency connection, and partly because the leaders of the poor states had been captured by the major capitalist powers and acted as a comprador bourgeoisie furthering the aims of the great powers. To this extent, the peripheral states were actively 'underdeveloped'. In fact, the literature on dependency and underdevelopment is very much more complex than this simplified summary might suggest; indeed, it is sometimes so complex as to defy understanding. But it clearly calls attention to some incontrovertible points: political independence does not bring with it complete economic autonomy; the rich industrialised nations dominate the world economy; the options open to small, undercapitalised states are severely limited. Whether it is more than a framework is open to question.

Some scholars have moved beyond a conceptual framework to an explanatory theory, arguing that the nature of international capital *causes* underdevelopment and the recreation of unequal class relationships in the peripheral countries. There is, however, no single theory which is accepted as *the* theory of dependency or underdevelopment and its explanatory value is increasingly being called into question (Nove, 1973–4; Jeffries, 1982). There are, too, doubts about the historical accuracy of some of its assertions (Smith, 1978–9); there are clearly instances of peripheral states breaking away from the dominance of the old metropolitan powers and establishing a local capitalism independent of outside forces (Warren, 1973); there has been a reaffirmation of that part of Marx's analysis which saw capitalism as having some progressive consequences in the realm of production (Warren, 1980); there is too much evidence in local studies of the political process, in consideration of welfare priorities or school curricula, or in competition for local office for more extreme claims of the theory as the ultimate talmud to hold up. 'Underdevelopment theory', Robin Cohen has written, 'is almost too powerful and too blunt a tool. Handled carelessly it can overwhelm the specificity of different concrete experiences or degenerate into a sterile determinism' (Cohen, 1976). Perhaps the least satisfactory part of this approach is the lack of autonomy granted to the local political leadership. The essentially manipulative linkages posited in the theory that the less developed countries are ruled by a local bourgeoisie who serve as the junior partners or executors of the bourgeoisie in the metropolis call for some examination. There is surely little doubt that the different economic paths followed by Tanzania and Kenya owe a great deal to the individual beliefs and convictions of Kenyatta and Nyerere respectively. Similarly, Touré in Guinea and Houphouet-Boigny in the Ivory Coast chose very different responses at independence. There is little doubt that the economic performances of the two countries have been intimately connected to these choices; but they were choices that could have been made differently. Political leaders in Africa are, indeed, constrained but they have a certain freedom within which to operate and the vast majority of them have the confidence and the courage to use that freedom as they see best. It is demeaning to African leaders to argue otherwise.

Many writers in the underdevelopment school tend to argue that the present development crisis in Africa is directly related to its contact with, and incorporation into, the already industrialised capitalist economic system (which seems entirely unexceptionable). However, they proceed further to give Western capitalism itself – in any case, a mammoth catchall phrase embracing cultural, economic and technical connotations – exclusive rights of paternity. To some extent, the underdevelopment school has set up an Aunt Sally to attack with vigour. The very concept of development is torn from its traditional ethnocentric environment, which is probably extremely healthy, and then transmogrified into a Prince Charming of 'rapid, self-sustained expansion, controlled and directed by and for the African people themselves' (Green and Seidman, 1969, p. 21) in which an egalitarian spread of rewards is seen as an integral part of the very concept. It is little wonder that capitalism and colonialism are cast as the ugly sisters; they must be. The new states, however, normally have to be linked to the rich states of the industrialised West who alone can purchase their products and provide their capital needs. These states are not (and, given their competitive electoral systems, cannot be) wholly altruistic sugar daddies to the poor world; the degree of specialisation involved in any form of technically more sophisticated modes of production in the poor states is likely to spawn inequalities. In short, unless the people of Africa want to forgo the material pleasures of consumer durables, clinics, permanent housing, education, and so on (and only the neo-imperialist idealist who has tasted of this fruit can expect the peasantries of The Third World to accept such self-abnegation), there will inevitably be inequities and there will inevitably be a degree of dependency.

The basic framework of the dependency theorists is sound. Because of their financial weaknesses and heavy dependence upon the rich industrialised world for capital, technology and markets, African states are driven to negotiate with the representatives of that world. The resources of each side are usually unequal. But that does not mean that the leaders of tropical Africa have no freedom of manoeuvre, no cards at all to bargain with, no chance to reject what is offered. They have; and some behave accordingly. All dyadic relations provide both partners with some bargaining resources, for the very fact of negotiating implies some interest on the part of both negotiating teams. When Tanzania refused to accept the terms of an IMF loan, the IMF bent its rules; when the Soviet Union overpressed Amin in Uganda, he expelled their diplomatic mission. What is more, it is conceivable that there is a mutuality of interest rather than an inevitably antagonistic relationship between the rich and the poor. This was certainly the view of the Brandt Commission (Brandt, 1980). There have been voices raised against the proposition, but they have largely been predicated on a fundamental antagonism to the kind of world economic system assumed by most of the commissioners. It should not be forgotten that in Africa, as in the rest of the world, there are leaders who genuinely believe that capitalism, tamed to some extent by state oversight, is the best path to improved standards of living.

But Africa is not an entirely passive actor. One response to weakness is to look for friends outside the state borders. The former imperial powers were the natural starting point; the ties of experience, language and personal contact pointed in that direction. Bilateral aid, economic and military, came disproportionately from the metropolitan country, except in the case of the former Portuguese colonies. In time of crisis, such as the 1964 mutinies in East Africa or potential disorder in Senegal, the old imperial troops returned. In terms of tangible contributions, whether good or ill, the primary link remained the imperial one. But it had two obvious drawbacks: it compounded a country's dependency by tying it too closely to a single outside power, and it derogated from that independence for which the nationalists had struggled.

One response was to spread the links with the capitalist powers and thus reduce a country's dependence. Canadians, Germans, Italians, Danes, Swedes and the army of international civil servants loosely associated with the United Nations began to fly into the African capitals and negotiate development projects and technical assistance programmes. There were costs involved in such a policy as well as the gains thought to flow from widening the company of friends. There were difficulties of language, of style, of matching new components with old machinery, and so on. The determination in English-speaking Africa to diversify in this way certainly introduced an element of competition into the new lucrative market of development planning and project work; but it also weakened, in places, the teaching at secondary and tertiary levels where linguistic difficulties added to the already existing problems of limited facilities. In French-speaking Africa, however, the drive to diversification was much less pronounced, partly because French governments' generosity was greater and more tied than British governments' and partly because the leaders of French-speaking Africa still valued the French language and the French connection very highly. Yet the diversification response was no answer to those who maintained that such a policy still tied the African countries firmly to the international capitalist system. It was not only the radical factions in the new leadership who felt this way; the liberals, too, saw a virtual identity between imperialism and capitalism and thus sought to loosen the ties with the old imperial powers and talk about socialism. Thus was born a widespread support for non-alignment.

The third response, therefore, was to make a public expression of a country's independence by establishing embassies, trading relations and cultural exchange schemes with the communist bloc. There were some, most notably Dr Banda of Malawi, who felt no need for such an assertion and, in any case, was so instinctively opposed to links with the East that he preferred the reality of South African rand to the chimera of Soviet roubles. The links with the communist bloc were more political than economic and hence, in the medium and long term, were less popular than the aid-producing associations with the capitalist West. The Sino-Soviet split ruffled some relations and the People's Republic of China became, for all the revisionist tags pinned on it by Moscow, a more popular model and aid-giver in peaceful times than the Soviet Union.

The fourth response was, in many ways, the true expression of non-alignment for it concentrated on the creation of African unity and African solutions to African problems. But there has been disappointingly little forthcoming from this source. Some border disputes have been eased by committees of reconciliation, but little has yet been done through regional and continental co-operation towards making the African states more economically self-sufficient or improving the transport and communications between states. There is too much competition, for leadership of the continent, for export crops. Where unity can usually be fostered is in bitter denunciation of the apartheid system of South Africa, the very antithesis of Pan-Africanism and African nationalism whose emotive powers remain remarkably strong.

To some extent, states cannot avoid international relations. Many initiatives, calling forth responses, emanate from outside. But states usually have aims to fulfil in their external activities and they try to prosecute them as best they can. For tropical Africa, the primary need is markets for its goods at decent prices, capital for its industrial infrastructure, technical assistance for its educational, agricultural, manufacturing and commercial sectors, and loans for development projects. That is the demand; the supply realistically can only come from the rich, industrialised nations, some of whom were the former imperial powers. Need and pride conflict. That is the context of international relations.

Interstate Relations within Africa

In the 1940s and 1950s neither the French nor the British attempted to integrate their African possessions into continent-wide organisations. The lines of communication continued to run from the African capital to the metropolitan capital; indeed, it was usually quicker to send a letter destined for another part of Africa through London or Paris rather than across the continent. There were, it is true, a few regional co-ordinating institutions like the East African Common Services Organisation or the two parts of the French African Empire, French Equatorial Africa and French West Africa, with their capitals in Brazzaville and Dakar respectively; but Africa remained essentially a geographic term rather than an entity with political and economic links. Nevertheless, many African leaders did manage to obviate the continent's disaggregated political structure, the French-speakers through a quasi-party with representation in the National Assembly, the Rassemblement Démocratique Africaine and the English-speakers through the Pan-African movement. The 1945 meeting in Manchester, at which leading nationalists like Jomo Kenyatta and Hastings Banda from Eastern Africa and Kwame Nkrumah, Joe Appiah, Chief Akintola and Wallace Johnson from West Africa, was replicated at other venues (Legum, 1962). The Pan-African Movement for East and Central Africa (PAFMECA) brought together nationalist politicians from all over English-speaking East and Central Africa for mutual support and for the planning of activities aimed at accelerating the route to independence (Cox, 1964). And there were other meetings, in Accra in 1958, in Addis Ababa in 1960, in Casablanca and Monrovia in 1961, in Lagos in 1962; but at all of these only some of the leaders came and the ideological divisions which were already conspicuous in West Africa largely dictated who attended and what conclusions emerged. By the early 1960s, therefore, there were several overlapping organisations and groups which were already fostering the ideal of continental unity; yet the membership of these organisations was predominantly (although not exclusively) either Francophone or Anglophone and they provided for nothing more positive than the holding of conferences.

The ideal of continental unity was the logical extension of African nationalism, once Africa had been wrested from Europeans for Africans. It was a matter of the heart; but it was also a pragmatic necessity. As the separate imperial possessions gained their political independence, discussions were held on how best to translate the ideals of Pan-Africanism into reality. To this end, towards the end of May 1963 the foreign ministers of thirty states met in Addis Ababa (Ethiopia, even more than Liberia, being thought to have no serious imperial legacy) to prepare agreed documents for their heads of government to sign. And on 25 May the Organisation of African Unity (OAU) was born (see, generally on the OAU, Cervenka, 1969). It was not, however, an easy birth for there were two opposed views on the proper nature of the organisation. The ideological splits which had created two West African groups, based upon Casablanca and Monrovia respectively, had not been resolved. Put simply, Nkrumah campaigned for a continental government from the outset, to which individual states would surrender their sovereignty; only in this way, he argued, could Africa mobilise what resources it had and preserve its independence from the pressures of outside powers. Nyerere, by contrast, was less ambitious, although his ultimate vision did not differ greatly from Nkrumah's; he felt that continental unity could only grow gradually and organically by the accretion of smaller federations (he was thinking very much of an East African Federation to which he, Kenyatta and Obote were then publicly committed). Nyerere's point of view prevailed. Ironically, Nyerere was himself largely responsible soon afterwards for the demise of an East African Federation and he came later to espouse Nkrumah's position (Mazrui, 1965; Agyeman, 1975).

The goals and principles of the OAU, as they emerged in

1963, were essentially of two types: those that regulated intra-African relations (such as the principles of sovereignty, non-interference, condemnation of subversion, peaceful solution of disputes) and those that set guidelines for relations between Africa and the rest of the world (commitment to the total decolonisation of the continent, struggle against racism, international co-operation, non-alignment). In some ways, these were essentially conservative principles for they underpinned the *status quo*, especially where state boundaries are concerned. Nkrumah had feared that, once political leaders gained control over the limited geographical space of a state, their primary instincts would be to conserve their own power and act with the narrow interests of the new state predominant. He was right. Nationalists who had inveighed against the unnatural boundaries of the imperial possessions now, with Somalia's noted exception, defended them with vigour; nationalists who had preached democracy and individual rights fought shy of allowing others to remind them of their failings; nationalists who had helped their friends in the progressive cause of removing the imperial power now frowned upon any attempt by other states to succour their own dissidents in exile.

The goals and principles of the OAU have largely survived, although there are clearly signs of fraying at the edges. The OAU itself put together a military force to assist in imposing an African solution to Chad's internal war, but it lacked the money and ultimately the will to enforce its remit. Somalia has never fully accepted that the boundaries inherited should be inviolate. And the Polisario, campaigning for an independent Saharan Republic against the carving up of the Spanish Sahara by Morocco and Mauritania, has divided the OAU so deeply that no quorum was found for the Tripoli Heads of Government meeting in 1982 and it had to be postponed.

The OAU has some successes to its name. In the early post-imperial years some border disputes were resolved by the intervention of a small number of African leaders acting on behalf of the OAU. In the 1970s the liberation committee based in Dar es Salaam undoubtedly did much, both morally and physically, to accelerate the decolonisation of southern Africa, although ultimately it was events in Portugal and

British intervention which resolved the struggles in Mozambique and Zimbabwe. In the 1970s, too, the OAU was used much more as a forum to co-ordinate economic demands and discuss international issues preparatory to action in the United Nations; and successive secretaries-general had attempted to push the Organisation along a more forthright path of economic concern. But, for the most part, the OAU has been very much an organisation to advance political views and garner political credit (Wolfers, 1976). Its resolutions are largely statements of principle, sometimes calls for action, but are rarely preludes to genuine co-operation. The dead hand of national sovereignty weighs too heavily upon it. Following the acknowledged enormities of the Amin regime in Uganda (and others, too), the OAU moved towards the establishment of a Charter of Human Rights for Africa, but it was aborted as governments came to realise that the fragility of their domestic positions might not stand its implementation. Disappointingly, therefore, the OAU has failed to provide African solutions for most African problems, has failed to overcome the inherited Balkanisation and replace it with a more integrated economy and has failed, notwithstanding the contribution of the African Development Bank, to do much for the development of the continent as a whole.

If Nkrumah's fear that self-interest would prevail has been proved largely correct, what, then, has happened to Nyerere's hope that regional associations would be the building bricks of continental unity? There has been no shortage of mergers, associations, putative federations and economic links. When these were essentially political in nature, they had a short life. While Ghaddafi's Libya must hold the record for the number of abortive federations, confederations and linkages entered into by any one state, West Africa has not been short of its examples. The union between Mali and Ghana was typical of the unconsidered nature of so many attempts to unite; the assumption of virtue associated with the creation of enlarged groupings was thought sufficient to turn an idea into a reality. Apart from some fraternal delegations enjoying brief visits to the capitals, however, the tangible signs of enlargement of scale were minimal.

Those regional associations which were essentially economic

in nature had a greater chance of success. The oldest English-speaking regional grouping was the East African Common Services Organisation which came into existence during the period of imperial rule to unify the currencies, transport systems, markets and other common services for the three East African states of Kenya, Tanganyika and Uganda. For a brief period in 1963 it looked as though this association might be translated into a political federation and, indeed, the leaders of the three territories committed themselves to such a union. But it did not materialise (Rothchild, ed., 1968). They settled instead for an essentially economic Community, not very dissimilar to the European Community in political form, but which continued to operate a wide number of common services. The economies of scale which this should have created, however, were offset by the consequent derogation of sovereignty and common interests were found to be weaker than parochial needs. Political forces were too strong; and the tendency for one state, in this case Kenya, to dominate the region economically itself had political repercussions. Tanzania's one-party system and socialist philosophy made it difficult to absorb into a single political unit the more open and capitalist polities of Uganda and Kenya, while Kenya's clearly greater affluence and Uganda's military awfulness under Idi Amin provided further arguments against closer association. With borders being closed, ships and aeroplanes being retained, and passionate words being exchanged, the Community died early in 1977 (Hodder-Williams, 1978). Economic inequalities were only one of the reasons; the political reality of sovereign independence unwilling to be diluted was the more potent cause.

In West Africa a new association was created some time after independence called the Economic Community of West African States (ECOWAS), whose membership had grown to sixteen by 1981. Learning from the experience of earlier unsuccessful attempts at regional associations, the leaders of the West African states involved moved cautiously to institute co-operative arrangements. There were obviously the problems of language, of valued sovereignty, of competitive economics, of different currencies and of political leadership. But Nigeria's lead, probably inevitable given its population and wealth, has been essential to the careful, even reticent, progress that has been steadily made. Nyerere's 1963 vision here seems to be taking some root; a regional association building on genuine common interests and a growing readiness to compromise promises an unspectacular success. A certain lack of ambition here may indeed be the price of acknowledging realities.

Farther south, during 1979 and 1980, another association was born, the Southern African Development Co-ordination Conference, or SADCC as it is usually termed (Nsekela, ed., 1981). This association involved nine states – Botswana, Angola, Mozambique, Tanzania, Zambia, Zimbabwe, Malawi, Lesotho and Swaziland – and it is expected that Namibia will join when it is independent. Although the impetus for this association was essentially political, in that the states wished to become less dependent upon the Republic of South Africa, its major concerns during the early discussions have been essentially economic and the establishment of regional specialisms. In this way, without actually having to introduce a common market in which traditionally the most developed and strongest economies have gained disproportionately, the region is practising something like the theory of comparative advantage in which the individual countries concentrate upon that economic activity in which they are best suited. The SADCC also acts as a channel for international aid, both from the European Community and from individual countries (Hill, 1983). The SADCC is still young and the optimism which gave it birth is still high; there are obviously conflicts of interests for the economies of the region are as competitive as they are complementary and the issue of personal leadership is by no means dead. Whether it can survive better than the East African Community remains to be seen, yet its acknowledgement of the primacy of political forces and individual sovereignty gives some cause for hope.

Only three regional associations have been mentioned here. There are, in fact, a great many more (Clark, 1979). Some are no more than shells and excuses for heads of government to meet; others are more productive; yet others in fact provide links with countries outside the continent which share common interests with some African states. It is difficult, after all, to describe and delineate anything so specific as 'the African interest', a fact which lies at the heart of the apparent failure of the OAU. The states of tropical Africa are politically independent and their governments attempt to employ whatever means are available to preserve that independence, to ensure their own survival, and to improve the lot of their people as they define it. Inevitably, therefore, their associations are varied. Given Africa's comparative lack of economic power – although it should not be ignored – and the continent's comparative lack of political significance to the great powers, she has to take the initiative to put her concerns on the international agenda.

Consequently, it is in groupings outside the continent altogether that Africa's voice is often most clearly heard. In the United Nations the numerical strength of the new and poorer states of the world has some impact – especially in the General Assembly – and African states see that institution as an important resource. The Group of 77 (although now comprising well over 100 states) with its 24-state executive does much to co-ordinate Third World politics generally, just as the African, Pacific and Caribbean (APC) group acts as a spokesman for many African interests in dealings with the European Community. In pressing for a New International Economic Order or a New World Information Order through UNESCO, African states have found non-African organisations invaluable.

This is due not only to the advantages provided by size when negotiations with the developed world are entered into. It is due also to the failure of the OAU to live up to its name. The postponement of the 1982 summit on Tripoli was symptomatic of the crisis in the OAU, where member states are reluctant to pay their dues and where political differences effectively destroy its capacity to act. The successful mediation of the early years and the important part played by its liberation committee in the decolonisation of Southern Africa have given way to a succession of failures, both economic and political. Zimbabwe's birth owes more to the *ad hoc* regional grouping of the so-called 'front line states' than to the OAU; it is the Western contact group which is negotiating with South Africa over Namibia; the Chad civil war was influenced more by Libyan and French soldiers than by the OAU peace force. Nevertheless, despite its failures and its political divisions, the spirit of Pan-Africanism remains a reality, most obviously at a rhetorical level but also in the unquestioned assumptions of most articulate Africans. They may not always behave like continental brothers, but the notion of continental brotherhood is still deeply felt, as much by the post-independence generation as by their African nationalist elders. Oppression in South Africa *is* a personal slight. Indeed, what unity the OAU has owes much to South African apartheid; if it did not exist, it would have to be invented.

The Great Powers and Tropical Africa

The most immediate external links after independence were necessarily with the former imperial powers. These links were of many kinds and of variable durability. In English-speaking Africa, the British connection remained strong; British advisers were at hand to assist governments in those ministries and parastatal organisations where local expertise was most lacking and British companies – manufacturers, traders, banks, accountants, mining houses – dominated the economies. In addition, the cultural links established through educational systems both in Africa and in Britain were continued, as the Inter University Council for Higher Education Overseas assisted in staffing the new universities, places were made available for Africans in home universities, the libraries, booksellers and film-distributors continued to look to Britain for their material, and a hundred and one other associations – from tourism to sporting links – continued to exist.

Yet this dominance was far from total. In part, successive British governments downplayed the African link, preferring to concentrate their attentions on Europe or the Atlantic Alliance; in part, the African governments themselves diversified their ties. Certainly, the capitals of the former British Empire began to be visited by technical experts from many countries and British products, most notably cars, began to be replaced by French, American and Japanese goods. Aid budgets in the metropolitan country were cut and student fees raised. The conscious shift of emphasis in British foreign policy from political calculations to economic calculations played its part as the British Council and the World Service of the BBC were cut and more attention and interest was paid to the oil-rich

Arabian states and the large American markets. The arms-length at which the empire had been kept thus had a consequential spillover effect into the post-imperial years. Certainly, there was not in London that mystical attachment to the former empire which continued in Paris.

Yet there was one institution which continued the old imperial links at a political level. The Commonwealth, so often prematurely assigned to the grave by uncomprehending commentators, flourished and played a significant part in international affairs. Behind the scenes, a web of associations dealing with a host of topics – communications, banking, parliamentarianism and law, for example – held meetings in various capitals of the Commonwealth. But it was at the heads of government meetings that the greatest benefits occurred. It is doubtful whether the transition to majority rule in Zimbabwe could have been achieved with such relatively little bloodshed had not the Commonwealth lent its approval to the negotiations of 1979; it is doubtful whether the British government would have taken notice at all of the North – South dialogue and the need to go to Cancún had not the Commonwealth and its active Secretary-General, Shridath Ramphal, pressed it. In this unique body, a microcosm of the international community is represented, white and black, rich and poor, countries from all continents and of most faiths. In their regular meetings at different Commonwealth capitals, African states used the opportunities to lobby on a wide range of issues, political as well as economic. The association is highly valued and the high commissions – as the embassies of Commonwealth countries in Commonwealth countries are called – with their regular meetings of high commissioners are a source of envy to non-Commonwealth diplomats.

French-speaking Africa has followed a different path. The Brazzaville repudiation of sovereign independence for overseas territories outside the French Empire remained the policy of consecutive French governments throughout the Fourth Republic. The events of 1958, however, which brought General de Gaulle to the Elysée Palace and inaugurated a new Constitution provided the opportunity for forging a fresh framework within which relations between metropolitan France and her imperial possessions could be conducted. The 28 September referendum on the new Constitution effectively invited the overseas territories to choose between membership of a federal Community (in which major powers would be retained in Paris but which offered the possibility, at some stage in the future, of sovereign independence) and immediate sovereign independence (which threatened the severance of all connections with France).

It was a difficult choice for the Africans. As the Malagasy leader Philibert Tsiranana put it: 'When I let my heart talk, I am a partisan of total and immediate independence; when I make my reason speak, I realise that it is impossible' (quoted in Mortimer, 1969, p. 314). Only in Guinea did the heart rule; and there Tsiranana's reason was shown to have rational foundations. De Gaulle's reaction to Sékou Touré's Guinea voting 'no' was immediate and unequivocal. Departing Frenchmen destroyed the files and removed much of the equipment, including typewriters; Guinea was excluded from the franc zone and denied technical and financial assistance. The economic consequences were immense. Despite comparatively rich natural resources, Guinea is now officially among the world's twenty-five poorest nations. A brief flirtation with Soviet aid – including one now famous consignment of snowploughs – and assistance from the United States' food aid programme have done little to satisfy the small country's inhabitants. Many plots have been hatched, one invasion of 300 mercenaries has been made, and perhaps 1 million of the country's 5·5 million inhabitants have emigrated. In 1982 Sékou Touré was in Paris hoping to mend fences, having already come in from the cold as far as his neighbours were concerned by joining ECOWAS. For the rest of the French West African and Equatorial empires, the ties with France were normally accepted and widely welcomed; even some of the more radical states, like the avowedly Marxist-Leninist Congo-Brazzaville, retained close economic and even political links.

Francophone West Africa was affected by the ideals of African nationalism just as Anglophone Africa was. Following Guinea's choice of 'freedom in poverty to riches in slavery', the two Francophone Trust Territories, Togo and Cameroon, sought and were granted their independence. These may have been special cases because their position in international law was clearly different from the states which had formed the French African Empire. But the pressures for independence, especially in what came to be called Mali, were great and the Community was increasingly seen to be little more than an appendage to a French state dominated by its new president. Although the Executive Council did meet from time to time, the more representative Senate of the Community only met twice, for its birth and its funeral as Georges Bidault's splendid jibe put it. De Gaulle's opposition to Guinea's independence was related more to Touré's repudiation of France than to his enthusiasm for sovereign status and the general's treatment of Algeria, whose bitter war spread its cancer into mainland France itself, was also based on the realisation that an *Algérie Francaise* was impracticable. Politicians in Africa, therefore, who sought independence were pushing at a door that was heavy rather than locked. In the face of widespread demands for independence, de Gaulle moved rapidly, the Constitution notwithstanding, to oversee the disintegration of the Community. The federal idea was dropped and confederal ideas took its place. Even Houphouet-Boigny, who had been the prime supporter of a federal French Community, opted for independence first and bilateral links with France thereafter. In 1960, therefore, Francophone Africa tumbled headlong into independence like a pack of cards, twelve states being admitted to membership of the United Nations that September.

De Gaulle, however, had no intention of weakening the bonds which tied these new states to France more than was absolutely necessary and the leaders of most of the new states, like Tsiranana, realised the benefits that might accrue by establishing bilaterally economic, technical and military links with France. For some, and Houphouet-Boigny was perhaps the prime example, links with France were positively desired because emotional attachment remained strong. At any rate, independence did not sever most links. In the immediate post-independence years, many Frenchmen served in the ministries and parastatal organisations of most states and even in the 1980s there are many more Frenchmen serving in sensitive policy-making positions than did so in Anglophone Africa even a decade after independence. A generous technical assistance programme has ensured that Frenchmen in considerable numbers do service in Africa just as Africans come to France for training and experience. In the very early days of independence, the treasuries of several states needed the advice of French experts and it was actually simpler for a research student wishing to study the budgets of many Francophone African states to interview a single consultant in Paris than the various ministers and senior civil servants in Africa. The extent of this dependence has markedly decreased but it has by no means been eliminated. Politically, too, the French governments have tried, and have largely succeeded, in cajoling or pressurising their former colonies into support for the metropolitan country's foreign-policy positions. The remarkably subdued reaction to French involvement in South Africa or in the Shaba Province of Zaire is evidence of this. The establishment in recent years of Franco-African summits, now sometimes held on African soil and including Francophone countries not part of the French Empire in former days, has begun to institutionalise common approaches (Nwokedi, 1982).

France's military presence in Africa is most notable. All the Francophone states, except Guinea, maintain military assistance agreements with France; and several – most notably, Senegal, Ivory Coast, Gabon, the Central African Republic and Cameroon – are protected by defence agreements, in addition. In five countries there are permanent French bases. Although the number of soldiers from France permanently in Africa has dropped in recent years, in 1981 nearly 7,000 were stationed in the continent, from Djibouti in the East to Senegal in the West. The Socialist government of Francois Mitterrand has tactfully rechristened Valérie Giscard d'Estaing's *force d'intervention*; it is now merely the *force d'assistance*, but its function is the same. On top of these numbers are perhaps 800 further serving officers who act as advisers and instructors to the armies of the newly independent states. Although these numbers are appreciably higher than British equivalents, they are major reductions from 1960 levels when there were more than 60,000 troops in 90 garrisons; while the number of French military advisers has decreased from a peak in the early 1960s of 3,000, the number of African officers and men trained in France has increased to beyond 2,000 in 1981 (Luckham, 1982). Mitterrand asked those countries where French military bases existed (Djibouti, Gabon, Ivory Coast, Senegal and the Central African Republic) whether they were still wanted; the answer was affirmative. In Djibouti – where 3,000 troops, many of them French *légionnaires*, are posted alongside a squadron of Mirage 3 interceptors and a ground force equipped with tanks, anti-aircraft artillery and howitzers – the French presence is accepted by radical countries such as Ethiopia and Libya. And it is not only a military presence which France has. There were, for instance, over 60,000 Frenchmen in the Ivory Coast in 1980 and more than 160,000 French residents in the whole of West Africa. Although Mitterrand's Socialist government is opposed to the kind of adventurism in which Giscard d'Estaing indulged and lacks the equivalent of a Jacques Foccart, whose manipulative skills in Africa were well used by de Gaulle in the 1960s, it is happy, nevertheless, to retain a visible presence abroad. The mystical attachment to the virtues of French civilisation are not alien to socialists; the cuisine and couture of France survives in remarkably good health in the distant capitals of what were once the giant federations of imperial West Africa.

There is also a strong economic dimension to the links between France and Francophone Africa. Many of the links which exist in the Anglophone world are also present in the Francophone world, although they seem more deeply entrenched within the French-language zone. Insurance arrangements, accounting practices, banking traditions and shipping lines all strengthen the more obvious continuation of trading links, whereby France imports primarily raw materials from her former empire and the French-speaking states import finished manufactured and investment goods from France. In the days before Britain metricated and became a member of the European Community (with its links to Africa through the various Yaoundé and Lomé Conventions), the dominance of France in the economies of her former possessions was almost absolute. And traditions die hard. Nearly 40 per cent of exports from Francophone Africa go to France which supplies 70 per cent of its imports; French business dominates, for France has supplied over 80 per cent of foreign investment in Francophone Africa (as opposed to the 30 per cent of foreign investment provided by Britain in Anglophone tropical Africa). The tangible links with the former imperial country are everywhere to behold and they have been much less diluted by American, or Scandinavian, or Japanese influence than is the case in English-speaking Africa.

Francophonie is self-conscious in a way Anglophone Africa is not. It can be seen in the organisations of multiple membership that grew in the late 1960s and 1970s to provide common trading markets or development funds for the member states and which were enlarged, almost exclusively, by the addition of French-speaking countries, such as Malagasy or Mauritius, rather than English-speaking ones. Apart from the associations born of African initiatives, there is also a powerful financial bond which ties most of Francophone Africa to France in membership of the franc zone. Apart from Guinea and Mauritania, all the countries that formerly comprised French West and Equatorial Africa are members and they agree to hold 65 per cent of their hard currency earnings in a special account at the French Treasury. Their currency, the CFA franc (which stands for Communauté Financière Africaine in West Africa and Coopération Financière en Afrique Centrale in the Central African area), is fixed to the value of the French franc – 2 centimes – and thus enjoys both its strengths and weaknesses. Two regional central banks, in Dakar and Yaoundé, have in recent years acquired their own African governors, but they remain monitored by French civil servants and ultimately subordinate to the Central Bank in Paris. Firm control of the expansion of credit and a general policy to avoid subsidising the price of farm produce has paid dividends for the local economies as a whole. Thus, although the visible signs of metropolitan French direction is much reduced, there remains a degree of dependency which is markedly higher than that which exists between Anglophone African states and either Britain or the United States.

There are voices raised in objection to this dependency. But they are the minority of those that are heard. The imperial heritage has clearly advantaged France in Africa. This advantage has been strengthened by the personal intimacies of participating in the same national political system in the 1950s, by the effects of the *civilisation francaise*, by the enduring élitism of French-speaking Africa (80 per cent of Gabon's population produces only 4 per cent of its monetary GDP, which gives it one of the greatest income distribution imbalances in sub-Saharan Africa), and by the realisation that the economies of many Francophone countries have been much less unsuccessful than broadly similar English-speaking states when gross growth figures, inflation rates and agricultural production are considered. And France undoubtedly reaps political benefits as well. She escapes the kind of censure heaped on Britain for neo-imperial business links or trading relations with South Africa; her allies remain loyal to her, happy to attend the Franco-African Conferences at which France (unlike Britain in the Commonwealth) is unquestionably the senior partner; at the OAU, the Francophone states frequently enter reservations if criticism of France, implicit or explicit, is voiced in resolutions, even when the issue is South Africa.

Although Britain and France initially dominated relations between Africa and the outside world, it was not long, however, before the two superpowers, neither of whom was as directly linked to Africa as France or Britain, began to eye the continent with a view to enhancing their political credit internationally. This was, in part, a response to African states' commitment to non-alignment which necessitated overtures to the Soviet bloc. But initiatives also came from the superpowers themselves. From the United States' point of view, Africa has always been of very much less significance than the Far East, the Middle East or Latin America and has been seen as the responsibility primarily of her allies. But the reality of a superpower is world-wide involvement. In the heyday of bipolarity, both superpowers were drawn into the Congo civil war and since then the temptation to intervene politically (the United States is deeply involved economically in Africa, as in all other parts of the globe) has never been entirely eschewed. Indeed, the competition between Moscow and Washington has, to some extent, been displaced from direct confrontation to proxy conflict in the continent. The involvement of the Soviet Union, first in Angola and then in Ethiopia in the late 1970s, was a new form of intrusion and worth extended comment.

A first general starting point is to observe that the Soviet leadership in Moscow believes as strongly in the superiority of socialism as an ideology controlling political, social and economic activity, as American politicians believe in the virtue of liberal democracy. Each great power attempts to help those whom it sees as its ideological friends; each great power attempts to strengthen the forces of greatest ideological compatibility in situations of doubt or confusion; the great powers are necessarily, therefore, often in conflict and dispute. But this does not mean that in each and every case the great powers will exercise their military muscle to the full. The reason for this, and this is the second fact, is that the two great powers have come to see that crusades aimed at world domination are impracticable dreams and that, given the destructive forces available to each side, to be drawn into every international squabble is to magnify the dangers of some apocalyptic thermonuclear war. The international relations competition is thus much more about scoring debating points and gathering friends than about territorial control. There is certainly a competition, but the rules are less clear than once they were. Present events in Africa have, to some extent, begun to clarify them and, perhaps, to reformulate them. The evidence suggests that, in Africa at any rate, the Soviet Union has not been following a 'grand design' so much as exploiting 'windows of opportunity'. There is evidence, indeed, that the domestic timetable of the Soviet Union's long-term economic plans has exerted a major influence upon the timing of Soviet arms deliveries to the Third World and that the ebb and flow of military aid is largely a function of the five-year planning cycle rather than positive political preferences (Hutchings, 1978).

The Soviet Union's relations with Africa have passed through three stages (see, generally, Albright, 1980). The first covered the early 1960s when a large number of African states achieved independence. During this period the Soviet leadership retained a bipolar view of the world. It was taken for granted, therefore, that the great powers would involve themselves, indeed had to involve themselves, in every conflict. The Congo civil war provides the classic example of this. It was not until the lessons of the Cuba confrontation had been digested, however, that the bipolar view of international relations began to weaken. As it did, the great powers – perhaps the United States more than the Soviet Union – accepted as one of the new rules of the international game that conflicts in the Third World did not necessitate the involvement of the two great powers.

Thus, war between India and Pakistan did not attract both powers into the action; and the Nigerian civil war, in fact, permitted both the United States and the Soviet Union to back the federal government against the Biafran secessionists.

Bipolarity was a legacy of the Cold War. So also was a certain ideological naïveté on both sides. Just as President Kennedy genuinely could not believe that people, all people, would not choose the capitalist path of development if given the chance, so the Soviet leadership assumed that the anti-colonial forces of African nationalism must be progressive and socialist by inclination. Although the ideologists at the Africa Institute in Moscow had problems in transplanting Marxist-Leninist analysis, developed in more industrialised situations, to Africa, they nevertheless believed that the new states of Africa were eager and willing to follow Soviet leadership. In this they were, of course, mistaken. But several countries, notably Guinea, Mali and Ghana in West Africa, developed close political and economic ties with Moscow and developed a rhetoric that sounded suitably progressive. In the early 1960s, therefore, it seemed to Moscow that Africa was ripe for the plucking, for their bipolar view of international relations implied that it had either to become part of their own orbit or part of the American informal empire and their naïve view of African nationalism persuaded them that, in the circumstances, Africans could only choose the socialist camp.

The second stage disabused them of this simplistic and naïve view. For one thing, it became increasingly clear that African states were not proving to be socialist in form or loyalty. The overthrow of Nkrumah in 1966 and the military coup in Mali in 1968 removed two of the more pro-Eastern leaders from the scene. The Russians were never likely to last long in favour except under special circumstances. They offered too little in the way of exciting consumer goods and their economic aid had virtually dried up by the 1980s; they were too dour and too suspicious of convivial parties for the extrovert Africans; they were arrogant and demanding as well, and were more condescending even than the former imperial masters towards African cultures and traditions. Changes in Moscow coincided with this rebuff on the African continent. The downfall of Khrushchev brought a new, and collective, leadership to power; and death provided the opening for new academics to rise to the top in the Africa Institute. A new ideological awareness grew up, an awareness which recognised the force of African nationalism and foresaw a longer road to socialism in Africa. It would be wrong to imagine that this reappraisal altered, in any fundamental way, the Russian leadership's commitment to assisting in the spread of socialism or weakened the expectation of ultimate success. What it did do, however, was to emphasise the pragmatic aspects of foreign policy more than in the past and to stress the importance of the specific conditions of different African states.

These years in the mid-1960s were years of reappraisal on many fronts. The end of bipolarity brought with it two complications. The first concerned the Soviet Union's relations with the People's Republic of China. The dominant fact in Soviet foreign policy increasingly became the Sino-Soviet split and, when advances were once more made to African groups, their links with Peking were a powerful determinant in the aid they received. After a disastrous foray into Africa by Chou En-lai in the early 1960s and the years of introspection epitomised by the Cultural Revolution, the People's Republic of China returned to the international scene in the 1970s. Her experience of developing an essentially peasant economy was thought by many to be a more appropriate model than either the capitalist West or the Soviet Union; besides, her aid programme was geared more to African needs and her personnel more physically involved in the hard labour of development (although hardly very approachable). In return for this more thoughtful policy, a sometimes embarrassing military support for those groups opposed to Moscow's clients, and the prestigious TAZARA project, China gained considerable support in Africa which was extremely useful in her efforts to be readmitted to the international community and her rightful place in the United Nations.

The second complication concerned the growth of middle-level powers, powers which were objectively weaker than their bloc leaders and yet partially independent of them. This was particularly evident in the Western bloc, where France, Iran, Israel, South Africa and even Japan acted in ways which offended the United States but which the United States could not control. But it was true also of the Eastern bloc; although the Soviet Union could, and did, force its satellite Czechoslovakia into line, it had manifestly failed with China and was clearly losing control over Jugoslavia, Egypt and even Romania. By the beginning of the 1970s, then, the world was a very much more complex place than it had been ten years earlier, and a very much more dangerous place, perhaps.

The third stage then covers the Soviet response to its initial rebuff in Africa and to the multipolarity of the 1970s. It seemed to many people that the United States and the Soviet Union now had much in common, for the *status quo* which they understood and had managed was in danger of being undermined by forces outside their control. Joint agreement not to escalate the Middle East impasse, or even to make much political capital out of it, was cited as the classic expression of mutual self-restraint. The Soviets had learned, it was said, that African leaders meant by non-alignment precisely what it said. They had not achieved independence from one set of imperial masters only to be subjected to another. Furthermore, the very instability of African governments meant that too close a relationship with specific individuals could often be counterproductive; the intimates of one regime were likely to become the enemies of its successor. Consequently, it seemed to many observers that the Soviet Union was beginning to act in ways not very dissimilar to those of the United States; it courted the more powerful or more strategically relevant countries in their capacity as powerful or strategic countries rather than the bearers of approved socialist orthodoxies. From time to time, the tradition of manipulation and the arrogant demand for agreement surfaced, as it did in both Egypt and the Sudan. The lessons learned from Soviet expulsion from these countries seemed clear. African states might befriend the Soviet Union for short periods of time, but ultimately the independent and nationalist spirit of all African leaders, whether radical or conservative, drove the Soviet Union out of the country once her agents began to interfere in internal affairs. Furthermore, it was felt that the Soviet Union would learn from these indiscretions and continue to develop her practices along traditional diplomatic lines.

There was one area where this analysis did not apply. The

Soviet Union remained an active supporter, both rhetorically in international forums and through the supply of arms, of selected liberation movements in southern Africa. Here there were no scruples about interfering with an existing *status quo*. It was in this area that the comparative complacency of Western powers and commentators was rudely shattered, for in 1975 and 1976 the Soviet Union went beyond the traditionally accepted practice of arming and training liberation forces. She now participated in the action herself by supporting the Popular Movement for the Liberation of Angola (MPLA) in Angola's civil war to an extent hitherto unprecedented on the continent. Despite the OAU's call to the three competing factions to create a leadership of national unity, the Soviet Union put all her diplomatic muscle into supporting the MPLA. Sometimes this was crude and unsuccessful; for example, General Amin was instructed by his Soviet military advisers to recognise the MPLA as the legitimate government of Angola at the beginning of 1976, but Amin, then Chairman of the OAU and intensely independent, promptly expelled the Russians from Ugandan soil. In other areas, the calmer relations of the early 1970s reaped dividends and Nigeria, particularly important now in African circles, quickly supported the MPLA.

The intensity of the Soviet Union's diplomatic activity was new. More significant, however, was a further factor: the commitment of Cubans to an active military rule. It was certainly an enormous risk, for the response of Africans to alien interference in their continent's affairs, of the Western Powers and of the South Africans was not known. But Moscow badly needed a diplomatic coup in Africa and committed allies. The late 1960s and early 1970s had been singularly unsuccessful with a whole succession of friends being overthrown or reverting to the West; and China, by contrast, had been building up slowly but surely a powerful coterie of friends who found her style of aid and her model of economic development less threatening and more relevant. It was also believed in Moscow, rightly as it turned out, that one consequence of the United States' involvement in Vietnam would be an instinctive unwillingness to get involved in another alien and unattractive part of the globe. The initial build up of American arms to Roberto's faction slowed perceptibly at this time and Kissinger's frantic efforts to importune Congress into granting funds came to nothing. In addition, naval leaders fancied the chance of using their growing fleet in the South Atlantic and Indian Ocean, if only to show the Americans its potential use. But the Soviet leadership knew that more would be needed to ensure the MPLA its victory than just the shipment of arms and materials. And there had to be victory; for this would show that friendship with the Soviet Union was worth having since they stood by their friends and helped them to win. Yet Russians themselves could not be the direct agents of this victory — the solution was as brilliant as it was simple.

The Cubans would make the revolution. This solution had many attractions. The Cubans were largely coloured; they spoke a language not very dissimilar from the Portuguese spoken in government circles in Angola; their defeat, if it should occur, would not reflect too much on the Soviet Union itself; they were, in any case, so indebted to the Soviet Union, which had been supporting its economy by as much as $2 million a day, that they could be forced to go. In fact, little pressure, if indeed any, was needed. Fidel Castro had always seen himself as a revolutionary leader and had often before promised to liberate Africa from its colonial chains; he was also a close friend of Agostinho Neto; he needed an international coup to deflate the growing disquiet about austerity at home; he had an army which would be more safely employed in stirring action in Africa than wondering where the next promotion would come from at home. Thus internal considerations and personal ideological factors persuaded Castro to enter the African continent as the defender of the true anti-imperial and anti-capitalist forces in Angola.

The 'windows of opportunity' of which the Soviet Union and Cuba have taken advantage, in Ethiopia as well as in Angola, provide the most observable forms of superpower involvement in tropical Africa. The United States enjoys a less obvious profile (once relations with South Africa are excluded), but the American presence cannot be ignored. To some extent, the British, and even the French, act as surrogates; the basic American interests are, in any case, elsewhere. But the financial contributions which the United States provides to most United Nations organisations and multilateral bodies, such as the

World Bank and the IMF, give a certain leverage to Washington which it is difficult to ignore. Furthermore, the main American presence consists of private corporations whose successful entrepreneurial activities are entirely conducive to American national interests. Clandestine operations by the Central Intelligence Agency have also taken place; by definition, the successful ones are not known, yet there is now enough evidence from memoirs and congressional hearings to be certain that American agents were not unprepared to participate actively in the domestic politics of some African states. United States officials are certainly very conscious of their national interests, which are pre-eminent. The recollections of some ambassadors in the continent make it quite clear that most Americans are confident in the virtues of a free enterprise and capitalist economy and are convinced of Africa's need for American enterprises and trade. It is little wonder, therefore, that they see little real conflict between American involvement in Africa and Africa's 'real' needs.

The emphasis in this chapter on state-to-state relations tends to disguise the significance of two further relations, those between multilateral organisations (such as the World Bank or the European Community) and African states, and those between transnational corporations (such as ICI or Gulf Oil) and individual African states. To some extent, the treatment of these relationships can be legitimately left to economic textbooks and works on development itself. There is little doubt that in the realm of economics their impact has been central and disputed. One plausible line of argument asserts that, without the capital provided by organisations such as the International Development Agency (IDA), or Directorate 8 of the European Community, or the Arab Bank for Economic Development in Africa, what infrastructural improvements that there have been in Africa would never have taken place. Much the same could be said for the capital, technology and managerial expertise introduced by the transnational corporations. However deeply Africa might lament the failure of the imperial powers to provide the skills needed for a modern manufacturing and industrial economy, lamentation cannot rewrite history. Outside assistance, therefore, may be personally humiliating, but it is economically essential.

There is, however, an alternative view which is stronger at chronicling and analysing the disadvantages of those links than providing a plausible alternative strategy. The argument here is much more a political and a normative one. In essence, it asserts that Africa's dependency upon the capitalist rich nations of the world leads to its own policies and priorities being distorted and, indeed, being controlled by outsiders. There are unquestionably examples of the multilateral bodies and major transnational corporations pushing through policies against the wishes of the host nation. Whether the focus is on the IMF's fiscal conservatism and its belief in 'realistic' currency valuations and controlled government expenditure, or on the activities of, say, soap manufacturers who use their enormous capital resources to undercut and so destroy a local competing soap company to ensure its monopoly of the market, the impact of such institutions cannot be gainsaid. It can be pointed out that the IDA lends to no country with a per capita income above $730, directs 80 per cent of its funds to those with per capita incomes below $400, asks for repayment over fifty years and demands no interest; at the same time, the European Community can take a very hard line against the Third World, as happened with the 1982 Multifibre Arrangement which let in United States and Swiss imports at more favourable terms. Trading points perhaps only serves to underline the three truths that the individual states of tropical Africa are deeply penetrated by external forces; that, without this penetration, for good or ill, the prospects for economic development are undeniably thin; and that, thirdly, the normative element in the discussion of external impact is extremely strong since it is essentially those who value equality and the equitable redistribution of wealth who are most critical of the role of multilateral agencies and transnational corporations. The debate is well encapsulated in the discussions over the Brandt Report (Brandt, 1980). Without giving the developed world a great many good points, the report argued that the interests of North and South were mutual in the long run. Its critics have not only worried away at some of its inconsistencies and fudging of controversial issues; they have attacked it precisely because they deny the existence of mutual interests. Liberal economists and neo-Marxist economists agree on development economics no more than on the economics of the industrialised world.

The political effects of these economic relationships come in two forms. In the first place, the economic environment in which African politicians have to operate is deeply affected, although not determined, by external economic links. Whether the disquiet which accompanies cumulative inequality and the spread of the ubiquitous Wabenzi is more serious than the disquiet which accompanies empty shops, low produce prices and unreliable services is a nice point. In the second place, any aspect of economics can be defined as political since, implicitly, some allocation of valued resources has taken place; there is virtually nothing which does not ultimately impinge on political attitudes and political behaviour. But the point that needs making is simply this: despite the constraints experienced by African leaders as a result of their poverty, there remains a range of options open to them when dealing with outside bodies, whether superpowers, multilateral agencies, or international companies. The choices are often purely political; Nyerere opted for minimal involvement of multinationals, Numeiry sent the Russians packing, Banda accepted Israeli aid at the price of being denied Arab assistance, Houphouet-Boigny encouraged French businesses to set up in the Ivory Coast, Amin frightened off most foreign entrepreneurs. These varieties are as real to African politics – and as fundamental to political argument – as is the limited range of choice open to political leaders.

Conclusion

A short chapter of this kind can hardly do justice to Africa's relations with the rest of the world. But it should at least provide a framework for further study. These relations are of two distinct kinds. One set of relations is unavoidable. The states of tropical Africa live in an interdependent world, in which trade and communications cross boundaries and governments' jurisdictions and in which no state is entirely self-sufficient. This interdependent world is a given. It is an unfortunate fact that its construction is largely balanced against the interests of the small and poor and in favour of the large and rich. African states naturally, therefore, attempt to alter the nature of that international system. At the same time, African states are the subject of outside interest which is often unwelcome; the visions of the world held by the leaders of the superpowers, and some of the intermediate powers also, are such that their national interests are deemed to necessitate involvement in the affairs of other states. The Congo crisis of the early 1960s is, perhaps, the classic instance; but in more recent years, Angola, Zaire and Ethiopia have witnessed the overt involvement of external forces, while covert involvement is less easy to quantify. The destabilisation policy of South Africa is a fine example of the readiness of an intermediate power to interfere in the political life of foreign countries. But there are also international relations which African leaders choose voluntarily to prosecute. The domestic spin-off of some policy positions is held to be important, for example, just as the universal condemnation of South Africa leads politicians to make statements and introduce policies which might, in a non-moral world, be distinctly against their self-interest. The foreign policies of the tropical African states are still in a state of flux (see, generally, Aluko, ed., 1977). There are two reasons for this: they are still malleable because there is no tradition of national interests which politicians and diplomats alike share; furthermore, the chief policy-maker *par excellence* is the head of government and, in many states, heads of government do not enjoy a long tenure of office. The presidential prerogative means that major initiatives, such as the amalgamation of Tanganyika with Zanzibar, can be consummated quickly on the authority of two presidents (Bailey, 1974 – 5). Policy, therefore, is not merely reactive, although much of it inevitably is (as is the case of most countries in the world); some of it represents a conscious programmatic decision of the independent state's government.

Stressing the possibility of local initiative should not hide the reality of an unequal international political system. Not only are states endowed with very different resources, few are truly sovereign, as the ubiquitous presence of transnational corporations and international organisations testify. Within a framework of penetrated and unequal states, there remains some room for individual choice. This freedom is very much enhanced if individual states come together into blocs, and the African states have learned over time to use their major asset, numbers, in those international fora where numbers are important. The United Nations is the obvious example of such a place. The regular meetings – both between representatives of the Commonwealth countries and between the OAU member countries and the increasingly institutionalised leadership of the Group of 77 – have resulted in a much more coherent set of demands being presented to international bodies, backed up with a greater unity and a greater weight of evidence than in earlier years. The reality of political solidarity created the illusion of political unanimity and, consequently, bedevils the agreement on details of international gatherings; but that solidarity has unquestionably brought its rewards. Combined with a weakening of confidence among the former imperial powers and, to some extent, the United States, the pressures for change in the international community have not been negligible. The North – South dialogue was forced on to the agenda of the international community, and largely kept there, by the unremitting determination of poor countries; a rethinking of the Bretton Woods institutions was not a voluntary decision taken by the rich industrialised nations; and the perceptible, if slight, changes in the normative rules of international relations (the strengthening of the democratic principle over the principle of strength) owe a great deal to the repeated requests and pressures of the Third World in which African states have played a major role.

So we all live in an interdependent world, in which absolute self-reliance is a delusion and in which inequalities abound. But the starting point for the study of foreign relations must still be the governments of the states themselves, the aims and ideas of their leaders, the resources at their disposal in terms of skills, will, strategic or economic importance, and the domestic forces which mould the final policy outcome. This is only a starting point, although it is one often omitted in discussions of Africa's foreign relations. One cannot ignore the political calculus of external power or the simple truth that few nations, or people, gratuitously throw away a position of advantage. Dyadic relations, as has already been stated, imply needs on both sides and skilful negotiators can play their hands more successfully than unskilled negotiators. Weakness cannot overnight be turned into strength nor poverty into riches; but the disadvantages of the tropical African states can be mitigated, and to some extent in many of them are being mitigated, by resourceful politicians and bureaucrats. The most realistic form of independence is the diversification of interdependence.

Envoi

There is no conclusion to this book. Indeed, it would be illogical to provide one. If it contains a single message, it is this: tropical Africa is an abstraction, the product of geographers and imperial historians rather than the description of an entity with common contemporary political characteristics. Most states have some things in common; but, both elephants and tables have legs. Furthermore, these states are still young and still in the experimental stage in which their inhabitants are developing their own means to resolve their own political conflicts. They lack that long shared historical experience and that shared set of institutions which distinguish the established states of Western Europe, and India too. In such a situation, conclusions are out of place.

Yet there is some value in restating several factors whose general incidence provides a theme on which the variations are constructed. The problem of order inevitably remains a central one. The stability which is represented by the regularity of transactions between politicians and people over time is still lacking (Ake, 1973). The trust which permits political actors reasonably to assume a set of self-restraining behaviour patterns by other actors has hardly anywhere been assured. The extractive and instrumental assumptions of the players in the political game are critical prerequisites for the unabashed readiness to use power to its full, which is such a predominant feature of tropical African politics. Ibo proverbs graphically illustrate this central facet of political life. 'I am against people reaping where they have sown', a character in Achebe's novel, *Things Fall Apart*, says. 'But we have a saying that if you want to eat a toad you should look for a fat one.' Yet one must not 'take away more than the owner can ignore'. The restraints which, in other systems, are provided by ideology or party loyalty are absent. The knowledge that the support of certain segments of society can be relied upon and that the state has limitations to its reach are both important for the smooth operation of political processes. It is little wonder, therefore, that the absence of so many of those central features of the developed and mature political systems of the Northern hemisphere – the Soviet Union as much as the United States – has been accompanied by chronic instability in much of Africa. Yet this emphasis on instability can be, and too often is, overstressed. There are many states – Tanzania, Kenya, Malawi and Zambia in English-speaking Eastern Africa; Senegal and the Ivory Coast in French-speaking West Africa – where there has been no putsch or coup and the level of political prisoners is comparatively low or even non-existent; their experiences cannot lightly be dismissed.

In any examination of tropical Africa in 1982, however, it would be absurd not to recognise the collapse, for instance, of the Ghanaian state. To some extent, Ghana is a state only because the outside world asserts that there is a Ghanaian state. The economy has largely ceased to be a monetary one; many traders buy and sell in neighbouring territories or resort to barter; many workers have voted with their feet by emigrating to the Ivory Coast or Togo; the value of the cedi is a matter for negotiation; the provision of education, health facilities and order itself cannot be assumed. In Uganda, too, over much of the country and for many months the writ of the central government did not run. The brigandage of undisciplined soldiers and the failure of successive governments to provide their citizens with the basic provisions of the state saw the withdrawal of a people with highly developed modern skills to subsistence living. Autarchy, if not anarchy in its pejorative sense, for much of the time prevailed.

There is a paradox here. In one sense, the state in Africa is immensely strong. It is monopolistic (Aron, 1966–7). The state is the major source of employment, the major source of finance and the major partner in most economic enterprises; the existence of well-armed and numerous police, paramilitary forces and the army itself adds to that appearance of strength. Yet, in another sense, the state is weak. It cannot always provide the people with what have become thought of as the necessities of life, such as education, health facilities, public transport networks, employment and the affluence associated with a leisure-time economy; that is an obvious sign of weakness. But, in many countries, the government cannot even implement its policies. It lacks the capacity to transform its rhetoric and paper policies into practical action in the rural areas or among the underprivileged peoples of the sprawling urban centres. There is a gulf between the theoretical power of the state, as expressed in constitutions and statutes or proclamations, and the real power of the state as represented by effective field officers, widespread political support and economies growing in line with governmental expectations.

Such a perspective raises again a set of issues which dominated the academic study of African politics in the early 1960s, but which fell into disrepute in the 1970s. The inability of the state to preserve order or to implement its development policies effectively reintroduces the problem of capacity; public administration in Kenya seems to have recognised this and has emphasised order even before development (Hyden *et al.*, 1970). The continuing friction between different tribes and the still ungeneralised attachment to the nation reintroduces the problem of national integration. The continuing existence of authoritarian governments and military autocracies, despite the welcome overthrow of Amin, Bokassa and Nguema in a single year, reintroduces the problem of democracy. The growth of corrupt practices and inefficient administrations reintroduces the problem of institutional transfer and bureaucratic values. There are, as has been argued, good reasons for many of these developments and their explanation does, indeed, partly lie in the constraints imposed upon governments by the external environment. This environment is both natural and structural. It should not be forgotten, as Brokensha noted when he returned after many years to that patch of Africa where he had once been the district officer, that 'the physical environment still exercises a dominating influence' over the lives of most Africans with its wilful excesses and shortages of rain and its profusion of diseases and bugs (Brokensha, 1971, p. 167). At the same time, as the dependency theorists argued, the world economic system and the political forces which underlie it continue to limit what the poor states of Africa can do. But the imperial intermission should be written off neither as dependency's only begetter nor as an unmitigated disaster for Africa. By the standards of the 1980s, what was done in the 1890s or the 1920s may seem indefensible or mean. But what strengths the new states do have in terms of skills, experience of the modern world, potential economic viability, and so on, derives from the metropolitan powers' creation of large states from many small polities and their administration of those states. Restraints on the post-independence governments there clearly are; yet these restraints are not absolute.

A central factor of the post-independence period is precisely that it follows independence. Political leaders moved into the decision-making positions and made decisions. They enjoyed a certain autonomy which permitted choices to be made, priorities to be ordered and policies to be chosen from a range of alternatives. There exists what might be called political space; that is to say, politicians have room within the constraints of underdeveloped economies and fragile polities to choose a wide range of policies. That they do not always choose as outside observers might wish or as rival politicians would prefer is evidence of this political space. It is idle to pretend that self-reliant and rapid growth can soon be achieved; people who imagine that this is a genuine possibility ignore the realities of the resources available to political leaders. These are piteously small; and they are not to be augmented from within Africa in the short term by any dramatic policy initiatives. The cruel truth is that there is a long haul ahead.

What makes the road to that idyllic ideal of development economists so hard is often the political system and the political forces of the tropical African countries themselves. The more open they are, the more the articulate and the well organised succeed in gaining for themselves a disproportionate slice of the small cake; the more instrumental and extractive the values of the participants in the political system, the more the decision-makers must yield to instant gratification and the short-term demands of élites and people alike. The inequalities which began in the imperial years have become cumulative; the competition for scarce resources remains liable to be structured along tribal lines; and the instrumental values of the polity reduce to a minimum that degree of party or national loyalty which enables unpopular measures to be accepted with a degree of equanimity. Any leader has a difficult task in the world of the 1980s where recession, efficient communications and ever-expanding expectations unmercifully press on the governments of the day. In Africa the problems are normally multiplied. At the same time, what has happened in much of Africa – the increasing level of malnutrition, the escalating violence both inside and between states, the growing cancer of corruption and graft, and the inequalities between rich and poor inside the states – has, in part, been caused by errors of judgement and personal failings of the African leaders themselves. Acton's adage that power tends to corrupt is not specific to Europe; it appears to be applicable to all humanity.

This pessimistic perspective is shared by many Africans themselves, as their novels eloquently testify. Some governments clearly dislike too open an expression of criticism, as Ngugi wa Thiong'o has found in Kenya, where he has been constantly harassed for his plays and books depicting a corrupt and self-satisfied élite dishonouring the revolution sought by the ordinary peasant farmers in their nationalist struggles. Sympathetic friends of Africa, like the French agronomist René Dumont, have criticised government policies and the tendency of the powerful to reward themselves and their friends too handsomely. The introduction to his famous book, *False Start in Africa* (1966), could well provide the conclusion to this book. There is expressed that mixture of disappointment and profound affection for Africa which I share. The heady optimism of the 1960s was clearly misplaced; the problems besetting Africa were too great and the continent's capability to manage and overcome them too slender. But the pessimism of the 1970s may well be misplaced, too. The discipline of debt, the slowly emerging patterns of stable political societies in some parts of Africa, and a growing awareness of the importance of less ambitious and more enduring development projects are positive indicators. But there is no escaping ultimately the truth that, when the world economic system catches a cold, Africa catches pneumonia. In 1982 there do not seem to be enough willing doctors armed with enough appropriate resources to ensure the patient's full recovery.

Bibliographical Note

The literature on tropical Africa is vast. History, social anthropology, geography and sociology are all relevant and necessary for an understanding of contemporary events. What is more, it is important both to have a general understanding of the relationships between the many factors that determine the precise form of politics practised in any country and also to have a detailed knowledge of at least a few parts of the continent to appreciate the rich diversity of patterns of political activity and gain a feel of the often exciting and complex nature of politics 'on the ground'. A large-scale conceptual map is required; but so, too, is a small-scale survey of selected parts. Inevitably, therefore, choosing a few books from the very large number cited in the Bibliography of this one is a difficult, and essentially personal, task. For what it is worth, therefore, here are the thirteen books, all of manageable length, which I would have in my library if that were all that was permitted to me.

I would need some historical background to start with and I would take Low, *Lion Rampant*; Rodney, *How Europe Underdeveloped Africa* (which I believe to be largely flawed, but certainly gives food for thought); a novel, such as Achebe *Things Fall Apart*; and a single-country study, such as Iliffe's magisterial *A Modern History of Tanganyika* (perhaps too long by my initial criteria, but easy to read); and a regional economic history, such as Hopkins, *An Economic History of West Africa*. General books about African society and the environment of African politics are a particularly difficult area to select from; I would probably opt for Goldethorpe, *The Sociology of the Third World*; Fanon, *The Wretched of the Earth*; and another novel, this time from East Africa, Ngugi wa Thiong'o, *Petals of Blood*. As for institutional studies of manageable length, the choice must again be very personal: my selection would include Decalo, *Coups and Army Rule in Africa: Studies in Military Style*; Jackson and Rosberg, *Personal Rule in Black Africa*; and Leys's fascinating account of local politics in Northern Uganda, *Politicians and Policies*. That only leaves two more: I think I would want a detailed account of the politics of the largest and richest state of Africa and would thus choose Post and Vickers, *Structure and Conflict in Nigeria* (although it only covers the First Republic) and one of the most challenging books on East Africa, although its relevance is much wider, Hyden, *Beyond Ujamaa in Tanzania*. Many will think this an idiosyncratic list and will regret the omission of this or that book. A year ago I might have chosen differently; a year hence I might again feel a different balance would be right.

One of the truths about African studies, however, is that much of the most informative and important literature appears in the journals. This is partly due to the decline, if not demise, of the monograph, especially on the British side of the Atlantic, and partly due to the plethora of conferences that now spawn a multitude of papers. The leading academic journals in English are *African Affairs* and the *Journal of Modern African Studies* (curiously the United States has no serious rival in this field). Much material, however, finds its way into print through journals not specifically focused on Africa, such as the *Journal of Development Studies* or *World Politics*. The day-to-day developments in the continent are difficult to monitor as the press is generally disinclined to give much space to tropical Africa (by contrast to South Africa) and, in any case, favours the bizarre ('crocodile eats child' or 'witch doctors fall foul of Tanzanian government' to name two recent ones). Britain has no equivalent to *Le Monde*, unfortunately, for African coverage. *Africa Report* appears six times a year out of Washington and has good general coverage at a reasonable rate; more expensive, more selective, but often more perceptive is *Africa Confidential*. The monthly magazines like *Africa* or *Africa Now* are useful. Otherwise, source material is very expensive to acquire or rather unreliable. There is no substitute, of course, to visiting Africa for a longish time and imbibing the ambience of politics there; but that, too, is now extremely expensive and difficult to find funds for. Keeping abreast of developments in the continent is, indeed, difficult.

References

Abraham, W. E. (1962), *The Mind of Africa* (London: Weidenfeld & Nicolson).

Abrahams, R. G. (1981), *The Nyamwezi Today: A Tanzanian People in the 1970s* (Cambridge: Cambridge University Press).

Achebe, Chinua (1964), *Things Fall Apart* (London: Heinemann).

Achebe, Chinua (1966), *A Man of the People* (London: Heinemann).

Adedeji, Adebayo (ed.) (1968), *Nigerian Administration and its Political Setting* (London: Hutchinson).

Adepoju, Aderanti (1982), 'The dimension of the refugee problem in Africa', *African Affairs*, vol. 81, pp. 21–35.

Adu, A. L. (1969), *The Civil Service in Commonwealth Africa* (London: Allen & Unwin).

Afrifa, A. A. (1967), *The Ghana Coup* (London: Frank Cass).

Agyeman, Opoku (1975), 'The *Osagyefo*, the *Mwalimu*, and Pan-Africanism: a study in the growth of a dynamic concept', *Journal of Modern African Studies*, vol. 13, pp. 653–75.

Ajayi, J. F. A. (1969), 'Colonialism: an episode in African history', in L. H. Gann and P. Duignan (eds), *Colonialism in Africa*, vol. 1 (Cambridge: Cambridge University Press), pp. 497–509.

Ajayi, J. F. A. (1982), 'Expectations of independence', *Daedalus*, vol. 3 (Spring), pp. 1–9.

Ake, Claude (1973), 'Explaining political instability in new states', *Journal of Modern African Studies*, vol. 11, pp. 347–59.

Albright, David E. (1980), *Africa and International Communism* (London: Macmillan).

Allen, Charles (ed.) (1979), *Tales from the Dark Continent: Images of British Colonial Africa in the Twentieth Century* (London: Deutsch and BBC).

Aluko, Olajide (ed.) (1977), *The Foreign Policies of African States* (London: Hodder & Stoughton).

Andreski, Stanislav (1968), *The African Predicament* (London: Michael Joseph).

Apter, David E. (1963), *Ghana in Transition* (Princeton, NJ: Princeton University Press).

Apter, David E. (1965), *The Politics of Modernisation* (Chicago: University of Chicago Press).

Arnold, Guy (1979), *Aid in Africa* (London: Kogan Page).

Aron, Raymond (1966–7), 'How non-monopolistic can a monopolistic party be?', *Government and Opposition*, vol. 2, pp. 165–71.

Arrighi, Giovanni (1969–70), 'Labour supplies in historical perspective: a study of the proletarianisation of the African peasantry in Rhodesia', *Journal of Development Studies*, vol. 6, pp. 197–234.

Austen, Ralph A. (1968), *Northwest Tanzania under German and British Rule: Colonial Policy and Tribal Politics, 1889–1939* (New Haven, Conn.: Yale University Press).

Austin, Dennis (1976), *Ghana Observed: Essays on the Politics of a West African Republic* (Manchester: Manchester University Press).

Austin, Dennis (1980), 'The transfer of power: why and how', in W. H. Morris-Jones and Georges Fischer (eds), *Decolonisation and Africa* (London: Frank Cass), pp. 3–34.

Austin, Dennis, and Luckham, Robin (eds) (1975), *Politicians and Soldiers in Ghana* (London: Frank Cass).

Bailey, Fred. G. (1959), *Politics and Social Change: Orissa in 1959* (Berkeley, Calif.: University of California Press).

Bailey, Martin (1974–5), 'Zanzibar's external relations', *International Journal of Politics*, vol. 4, pp. 35–57.

Barkan, Joel D. (1979), 'Legislators, elections, and political linkage', in Joel D. Barkan and John J. Okumu (eds), *Politics and Public Policy in Kenya and Tanzania* (New York: Praeger), pp. 64–93.

Barton, Frank (1979), *The Press of Africa: Persecution and Perseverance* (London: Macmillan).

Bates, Robert H. (1971), *Unions, Parties and Political Development: A Study of Mineworkers in Zambia* (New Haven, Conn.: Yale University Press).

Bennett, George (1969), 'Tribalism in politics', in Philip Gulliver (ed.), *Tradition and Transition in East Africa: Studies of the Tribal Element in the Modern Era* (London: Routledge & Kegan Paul).

Berry, Sara S. (1975), *Cocoa, Custom and Socio-Economic Change in Rural Western Nigeria* (Oxford: Clarendon Press).

Bienefeld, M. A. (1979), 'Trade unions, the labour process, and the Tanzanian state', *Journal of Modern African Studies*, vol. 17, pp. 553–93.

Bienen, Henry S. (ed.) (1968), *The Military Intervenes* (New York: Russell Sage Foundation).

Bohannan, Paul, and Curtin, Philip (1971), *Africa and Africans* (Garden City, NY: Natural History Press).

Brandt, Willy (1980), *North-South: A Programme for Survival* (London: Pan Books).

Bretton, H. L. (1973), *Power and Politics in Africa* (London: Longman).

Brokensha, David (1971), 'Handeni revisited', *African Affairs*, vol. 70, pp. 159–68.

Brooks, George E. (1975), 'Peanuts and colonialism: consequences of commercialisation of peanuts in West Africa, 1830–1870', *Journal of African History*, vol. 16, pp. 29–54.

Brunschwig, Henri (1974), 'De la résistance africaine à l'impérialisme européen', *Journal of African History*, vol. 15, pp. 47–64.

Bryceson, Deborah Fahy (1982), 'Peasant commodity production in post-colonial Tanzania', *African Affairs*, vol. 81, pp. 547–67.

Buell, Raymond Leslie (1928), *The Native Problem in Africa*, 2 vols (New York: Macmillan).

Busia, K. A. (1967), *Africa in Search of Democracy* (London: Routledge & Kegan Paul).

Cameron, Sir Donald (1939), *My Tanganyika Service and Some Nigeria* (London: Allen & Unwin).

Cervenka, Zdenek (1969), *The Organisation of African Unity and its Charter*, 2nd edn (London: Hurst).

Chazan, Naomi (1981–2), 'The new politics of participation in tropical Africa', *Comparative Politics*, vol. 14, pp. 169–89.

Clapham, Christopher (1970), 'The context of African political thought', *Journal of Modern African Studies*, vol. 8, pp. 1–14.

Clapham, Christopher (ed.) (1982), *Private Patronage and Public Power: Political Clientèlism in the Modern State* (London: Frances Pinter).

Clark, John F. (1979), 'Patterns of support for international organisations in Africa', in Timothy M. Shaw and Kenneth A. Heard (eds), *The Politics of Africa: Dependence and Development* (London: Longman).

Cliffe, Lionel (ed.) (1967), *One Party Democracy: The 1965 Tanzania General Elections* (Nairobi: East African Publishing House).

Cobbing, Julian (1977), 'The absent priesthood: another look at the Rhodesian risings of 1896–1897', *Journal of African History*, vol. 18, pp. 61–84.

Cohen, Sir Andrew (1959), *British Policy in Changing Africa* (London: Routledge & Kegan Paul).

Cohen, Robin (1976), 'The state in Africa', *Review of African Political Economy*, no. 5, pp. 1–2.

Cohen, William B. (1971), *Rulers of Empire: The French Colonial Service in Africa* (Stanford, Calif.: Hoover Institution Press).

Coleman, J. S., and Rosberg, C. G. (eds) (1964), *Political Parties and National Integration in Tropical Africa* (Berkeley, Calif.: University of California Press).

Colson, Elizabeth (1969), 'African society at the time of the scramble', in L. H. Gann and P. Duignan (eds), *Colonialism in Africa*, vol. 1 (Cambridge: Cambridge University Press), pp. 27–65.

Comaroff, John L. (1974–5), 'Chiefship in a South African Homeland', *Journal of Southern African Studies*, vol. 1, pp. 36–51.

Coulson, Andrew (ed.) (1979), *African Socialism in Practice: The Tanzanian Experience* (Nottingham, Notts.: Spokesman).

Cox, Richard (1964), *Pan-Africanism in Practice: PAFMECSA 1958–1964* (London: Oxford University Press).

Davidson, Basil (1964), *The African Past: Chronicles from Antiquity to Modern Times* (London: Longman).

Decalo, Samuel (1976), *Coups and Army Rule in Africa: Studies in Military Style* (New Haven, Conn.: Yale University Press).

de Smith, S. A. (1964), *The New Commonwealth and its Constitutions* (London: Stevens).

Dore, Ronald (1976), *The Diploma Disease: Education, Qualification and Development* (London: Allen & Unwin).

Dumont, René (1966), *False Start in Africa* (London: Deutsch).

Dunn, J., and Robertson, A. F. (1973), *Dependency and Opportunity: Political Change in Ahafo* (Cambridge: Cambridge University Press).

Duverger, Maurice (1954), *Political Parties: Their Organisation and Activity in the Modern State* (London: Methuen).

Easton, David (1956–7), 'An approach to the analysis of political systems', *World Politics*, vol. 9, pp. 383–400.

Eckstein, Harry (1965), 'On the etiology of internal wars', *History and Theory*, vol. 4, pp. 133–63.

Elias, T. O. (1961), *Government and Politics in Africa* (Delhi: Asia Publishing House).

Enloe, Cynthia H. (1980), *Ethnic Soldiers: State Security in a Divided Society* (Harmondsworth, Middx.: Penguin).

Epstein, Arnold L. (1958), *Politics in an Urban African Community* (Manchester: Manchester University Press).

Etherington, Norman (1982), 'Theories of imperialism in southern Africa revisited', *African Affairs*, vol. 81, pp. 385–407.

Fallers, Lloyd (1955), 'The predicament of the modern African chief: an instance from Uganda', *American Anthropologist*, vol. 57, pp. 290–305.

Fanon, Frantz (1965), *The Wretched of the Earth* (London: MacGibbon & Kee).

Fanon, Frantz (1968), *Black Skin, White Masks* (London: MacGibbon & Kee).

Finer, S. E. (1962), *Man on Horseback: The Role of the Military in Politics* (London: Pall Mall).

First, Ruth (1970), *The Barrel of a Gun: Political Power in Africa and the Coup d'Etat* (Harmondsworth, Middx.: Penguin).

Fisher, Humphrey, J. (1969), 'Elections and coups in Sierra Leone, 1967', *Journal of Modern African Studies*, vol. 7, pp. 611–36.

Frank, André Gundar (1969), *Capitalism and Underdevelopment in Latin America: Historical Studies of Chile and Brazil* (New York: Monthly Review Press).

Frey, Frederick W. (1968), 'Socialisation to national identification among Turkish peasants', *Journal of Politics*, vol. 30, pp. 934–65.

Friedland, William H. (1969), *Vuta Kamba: The Development of Trade Unions in Tanganyika* (Stanford, Calif.: Hoover Institution Press).

Friedland, William H., and Rosberg, Carl G. (eds) (1964), *African Socialism* (Stanford, Calif.: Stanford University Press).

Furedi, Frank (1974), 'The development of anti-Asian opinion among Africans in Nakuru District, Kenya', *African Affairs*, vol. 73, pp. 347–58.

Gallagher, John, and Robinson, Ronald (1953), 'The imperialism of free trade', *Economic History Review*, vol. 6, pp. 1–15.

Gann, Lewis Henry, and Duignan, Peter (1968), *Burden of Empire: An Appraisal of Western Colonialism South of the Sahara* (London: Pall Mall).

Gertzel, Cherry (1966), 'The provincial administration in Kenya', *Journal of Commonwealth Political Studies*, vol. 4, pp. 201–15.

Giles, Bryn G. (1978–9), 'Economists in government: the case of Malawi', *Journal of Development Studies*, vol. 15, pp. 216–32.

Gillett, Simon (1973), 'The survival of chieftaincy in Botswana', *African Affairs*, vol. 72, pp. 179–85.

Glickman, Harvey (1967), 'Dilemmas of political theory in an African context: the ideology of Julius Nyerere', in J. Butler and A. A. Castagno (eds), *Transition in African Politics* (New York: Praeger).

Golan, Tamar (1981), 'A certain mystery: how can France do everything that it does in Africa − and get away with it?', *African Affairs*, vol. 80, pp. 3−12.

Goldsworthy, David (1981), 'Civilian control of the military in Black Africa', *African Affairs*, vol. 80, pp. 49−74.

Goldthorpe, J. E. (1975), *The Sociology of the Third World: Disparity and Involvement* (Cambridge: Cambridge University Press).

Goody, Jack (1968), 'Consensus and dissent in Ghana', *Political Science Quarterly*, vol. 83, pp. 337−52.

Goody, Jack (1971), *Technology, Tradition and the State in Africa* (London: Oxford University Press).

Green, Reginald, and Seidman, Ann (1969), *Unity or Poverty?* (Harmondsworth, Middx.: Penguin).

Greenstone, J. David (1965−6), 'Corruption and self-interest in Kampala and Nairobi: a comment on local politics in East Africa', *Comparative Studies in Society and History*, vol. 8, pp. 199−210.

Gregor, A. James (1967), 'African socialism, socialism and fascism: an appraisal', *Review of Politics*, vol. 29, pp. 324−53.

Hachten, William A. (1971), *Muffled Drums: The News Media in Africa* (Ames, Iowa: Iowa State University Press).

Hailey, Lord ([1942] 1957), *Native Administration and Political Development in British Tropical Africa*, 2nd edn (London: Oxford University Press).

Hansen, Emmanuel, and Collins, Paul (1980), 'The army, the state, and the "Rawlings Revolution" in Ghana', *African Affairs*, vol. 79, pp. 3−23.

Hargreaves, John D. (1967), *West Africa: The Former French States* (Englewood Cliffs, NJ: Prentice-Hall).

Hayter, Teresa (1971), *Aid as Imperialism* (Harmondsworth, Middx.: Penguin).

Hill, Christopher R. (1983), 'Regional co-operation in Southern Africa', *African Affairs*, vol. 82, pp. 215−39.

Hill, Polly (1963), *The Migrant Cocoa-farmers of Southern Ghana: A Study in Rural Capitalism* (Cambridge: Cambridge University Press).

Hodder-Williams, Richard (1977), 'The Mashona uprising of 1896−1897: some observations from the Marandellas District', in Christopher R. Hill and Peter Warwick (eds), *Collected Papers*, vol. 2 (York: Centre for Southern African Studies), pp. 40−60.

Hodder-Williams, Richard (1978), 'Changing perspectives in East Africa', *World Today*, vol. 34, pp. 166−74.

Hodder-Williams, Richard (1979), 'Support in eastern Africa: some observations from Malawi', in Timothy M. Shaw and Kenneth A. Heard (eds), *The Politics of Africa: Dependence and Development* (London: Longman), pp. 153−82.

Hodgkin, Thomas (1957), *Nationalism in Colonial Africa* (New York: New York University Press).

Hodgkin, Thomas (1961), 'A note on the language of African nationalism', in K. Kirkwood (ed.), *St Antony's Papers*, no. 10, pp. 22−40.

Holleman, J. F. (1969), *Chief, Council and Commissioners* (London: Oxford University Press).

Hopkins, Anthony G. (1973), *An Economic History of West Africa* (London: Longman).

Hopkins, Anthony G. (1979), *Two Essays on Underdevelopment* (Geneva: Institut Universitaire des Hautes Etudes Internationales).

Hopkins, Nicholas S. (1972), *Popular Government in an African Town: Kita, Mali* (Chicago: University of Chicago Press).

Hopkins, Raymond F. (1971), *Political Roles in a New State: Tanzania's First Decade* (New Haven, Conn.: Yale University Press).

Hughes, Arnold, and Cohen, Robin (1978), 'An emerging Nigerian working class: the Lagos experience, 1897 – 1939', in Peter C. W. Gutkind, Robin Cohen and Jean Copans (eds), *African Labour History* (Beverly Hills, Calif.: Sage).

Hughes, Arnold, and Kolinsky, Martin (1976), '"Paradigmatic fascism" and modernisation: a critique', *Political Studies*, vol. 24, pp. 371 – 96.

Hunt, R. N. Carew (1950), *The Theory and Practice of Communism* (London: Geoffrey Bles).

Hunter, Guy (1962), *The New Societies of Tropical Africa: A Selective Study* (London: Oxford University Press for Institute of Race Relations).

Hutchings, Raymond (1978), 'Soviet arms exports to the Third World: a pattern and its implications', *World Today*, vol. 34, pp. 378 – 89.

Hyden, Göran (1968), *TANU Yajenga Nchi: Political Development in Rural Tanzania* (Lund: Uniskol).

Hyden, Göran (1980), *Beyond Ujamaa in Tanzania: Underdevelopment and an Uncaptured Peasantry* (London: Heinemann).

Hyden, Göran *et al.* (1970), *Development Administration: The Kenyan Experience* (Nairobi: Oxford University Press).

Hyden, Göran, and Leys, C. T. (1972), 'Elections and politics in single-party systems: the cases of Kenya and Tanzania', *British Journal of Political Science*, vol. 2, pp. 389 – 420.

Iliffe, John (1979), *A Modern History of Tanganyika* (Cambridge: Cambridge University Press).

Ingle, Clyde R. (1972), *From Village to State in Tanzania: The Politics of Rural Development* (Ithaca, NY: Cornell University Press).

International Labour Office (ILO) (1972), *Employment, Incomes and Equality: A Strategy for Increasing Productive Employment in Kenya* (Geneva: ILO).

Jackson, Dudley (1979), 'The disappearance of strikes in Tanzania: incomes policy and industrial democracy', *Journal of Modern African Studies*, vol. 17, pp. 219 – 51.

Jackson, Robert H., and Rosberg, Carl G. (1982), *Personal Rule in Black Africa: Prince, Autocrat, Prophet, Tyrant* (Berkeley, Calif.: University of California Press).

Jeffries, Richard (1978), *Class, Power and Ideology in Ghana: The Railwaymen of Sekondi* (Cambridge: Cambridge University Press).

Jeffries, Richard (1982), 'Rawlings and the political economy of underdevelopment in Ghana', *African Affairs*, vol. 81, pp. 307 – 18.

Johnson, Douglas H. (1982), 'Evans-Pritchard, the Nuer, and the Sudan political service', *African Affairs*, vol. 81, pp. 231–46.

Jolly, Richard (1971), 'The skilled manpower constraint', in Charles Elliot (ed.), *Constraints on the Economic Development of Zambia* (Oxford: Clarendon Press) pp. 21–56.

Jones, W. I. (1972), 'The mise and demise of socialist institutions in rural Mali', *Genève-Afrique*, vol. 11, pp. 19–44.

Joseph, Richard A. (1981–2), 'Democratisation under military tutelage: crisis and consensus in the Nigerian 1979 elections', *Comparative Politics*, vol. 14, pp. 75–100.

Kasfir, Nelson (1978–9), 'Explaining ethnic political participation', *World Politics*, vol. 31, pp. 365–88.

Kedourie, Elie (1960), *Nationalism* (London: Hutchinson).

Kidron, Michael, and Segal, Ronald (1981), *The State of the World Atlas* (London: Pan Books).

Killick, Tony (1978), *Development Economics in Action* (London: Heinemann).

Kirk-Greene, A. H. M. (1966), *The Principles of Native Administration in Nigeria: Selected Documents, 1900–1947* (Oxford: Clarendon Press).

Kirk-Green, A. H. M. (1972), 'The new African administrator', *Journal of Modern African Studies*, vol. 10, pp. 93–107.

Kirk-Greene, A. H. M. (1980), 'The thin white line: the size of the British colonial service in Africa', *African Affairs*, vol. 79, pp. 25–44.

Kirk-Greene, A. H. M. (1981), *Stay by Your Radios: Documentation for a Study of Military Government in Tropical Africa* (Cambridge: African Studies Centre).

Kitching, Gavin N. (1980), *Class and Economic Change in Africa: The Making of an African Petite Bourgeoisie, 1905–1970* (London: Methuen).

Kitching, Gavin, N. (1982), *Development and Underdevelopment in Historical Perspective* (London: Methuen).

Kopytoff, Igor (1964), 'Socialism and traditional African societies', in William H. Friedland and Carl G. Rosberg (eds), *African Socialism* (Stanford, Calif.: Stanford University Press), pp. 53–62.

Kornhauser, William (1971), *The Politics of Mass Society* (London: Routledge & Kegan Paul).

Lamb, Geoff (1974), *Peasant Politics: Conflict and Development in Murang'a* (Lewes, Sussex: Julian Friedman).

Lee, J. M. (1969), *African Armies and Civil Order* (London: Chatto & Windus).

Legum, Colin (1962), *Pan-Africanism: A Short Political Guide* (New York: Praeger).

Lemarchand, René (1972), 'Political clientilism and ethnicity in tropical Africa: competing solidarities in nation-building', *American Political Science Review*, vol. 66, pp. 68–90.

Lewis, M. D. (1962–3), 'The assimilation theory in French colonial policy', *Comparative Studies in Society and History*, vol. 4, pp. 129–53.

Lewis, Sir William Arthur (1965), *Politics in West Africa* (London: Allen & Unwin).

Leys, Colin T. (1965), 'What is the problem about corruption?', *Journal of Modern African Studies*, vol. 3, pp. 215 – 30.

Leys, Colin T. (1967), *Politicians and Policies: An Essay on Politics in Acholi, Uganda, 1962 – 1965* (Nairobi: East African Publishing House).

Leys, Colin T. (1973), 'Interpreting African underdevelopment: reflections on the ILO report on employment, incomes and equality in Kenya', *African Affairs*, vol. 72, pp. 419 – 29.

Leys, Colin T. (1975), *Underdevelopment in Kenya: the political economy of neo-colonialism* (London: Heinemann).

Lipset, Seymour Martin (1964), *The First New Nation: The United States in Historical and Comparative Perspective* (London: Heinemann).

Lloyd, P. C. (1966), *The New Elites of Tropical Africa* (Harmondsworth, Middx.: Penguin).

Lofchie, Michael Frank (1971), 'Political constraints on African development', in M. F. Lofchie (ed.), *The State of the Nations: Constraints on Development in Independent Africa* (Berkeley, Calif.: University of California Press), pp. 9 – 18.

Lonsdale, John M. (1968), 'Some origins of nationalism in East Africa', *Journal of African History*, vol. 9, pp. 119 – 46.

Low, D. Anthony (1964), 'Lion rampant', *Journal of Commonwealth Political Studies*, vol. 2, pp. 235 – 52.

Low, D. Anthony (1971), *Buganda in Modern History* (London: Weidenfeld & Nicolson).

Low, D. Anthony (1973), *Lion rampant: Essays in the Study of British Imperialism* (London: Frank Cass).

Low, D. Anthony, and Lonsdale, John (1976), 'Introduction: towards the new order, 1945 – 1963', in D. A. Low and Alison Smith (eds), *History of East Africa* (Oxford: Clarendon Press), pp. 1 – 63.

Luckham, Robin (1982), 'French militarism in Africa', *Review of African Political Economy* no. 24, pp. 55 – 84.

McCracken, John (1982 – 3), 'Planters, peasants and the colonial state: the impact of the Native Tobacco Board in the Central Province of Malawi', *Journal of Southern African Studies*, vol. 9, pp. 72 – 92.

McKenzie, John (1975 – 6), 'Sambo and economic determinism: a comment on Charles van Onselen's "Black Workers in Central African Industry"', *Journal of Southern African Studies*, vol. 2, pp. 98 – 101.

Mackintosh, John P. (1962), 'Electoral trends and the tendency to a one party system in Nigeria', *Journal of Commonwealth Political Studies*, vol. 1, pp. 194 – 210.

Macpherson, C. B. (1966), *The Real World of Democracy* (Oxford: Clarendon Press).

Mafeje, Archie (1971), 'The ideology of tribalism', *Journal of Modern African Studies*, vol. 9, pp. 253 – 62.

Mannoni, Jacques Dominique Octave (1964), *Prospero and Caliban: The Psychology of Colonisation* (New York: Praeger).

Maquet, J. J. M. (1961), *The Premise of Inequality in Ruanda: A Study of Political Relations in a Central African Kingdom* (London: Oxford University Press).

Marnham, Patrick (1980), *Fantastic Invasion: Despatches from Contemporary Africa* (London: Cape).

Mawhood, Philip, and Davey, Ken (1980), 'Anglophone Africa', in Donald C. Rowat (ed.), *International Handbook on Local Government Reorganisation: contemporary developments* (London: Aldwych Press), pp. 404–14.

Mazrui, A. A. (1965), 'Tanzania *versus* East Africa, *Journal of Commonwealth Political Studies*, vol. 3, pp. 224–42.

Mazrui, A. A. (1967a), 'The monarchical tendency in African political culture', *British Journal of Sociology*, vol. 18, pp. 231–50.

Mazrui, A. A. (1967b), *Towards a Pax Africana: A Study of Ideology and Ambitions* (London: Weidenfeld and Nicolson).

Mbilinyi, Marjorie J. (1972), 'The "new woman" and traditional norms in Tanzania', *Journal of Modern African Studies*, vol. 10, pp. 57–72.

Mboya, Tom (1963), *Freedom and After* (London: Deutsch).

Melson, Robert, and Wolpe, Howard (1970), 'Modernisation and the politics of communalism: a theoretical perspective', *American Political Science Review*, vol. 64, pp. 1112–30.

Miller, Norman N. (1969), 'The survival of traditional leadership', *Journal of Modern African Studies*, vol. 6, pp. 183–207.

Mohan, Jitendra (1966), 'Varieties of African socialism', in Ralph Miliband and John Saville (eds), *The Socialist Register, 1966* (London: Merlin Press), pp. 220–66.

Mohan, Jitendra (1968), 'A Whig interpretation of African nationalism', *Journal of Modern African Studies*, vol. 6, pp. 389–410.

Mohiddin, Ahmed (1981), *African Socialism in Two Countries* (London: Croom Helm).

Morris, James (1968), *Pax Britannica: The Climax of an Empire* (London: Faber).

Mortimer, Edward (1969), *France and the Africans, 1944–1960: A Political History* (London: Faber).

Muller, Mike (1981), *The Health of Nations: A North–South Investigation* (London: Faber).

Murray, D. J. (1970), 'The Western Nigerian civil service through political crises and military coups', *Journal of Commonwealth Political Studies*, vol. 8, pp. 229–40.

Naipaul, V. S. (1979), *A Bend in the River* (New York: Knopf).

Nasser, Abdul Gamal (1955), *Egypt's Liberation: The Philosophy of the Revolution* (Washington, DC: Public Affairs Press).

Nellis, J. R. (1973), 'Expatriates in the government of Kenya', *Journal of Commonwealth Political Studies*, vol. 11, pp. 251–64.

Ngugi wa Thiong'o (1977), *Petals of Blood* (London: Heinemann).

Nkrumah, Nkwame (1968), *Dark Days in Ghana* (London: Lawrence & Wishart).

Nolutshungu, Sam C. (1982), *Changing South Africa: Political Considerations* (Manchester: Manchester University Press).

Nove, Alec (1973–4), 'On reading André Gunder Frank', *Journal of Development Studies*, vol. 10, pp. 445–55.

Nsekela, Amon J. (ed.) (1981), *Southern Africa: Toward Economic Liberation* (London: Rex Collings).

Nwabueze, B. O. (1975), *Presidentialism in Commonwealth Africa* (London: Hurst).

Nwokedi, Emeka (1982), 'Franco-African summits: a new instrument for France's African strategy?', *World Today*, vol. 38, pp. 478–82.

Nye, J. S. (1967), 'Corruption and political development: a cost-benefit analysis', *American Political Science Review*, vol. 61, pp. 417–27.

Nyerere, Julius K. (1966), *Freedom and Unity: Uhuru na Umoja* (Dar es Salaam: Oxford University Press).

Nyerere, Julius K. (1968), *Freedom and Socialism: Uhuru na Ujamaa* (Dar es Salaam: Oxford University Press).

Oberschall, A. R. (1969–70), 'Rising expectations and political turmoil', *Journal of Development Studies*, vol. 6, pp. 5–22.

O'Brien, Donal Cruise (1966–7), 'Political opposition in Senegal, 1960–1967', *Government and Opposition*, vol. 2, pp. 557–66.

O'Brien, Donal Cruise (1972), 'Modernisation, order and the erosion of a democratic ideal: American political science, 1960–1970', *Journal of Development Studies*, vol. 8, pp. 351–78.

O'Brien, Donal Cruise (1975), *Saints and Politicians: Essays in the Organisation of a Senegalese Peasant Society* (Cambridge: Cambridge University Press).

O'Brien, Rita Cruise (1972), *White Society in Black Africa: the French of Senegal* (London: Faber).

O'Connell, James (1967), 'The inevitability of instability', *Journal of Modern African Studies*, vol. 5, pp. 181–92.

O'Connor, James R. (1973), *The Fiscal Crisis of the State* (New York: St Martin's Press).

Odinga, Ajuma Oginga (1967), *Not Yet Uhuru: The Autobiography of Oginga Odinga* (London: Heinemann).

Okoth-Ogendo, H. W. (1972), 'The politics of constitutional change in Kenya since independence, 1963–1969', *African Affairs*, vol. 71, pp. 9–34.

Owusu, Maxwell (1970), *Uses and Abuses of Political Power: A Case Study of Continuity and Change in the Politics of Ghana* (Chicago: Chicago University Press).

Palmer, Robin H. (1977), 'The agricultural history of Rhodesia', in R. H. Palmer and Neil Parsons (eds), *The Roots of Rural Poverty in Central and Southern Africa* (London: Heinemann), pp. 221–54.

Panter-Brick, Keith (ed.) (1970), *Nigerian Politics and Military Rule: Prelude to Civil War* (London: Athlone Press).

p'Bitek, Okot (1966), *Song of Lawino* (Nairobi: East African Publishing House).

Peil, Margaret (1976), *Nigerian Politics: The People's View* (London: Cassell).

Perham, Margery (1960), *Lugard: The Years of Authority, 1898–1945* (London: Collins).

Perham, Margery (1961), *The Colonial Reckoning* (London: Collins).

Phillips, Ann (1977), 'The concept of "development"', *Review of African Political Economy*, no. 8, pp. 7 – 20.

Picard, Louis A. (1979), 'District councils in Botswana – a remnant of local autonomy', *Journal of Modern African Studies*, vol. 17, pp. 285 – 308.

Post, K. W. J. (1963), *The Nigerian Federal Election of 1959: Politics and Administration in a Developing Political System* (London: Oxford University Press).

Post, K. W. J., and Vickers, Michael (1973), *Structure and Conflict in Nigeria* (London: Heinemann).

Potter, David M. (1954), *People of Plenty: Economic Abundance and the American Character* (Chicago: University of Chicago Press).

Powell, John Duncan (1970), 'Peasant society and clientilist politics', *American Political Science Review*, vol. 64, pp. 411 – 25.

Prewitt, Kenneth (ed.) (1971), *Education and Political Values: An East African Case Study* (Nairobi: East African Publishing House).

Proctor, John H. (1969), 'Building a constitutional monarchy in Lesotho', *Civilisations*, vol. 19, pp. 64 – 84.

Proctor, John H. (1973), 'Traditionalism and parliamentary government in Swaziland', *African Affairs*, vol. 72, pp. 273 – 87.

Rathbone, Richard (1981), *Nationalism in Africa* (London: Macmillan).

Ridley, Fred F., and Blondel, Jean (1964), *Public Administration in France* (London: Routledge & Kegan Paul).

Riggs, Fred W. (1964), *Administration in Developing Societies: The Theory of Prismatic Society* (Boston, Mass.: Houghton Mifflin).

Robinson, Joan (1964), *Economic Philosophy* (Harmondsworth, Middx.: Penguin).

Robinson, Kenneth (1961), 'Constitutional autochthony in Ghana', *Journal of Commonwealth Political Studies*, vol. 1, pp. 41 – 55.

Robinson, Kenneth (1965), *The Dilemmas of Trusteeship: Aspects of British Colonial Policy between the Wars* (London: Oxford University Press).

Robinson, Ronald (1972), 'Non-European foundations of European imperialism: a sketch for a theory of collaboration', in Roger Owen and Bob Sutcliffe (eds), *Studies in the Theory of Imperialism* (London: Longman), pp. 117 – 42.

Robinson, Ronald E., and Gallagher, John, with Denny, Alice (1961), *Africa and the Victorians: The Official Mind of Imperialism* (London: Macmillan).

Rodney, Walter (1972), *How Europe Underdeveloped Africa* (Dar es Salaam: Tanzania Publishing House).

Rosberg, Carl Gustav, and Nottingham, John Cato (1966), *The Myth of 'Mau Mau': Nationalism in Kenya* (London: Pall Mall).

Roston, Walt W. (1960), *The Stages of Economic Growth: An Anti-Communist Manifesto* (Cambridge: Cambridge University Press).

Rothchild, Donald (ed.) (1968), *Politics of Integration: An East African Documentary* (Nairobi: East African Publishing House).

Sandbrook, Richard (1972), 'Patrons, clients and factions: new dimensions of conflict analysis in Africa', *Canadian Journal of Political Science*, vol. 5, pp. 104 – 19.

Saul, John (1969), 'Africa', in Ghita Ionescu and Ernest Gellner (eds),

Populism: Its Meanings and National Characteristics (London: Weidenfeld & Nicolson), pp. 122 – 50.

Schatz, Sayre P. (1969), 'Crude private neo-imperialism: a new pattern in Africa', *Journal of Modern African Studies*, vol. 7, pp. 677 – 88.

Schmidt, S. W. *et al.* (1977), *Friends, Followers and Factions: A Reader in Political Clientilism* (Berkeley, Calif.: University of California Press).

Seeley, Sir John (1883), *The Expansion of England: Two Courses of Lectures* (London: Macmillan).

Selassie, Bereket H. (1974), *The Executive in African Governments* (London: Heinemann).

Sembene, O. (1970), *God's Bits of Wood* (New York: Doubleday).

Shaffer, B. B. (1965 – 6), 'The concept of preparation: some questions about the transfer of systems of government', *World Politics*, vol. 18, pp. 42 – 67.

Smith, Anthony D. (1978), 'A comparative study of French and British Decolonization', *Comparative Studies in Society and History*, vol. 20, pp. 70 – 102.

Smith, Anthony D. (1978 – 9), 'The underdevelopment of development literature', *World Politics*, vol. 31, pp. 247 – 88.

Stevens, Christopher and Speed, John (1977), 'Multi-partyism in Africa: the case of Botswana revisited', *African Affairs*, vol. 76, pp. 381 – 7.

Sylla, Lancinné (1982), 'Succession of the charismatic leader: the gordian knot of African politics', *Daedalus*, vol. 3 (Spring), pp. 11 – 28.

Symonds, Richard (1966), *The British and their Successors: A Study in the Development of Government Services in the New States* (London: Faber).

Thornton, A. P. (1959), *The Imperial Idea and its Enemies: A Study in British Power* (London: Macmillan).

Tordoff, William (1973), 'Local administration in Botswana – part I', *Journal of Administration Overseas*, vol. 12, pp. 172 – 83.

Tordoff, William (1980), 'Ghana', in Donald C. Rowat (ed.), *International Handbook on Local Government Reorganisation: Contemporary Developments* (London: Aldwych), pp. 379 – 92.

Turok, Ben (1981), 'Control in the parastatal sector of Zambia', *Journal of Modern African Studies*, vol. 19, pp. 421 – 45.

UNESCO (1957), *World Illiteracy at Mid-Century* (Paris: UNESCO).

University of Dar es Salaam (1974), *Socialism and Participation: Tanzania's 1970 National Elections* (Dar es Salaam: Tanzania Publishing House).

Vail, Leroy (1975), 'The making of an imperial slum: Nyasaland and its railways, 1895 – 1935', *Journal of African History*, vol. 16, pp. 89 – 112.

van Onselen, Charles (1976), *Chibaro: African Mine Labour in Southern Rhodesia, 1900 – 1933* (London: Pluto Press).

Vaughan, Megan Ann (1981), 'Social and economic change in Southern Malawi: a study of rural communities in the Shire Highlands and Upper Shire Valley from the mid-nineteenth century to 1915', unpublished PhD thesis, University of London.

Vickers, Michael (1970), 'Competition and control in modern Nigeria: origins of the war with Biafra', *International Journal*, vol. 25, pp. 603 – 33.

Vincent, Joan (1970), 'Local co-operatives and parochial politics in Uganda:

problems of organisation, representation, and communication', *Journal of Commonwealth Political Studies*, vol. 8, pp. 3–17.

Wallerstein, Immanuel (1964), 'Voluntary associations', in J. S. Coleman and C. G. Rosberg (eds), *Political Parties and National Integration in Tropical Africa* (Berkeley, Calif.: University of California Press), pp. 318–39.

Wallerstein, Immanuel (1971), 'The range of choice: constraints on the policies of governments of contemporary African states', in M. F. Lofchie (ed.), *The State of the Nations: Constraints on Development in Independent Africa* (Berkeley, Calif.: University of California Press), pp. 19–33.

Warren, Bill (1973), 'Imperialism and capitalist industrialisation', *New Left Review*, no. 81 (September–October), pp. 3–44.

Warren, Bill (1980), *Imperialism: Pioneer of capitalism* (London: New Left Books).

Wasserman, Gary (1976), *Politics of Decolonisation: Kenya Europeans and the Land Issue, 1960–1965* (Cambridge: Cambridge University Press).

Weinrich, A. K. H. (1971), *Chiefs and Councils in Rhodesia* (London: Heinemann).

Weinstein, Brian (1970), 'Felix Eboué and the chiefs: perceptions of power in early Oubangui Chari', *Journal of African History*, vol. 11, pp. 107–26.

Welch, Claude E. (1974), 'The dilemmas of military withdrawal from politics: some considerations from tropical Africa', *African Studies Review*, vol. 17, pp. 213–29.

Were, Gideon (1981), *History, Public Morality and Nation-Building: A Survey of Africa since Independence* (Nairobi: University of Nairobi).

Werlin, Herbert H. (1972), 'The roots of corruption: the Ghanaian enquiry', *Journal of Modern African Studies*, vol. 10, pp. 247–66.

Werlin, Herbert H. (1974), *Governing an African City: A Study of Nairobi* (New York: Africana Publishing House).

Wheare, Sir Kenneth (1960), *The Constitutional Structure of the Commonwealth* (London: Oxford University Press).

Wilcox, Dennis L. (1975), *Mass Media in Black Africa* (New York: Praeger).

Wiseman, John (1977), 'Multi-partyism in Africa: the case of Botswana', *African Affairs*, vol. 76, pp. 70–9.

Wolfers, Michael (1976), *Politics in the Organisation of African Unity* (London: Methuen).

World Bank (1981), *Accelerated Development in Sub-Saharan Africa: An Agenda for Action* (Washington, DC: World Bank).

Wraith, Ronald, and Simpkins, Edgar (1963), *Corruption in Developing Countries* (London: Allen & Unwin).

Young, Hugo, and Sloman, Anne (1982), *No, Minister: An Enquiry into the Civil Service* (London: BBC).

Appendices

The information contained in the following tables *must* be treated with great caution. Statistics from any country need careful interpretation (what counts as part of the defence budget, for instance, differs from state to state), and they too often give a sense of spurious accuracy. Statistics from Africa should be treated with even greater caution than usual; they are normally prepared by overworked bureaucats, often with little statistical knowledge, operating with incomplete (or sometimes fabricated) figures from subordinates. On occasions, either for internal political reasons or effect abroad, they are the consequence of creative imaginations. But we do need some attempt at quantification, at providing hard data on which analysis can be built; and these tables are about as hard as it is possible to get. They are taken from the World Bank's report *Accelerated Development in Sub-Saharan Africa: An Agenda for Action* (1981) in which there is an extremely useful glossary on the tables explaining the problems encountered in producing them (pp. 187–96). But do remember that the margin of error in many of these apparently definitive numbers is likely to be considerable.

Appendix I   Basic Indicators

	Population (millions) mid–1979	Area (thousands of square kilometers)	GNP per capita — Dollars 1979	GNP per capita — Average annual growth rate (per cent) 1960–79	Average annual rate of inflation (per cent) 1960–70	Average annual rate of inflation (per cent) 1970–9	Adult literacy (per cent) 1976	Life expectancy at birth (years) 1979	Average index of food production per capita (1969–71 = 100) 1977–9
Low-Income Countries	**187·1**	**15,718**	**239**	**0·9**	**2·8**	**10·2**	**25**	**46**	**91**
Low-income, semi-arid	28·0	5,745	187	0·0	3·3	10·0	17	43	88
1 Chad	4·4	1,284	110	−1·4	4·6	7·9	15*	41	91
2 Somalia	3·8	638	110	−0·5	4·5	11·3	60	44	85
3 Mali	6·8	1,240	140	1·1	5·0	9·7	10	43	88
4 Upper Volta	5·6	274	180	0·3	1·3	9·8	5*	43	93
5 Gambia	0·6	11	250	2·6*			10*	42	77
6 Niger	5·2	1,267	270	−1·3	2·1	10·8	8	43	89
7 Mauritania	1·6	1,031	320	1·9	1·6	10·1	17*	43	75
Low-income, other	159·1	9,973	247	1·0	2·8	10·7	27	47	91
8 Ethiopia	30·9	1,222	130	1·3	2·1	4·3	15*	40	84
9 Guinea-Bissau	0·8	36	170				7*	42	94
10 Burundi	4·0	28	180	2·1	2·8	11·2	25	42	105
11 Malawi	5·8	118	200	2·9	2·4	9·1	25*	47	100
12 Rwanda	4·9	26	200	1·5	13·1	14·6	—	47	107
13 Benin	3·4	113	250	0·6	1·9	9·2	7*	47	97
14 Mozambique	10·2	783	250	0·1	2·8	11·0	—	47	75
15 Sierra Leone	3·4	72	250	0·4	2·9	11·3	—	47	87
16 Tanzania	18·0	945	260	2·3	1·8	13·0	66*	52	94
17 Zaire	27·5	2,345	260	0·7	29·9	31·4	15	47	90
18 Guinea	5·3	246	280	0·3	1·5	4·4	20*	44	86
19 Central African Republic	2·0	623	290	0·7	4·1	9·1	—	44	102

20 Madagascar	8·5	587	290	−0·4	3·2	10·1	30*	47	94
21 Uganda	12·8	236	290	−0·2	3·0	28·3	−	54	90
22 Lesotho	1·3	30	340	6·0	2·5	11·6	52*	51	100
23 Togo	2·4	57	350	3·6	1·1	10·3	18	47	81
24 Sudan	17·9	2,506	370	0·6	3·7	6·8	20*	47	105
Middle-Income Oil Importers	65·2	3,690	532	1·5	2·4	9·9	34	50	95
25 Kenya	15·3	583	380	2·7	1·5	11·1	45*	55	92
26 Ghana	11·3	239	400	−0·8	7·6	32·4	−	49	82
27 Senegal	5·5	197	430	−0·2	1·7	7·6	10*	43	88
28 Zimbabwe	7·1	391	470	0·8	1·3	8·4	−	55	100
29 Liberia	1·8	111	500	1·6	1·9	9·4	30	54	101
30 Zambia	5·6	753	500	0·8	7·6	6·8	39*	49	99
31 Cameroon	8·2	475	560	2·5	4·2	10·3	−	47	110
32 Swaziland	0·5	17	650	7·2*	−	−	65*	47	109
33 Botswana	0·8	600	720	9·1*	−	−	35*	49	89
34 Mauritius	0·9	2	1,030	2·3*	−	−	80*	65	100
35 Ivory Coast	8·2	322	1,040	2·4	2·8	13·5	20	47	102
Middle-Income Oil Exporters	91·6	2,781	669	3·2	3·3	19·0	−	48	86
36 Angola	6·9	1,247	440	−2·1	3·3	21·6	−	42	85
37 Congo	1·5	342	630	0·9	5·4	10·9	−	47	81
38 Nigeria	82·6	924	670	3·7	2·6	19·0	−	49	87
39 Gabon	0·6	268	3,280	6·1*	−	−	12*	45	94
Sub-Saharan Africa	343·9	22,189	411	1·6	2·8	10·3	27	47	91
All low-income countries	2,260·2	33,778	230	1·6	3·0	10·8	51	57	105
All middle-income countries	985·0	38,705	1,420	3·8	3·0	13·3	72	61	107
Industrialised countries	671·2	30,430	9,440	4·0	4·3	9·4	99	74	110

* indicates years other than 1976.

n.a. = not available.

Source: World Bank (1981), p. 143.

Appendix II Selected Characteristics of Tropical African Countries

	(1) GDP attributable to agriculture (per cent)	(2) GDP attributable to services (per cent)	(3) Govt. expenditure on agriculture (per cent)	(4) Govt. expenditure on education (per cent)	(5) Govt. expenditure on defence (per cent)	(6) Primary school age children in school (per cent)	(7) Secondary school age children in school (per cent)	(8) Share of total exports from three sources (per cent) 1976–8 av.	(9) Net flow of resources per capita 1979	(10) Debt service as percentage of exports 1979
Low-income Countries										
Low-income, semi-arid										
1 Chad	70	19	20·9	13·5	25·8	35*	3*	82·1	19·6	14·4
2 Somalia	60*	29*	13·6	14·0	20·1	44*	4*	90·6	67·6	1·1
3 Mali	42	47	n.a.	21·6	18·6	28	9*	86·4	29·9	8·5
4 Upper Volta	38	42	1·7	15·6	21·8	17	2	43·6	38·5	3·8
5 Gambia	46	46	22·0	6·5	0·0	37	12	79·7	67·0	n.a.
6 Niger	44	24	6·6	23·3	6·1	23	3*	79·5	51·5	3·6
7 Mauritania	27	40	n.a.	n.a.	n.a.	26*	5*	86·1	133·6	32·4
Low-income, other										
8 Ethiopia	46	39	10·4	11·5	n.a.	38*	9*	81·5	7·2	4·9
9 Guinea-Bissau	54	34	5·1	15·6	24·0	112	10	76·6	71·4	59·0
10 Burundi	55	30	12·0	20·6	11·2	21	3	95·2	22·8	3·1
11 Malawi	43	37	11·5	11·8	11·3	59*	4*	83·1	31·5	9·4
12 Rwanda	42	37	10·3	18·8	12·4	64*	2*	86·5	29·9	0·6
13 Benin	43	45	n.a.	n.a.	n.a.	60*	12*	32·0	30·4	5·1
14 Mozambique	44	40	n.a.	n.a.	n.a.	n.a.	n.a.	25·6	15·5	n.a.
15 Sierra Leone	36	41	5·4	16·0	7·8	37*	12*	79·1	15·7	22·2
16 Tanzania	54	33	8·9	12·5	10·5	70*	4*	55·4	40·4	7·4
17 Zaire	33	43	0·2	15·1	10·8	90*	19*	91·1	26·4	9·1
18 Guinea	41	33	n.a.	n.a.	n.a.	34*	16*	72·9	11·8	22·2
19 Central African Republic	37	45	n.a.	n.a.	n.a.	78*	9*	54·0	45·9	0·1

20 Madagascar	34	46	14·4	15·3	4·1	94*	12*	48·1	25·8	3·9
21 Uganda	55	38	n.a.	n.a.	n.a.	50*	5*	96·0	2·7	7·4
22 Lesotho	36	49	18·5	21·3	0·0	101*	17*	100·0	47·7	0·6
23 Togo	25	52	6·4	13·7	9·6	102*	25*	81·4	91·0	24·4
24 Sudan	38	49	9·0	5·2	13·6	50	16	70·6	36·0	33·0
Middle-Income Oil Importers										
25 Kenya	34	45	8·5	18·7	16·0	99	18	52·5	29·4	7·5
26 Ghana	66	13	12·2	15·6	5·3	71*	32*	62·8	17·6	4·2
27 Senegal	29	47	5·2	19·0	10·7	41*	10*	49·7	63·3	13·7
28 Zimbabwe	12	49	n.a.	n.a.	n.a.	97*	9*	21·9	1·5	n.a.
29 Liberia	35	39	2·9	11·3	2·7	64	20	82·1	185·4	13·8
30 Zambia	15	44	n.a.	16·8	n.a.	98*	16*	96·2	45·3	19·7
31 Cameroon	32	52	7·1	16·8	8·3	101*	16*	62·8	68·2	9·5
32 Swaziland	n.a.	n.a.	13·1	21·4	6·5	92	32	58·9	147·2	n.a.
33 Botswana	21	49	10·5	20·5	0·0	89	20	99·1	164·8	n.a.
34 Mauritius	25	47	9·7	14·2	0·6	104	51	71·9	64·0	n.a.
35 Ivory Coast	26	51	2·9	35·7	7·2	71*	14	68·1	65·6	15·2
Middle-Income Oil Exporters										
36 Angola	48	29	n.a.	n.a.	n.a.	n.a.	n.a.	60·9	16·1	n.a.
37 Congo	13	51	n.a.	n.a.	n.a.	156	69	82·4	40·2	7·3*
38 Nigeria	22	33	2·6	9·6	17·9	62*	13*	97·1	3·5	1·5
39 Gabon	6	29	n.a.	n.a.	n.a.	202	34	87·8	−90·8	n.a.
Sub-Saharan Africa	32	37	9·0	15·6	10·5	63	13	79·1	24·6	6·9
All Low-Income Countries	34	30	10·3	14·0	11·3	83	36	n.a.	n.a.	10·8
All Middle-Income Countries	14	48	4·0	14·1	11·5	95	41	n.a.	n.a.	14·2
Industrialised Countries	4	59	2·6	10·9	6·9	100	89	n.a.	n.a.	n.a.

* indicates a year other than that indicated.

n.a. = not available.

Source: World Bank (1981), pp. 145, 184, 181, 164, 159.

Index